AN INTRODUCTION
TO CHRISTIAN PHILOSOPHY

AN INTRODUCTION TO CHRISTIAN PHILOSOPHY

BY
J. M. SPIER

Translated by
DAVID HUGH FREEMAN
*Professor of Philosophy,
University of Rhode Island*

Second Edition

THE CRAIG PRESS
Nutley, New Jersey
1979

UNIVERSITY SERIES, Philosophical Studies
Dr. Gordon H. Clark, Editor

COPYRIGHT 1954
BY THE PRESBYTERIAN AND REFORMED PUBLISHING COMPANY
PHILADELPHIA, PA.

ISBN: 0-934532-25-7
Library of Congress Catalog Card Number 53-12296

TRANSLATOR'S NOTE

THIS work was originally published in Dutch under the title, *Een Inleiding tot de Wijsbegeerte der Wetsidee*. It is largely a popular exposition of the philosophy systematically developed by Hermann Dooyeweerd in his four volume work, *A New Critique of Theoretical Thought*.[1]

The critical reader may be annoyed by the fact that Spier does not always argue points which are philosophically disputable. For such argument the reader is referred to the above mentioned work by Dooyeweerd.

Those interested in a critical study of Christian philosophy will find that Spier provides an excellent introduction to the study of Dooyeweerd and his school.

In the Netherlands this school of philosophy has attracted considerable attention. In addition to the Free University of Amsterdam where Dooyeweerd is a professor of Law and Vollenhoven of philosophy, the Universities of Utrecht, Leiden, and Groningen, the Technical School of Delft, and The School of Economics in Rotterdam all have special chairs of philosophy held by members of the *Dooyeweerdian* school.

Christians of all persuasions may find much in this movement with which they can be in sympathy. Those not sympathetic with Christianity but interested in philosophy will find much of interest from an historical and critical point of view.

It should be needless to say that this movement of Christian philosophy cannot be evaluated on the basis of this book alone. Spier's work must be taken in conjunction with the major works of Dooyeweerd.

In the work of translation I have tried to give as literal a translation of the original as is in keeping with ordinary

[1]Originally published in Dutch in the three volume work entitled *De Wijsbegeerte Der Wetsidee*.

v

English usage. I would like to express my gratitude to Miss Sybil Chance, Mrs. Helen Ward, Professor John Murray, and Professor John Skilton, whose criticism and suggestions on matters of English style were most valuable to me; to Mr. J. M. Spier, for reading and correcting the manuscript; and to Miss Gloria Ericson for her assistance with the typing. I especially want to thank Mr. Joseph Zimbrolt for his encouragement and friendly advice on style in translation work.

It would be most ungrateful of me if I neglected to mention the generous interest shown by the Presbyterian and Reformed Publishing Company whose relationship to this work is not so much a business one as that of appreciation.

DAVID HUGH FREEMAN

University of Rhode Island
Kingston, Rhode Island

PUBLISHER'S NOTICE

In view of the continuing and increased interest in the system of philosophy developed by Dr. Herman Dooyeweerd, The Craig Press has included J. M. Spier's *An Introduction to Christian Philosophy* in the University Series of paperbacks. The author himself, writing in English, has thoroughly revised his work for this second United States edition, which remains the only popular exposition of this school of philosophy in the English language. Dr. Gordon H. Clark, Chairman of the Philosophy Department at Butler University, is editor of this series.

AUTHOR'S PREFACE

It is a great joy to me that my book, *An Introduction to Christian Philosophy*, is now published in English. I am not primarily pleased with the success of a Dutch best seller, but I am thankful that this system of Christian philosophy can be read and studied in the English-speaking world.

The first Dutch edition of this book was published in 1938. This English edition is a revised and supplemented translation of the fourth Dutch edition published in 1950.

I have great respect for the manner of translation by Mr. David H. Freeman. The work was not easy, but he has done it excellently.

This movement is sometimes misunderstood. It is wrongly thought that I am contending that this system of Christian philosophy is the only possible approach open to Christian philosophers. I would like to take this opportunity to remove this misunderstanding. This approach to Christian philosophy is only a first attempt to construct a philosophy which is in keeping with Christianity. The movement of the so-called "Calvinistic philosophy" — originated from the Netherlands about forty years ago — has soon become an international philosophic movement with followers in many countries of the world, for instance South Africa, Prof. Dr. H. G. Stoker, Potchefstroom; the United States of America, Prof. Dr. H. Evan Runner, Grand Rapids, Mich.; Canada, and so on.

My desire is that God will bestow His blessing upon this book. I hope it may encourage the further development of Christian philosophy and science, and may God receive all honor and glory.

J. M. SPIER

Sneek, Holland

CONTENTS

Translator's Note v

Author's Preface vii

CHAPTER		PAGE
I.	An Introduction to Christian Philosophy . .	1
II.	The Theory of Cosmic Modalities or Law-Spheres	30
III.	The Theory of Knowledge	131
IV.	The Theory of the Structures of Temporal Things	164
V.	The Theory of the Structure of Human Society	189
VI.	The Theory of Structural Interrelations .	244
VII.	Final Remarks	257

CHAPTER I

AN INTRODUCTION TO CHRISTIAN PHILOSOPHY

1

Preliminary Questions

Before we can enter into an examination of the philosophical system before us, we must answer the question: "What is philosophy?" The word philosophy is commonly employed in a dual sense. It can denote the *result* of philosophic activity, and it is in this sense that one speaks of the philosophy of Plato and of Kant. In this case one refers to their philosophical *system,* which still exists though these men have long since ceased to be active philosophically.

Philosophy can also designate *philosophic activity* itself, the act of philosophizing, which is a human activity bound to our temporal life. We shall employ the term in its second sense.

Now what does a philosopher do? What does it mean to philosophize? First of all to be philosophically active is to be engaged *in thought.* We can also devote ourselves to other actions, i.e., eating, sleeping, and so on. However, all cogitation is not necessarily philosophical. While making a suit of clothes a tailor thinks but does not philosophize. To be active philosophically is to engage in a specific form of *scientific* thought. Before we can answer the question, What is philosophy? we must, therefore, first answer the question, What is science?

Science, and thus also philosophy, is a particular form of cogitative activity. To think scientifically is to think analytically. *Science* is *analytical* and *antithetical* systematic thought.

To understand this definition thoroughly we must contrast our *naive everyday manner of thinking* with scientific thought. In our *naive* everyday experience, if we observe a beautiful table, for example, we examine it precisely, think about its style, and estimate its age and value. We think naively and uncritically. Giving free play to our mind, we unconsciously pass from one domain to another. Our whole person is bound to the object of our thought and we experience concrete reality.

A scientist, in contrast, commences by making sharp distinctions and separately examining various aspects of the same object. He considers a table's dimensions, weight, age, style, type of wood, and so on. A scientist analyzes these different aspects separately and disassociates them from each other. A physicist or a chemist is interested only in the type and nature of the material which constitutes the table. And, the historian of art is, for the moment, concerned only with its style and period.

Scientific thought is *discriminative, analytical,* and *antithetical.* In our naive experience we are closely in touch with *life-in-its-totality* or *fulness.* In science we maintain a certain distance between ourselves and the object of our investigations. A scientist does not permit his thought to wander undisciplined; he is very zealous not to pass from one aspect to another. He conducts his examination logically and systematically and is not satisfied until he has examined his field of investigation exhaustively.

Philosophy is a science. It is systematic, analytical, and antithetical. Each branch of what we usually call science investigates a particular aspect of reality. Law, sociology, history, and the natural sciences differ because they investigate different fields. An historian and a naturalist examine different aspects of reality. What aspect of reality does a philosopher examine?

A philosopher does not concentrate his scientific cogitative activity upon any single aspect, but is concerned with all created reality. He views no aspect in isolation; his field is the cosmos in its entirety.¹ Philosophy seeks to acquire a view of *totality* which is exhaustive and integral in character. The special sciences are concerned with only one aspect of reality.²

No single aspect of reality exists in itself. Each points beyond itself to the other aspects with which, according to the will of the Creator, it is indissolubly connected. In the coherence of the world nothing exists by itself. And this is why science must have a philosophical basis. Each particular science requires a careful systematic consideration of the relationship between the aspect which it examines and the remaining aspects. Philosophy is, therefore, the necessary foundation of all other sciences. Consciously or unconsciously every science is based upon certain philosophical presuppositions. Consequently, philosophy is concerned with the cosmos in its entirety. As a part of theoretical thought it enriches and deepens naive thought.

Now some scientists do not raise certain ultimate questions which they ought to pose. Some natural scientists, at least while engaged in their own particular field, are not interested in how nature came into existence. They are not interested in the origin, meaning, or end of nature. The philosopher, however, should be interested in such questions since he ought to focus his thought (scientifically) on the totality of temporal reality. The various aspects of temporal reality and the cosmos in its entirety do not exist independently, but point toward their origin. Consequently, the philosophy which desires to fulfil its task completely must be directive in character and point toward God, the

[1] Only earthly reality can be the object of scientific research. Our knowledge of heaven and hell, for example, depends exclusively upon divine revelation in the Holy Scripture and faith.

[2] This distinction between philosophy and the special sciences has been made by Abraham Kuyper in *Encyclopaedie der Heilige Godgeleerdheid II*, p. 586. ". . . The second task of philosophy, on the other hand, is entirely different, for it is not directed toward the conscious thinking man, but it is the attempt of the thinking man to reflect in the mirror of his consciousness the cosmos which confronts him, as an organic whole."

final end and origin of creation. Real philosophy is Christian philosophy; all things are from Him and through Him.

Philosophy is scientific thought occupied with the entire temporal cosmos in such a manner that the latter is viewed in direct relation to its origin.

2

Philosophy and Religion

The second preliminary question deals with the relationship between philosophy and religion. Philosophy must be more than a mere pastime or a hobby if it is to be *significant* as a basic science. A philosopher must labor in full awareness of his "Divine Calling" and must know that philosophy belongs to the task which God assigned to humanity in His covenant. Philosophy is a part of the cultural mandate which God has given and never has abrogated. The life of the whole human race ought to be dedicated to the service of God (Heidelberg Catechism, question 6).

God has instituted His Covenant with humanity and by prescribing duties for man to perform in keeping it, He has called man to perform a task. Humanity in Adam, the first covenant head, terminated its obedience to God, thereby losing the promise of the Covenant and invoking its curse. However, by His grace, God kept His Covenant and made it again possible to acquire the Covenant promise, through Jesus Christ, the second Adam. By His obedience Christ bore the curse of the Covenant and saved His Church from the penalty of the Fall. And, in principle, He re-established man, within the Church, in the service of God with all his heart.

To serve God through Jesus Christ, man must keep the Covenant, and the Covenant embraces all of human life. It includes the full man in all his relationships and activities. We must emphasize to the fullest the fact that according to Scripture not *only* our soul is redeemed. It is not only a spiritual nucleus of the believer that belongs to the

Covenant but his full self. We belong to it with our heart and our life, with our soul and body, and with every thing we have and do. Our hopes, and our goals, our past, present, and our future all belong to the Covenant. Therefore the Biblical philosopher cannot agree with the thomistic (Roman-Catholic) distinction of life in the two sections of nature and grace. For the Scripture says, that God's grace in Jesus Christ renews and redeems the whole life and ultimately the world in its totality.

This service of the God of the Covenant with our whole life through faith in Jesus Christ we call *religion*. Irrespective of who one is, or what he does, everyone is called by God to serve Him. The worker in the factory must serve God to the same extent as the minister in his study and the natural scientist in his laboratory. The office worker and the housewife must serve Him as well as the scientist. Nothing may be withdrawn from religion, and religion is the service of God with all one's heart. Whether we eat or drink, sleep or think, laugh or pray, go shopping or read a book, all our activities are a part of our religious life, and are religious in character.

Religion is distinct from worship. Religion encompasses our whole life, whereas worship is only a small part of it. We are active in worship when we pray, participate in a church service, or take the sacraments. We also have a divine calling outside of the narrow sphere of worship. We are to perform our tasks for the Lord through faith and to seek to attain His honor and glory by walking in the Covenant and withdrawing nothing from Him. The entire life of the believer is religious. Prayer is therefore no more pious than work. To worship is not any more pleasing to God than to be engaged in science. In His Covenant God demands that His people pray and work. Man ought to praise God in science; it is a God-given task. And philosophy, as a part of science, is therefore included in the task given by God to man. Philosophy belongs to religion or to the service of God with all one's heart. However, philosophy is not a temple or a shrine. It does not take the place of worship. Non-Christian philosophers often exchange worship for philosophy, and in the temple of the latter bow down before an idol erected to sovereign reason.

Philosophy is not the worship of God, but it is a part of religion, a part of our earthly calling to serve the Lord and to fight against other gods. There is a conflict in philosophy with false gods, against the kingdom of darkness, a struggle with all scientific thought which is apostate and does not recognize Christ's *sovereignty* in heaven and upon the earth.

The philosophy which recognizes God may be assured of the rich blessings of the Covenant. Those who keep the Covenant in the field of science are benefited by the illumination and direction of the Holy Spirit.

3

PHILOSOPHY AND THE EVERYDAY CHRISTIAN

THE question may be asked, What concern is philosophy to the everyday believer? The simple Christian is not trained in science. Of what interest is philosophy to him? Philosophy is much too "high-brow" for the common man. It is the enterprise of scholars who are elevated above the "masses." Such notions are wrongly prevalent among believing church members. The exaltation of the man of science above the common people is the result of the deification of science which occurred in former centuries among those who no longer lived by the light of the revealed Word of God, but lived by the glimmer — the false light — of human reason and proclaimed science to be self-sufficient. A man of science, especially a philosopher, was elevated above the people; he received great respect, and his word was law. Ordinary mortals were not to be concerned with his work. They had to be content with the few blessings which descended upon them from the lofty regions in which science and philosophy dwelt.

Do simple believers really have anything to do with *Chris-*

tian science?¹ Recall the well-known statement of Scripture: "All things are thine, but ye are of Christ, and Christ is of God." Do not make this text powerless by restricting it to a pious utterance. Understand it as it is meant to be understood, in its concrete fulness and you can only conclude that the church of Jesus Christ² is actually concerned with Christian science and philosophy.

The people of God are concerned with everything pertaining to their heavenly Father and with everything by which the Lord can be served — that is, they are concerned with everything which is redeemed and renewed by Christ. Christ is sovereign in the sphere of science too. Christian science seeks His glory and is a God-given task whose fulfillment serves and advances the Kingdom of God. In the final analysis, the scientific task is given to humanity and is not the isolated endeavor of a few scholars. Consequently, the whole church, the entire people of God — who are in principle the new humanity — should know that they are called to confess God's name and to exalt His greatness in all things, including science.

Not that each believer must actually engage in scientific activity and in philosophy. There is a division of labor in the Kingdom of God, but no single believer may be indifferent to any enterprise concerned with the honor of God. Every Christian must be interested in that which is from the Father and is for His glory.

The Christian people in Holland who nearly a century ago prayed and sacrificed in order to erect their own Christian University, will no doubt agree with what I have just said.³ And when this agreement is reached it is not difficult to indicate the connection between philosophy and the everyday believer. Only a few are called to be philos-

¹Tr. Note: The reference here is not to the sect of Christian Science. —D.H.F.
²Tr. Note: The author here is referring to the church as an organism and not as an institution, as the Roman Catholic Church teaches.—D.H.F.
³Tr. Note: The author is referring to the Free University of Amsterdam founded in 1880 by Dr. Abraham Kuyper. This University endeavors to teach from a Christian point of view in all fields of science.—D.H.F.

ophers, and these are in no respect elevated above their fellow believers. Scientific activity is not more pleasing to God than business, factory or farm work. The majority of people are not called to engage in science, but they are called to possess a real interest in the progress of Christian science. And for this they must pray, a thing which they actually do when they utter the words, "Thy Kingdom come."

Christian science and philosophy yield fruit for the life of all believers. The people of God, including those not scientifically trained, ought to assimilate the results of Christian science so that they will be in a better position to observe and judge the connections and relationships in the everyday experience of the reality of life. Christian science will enable them to perceive the richness of God's works and the wisdom which they display. A knowledge of the results of Christian science and philosophy aids the people of God to be on guard against all movements which are of the "world," and which constantly seek to deify an aspect of created reality. When they have gained an insight into the force of an error which originates in a non-Christian or anti-Christian system, they will not so easily be led astray by false spirits but will draw the right lines in all Christian action. They will walk the path which is directed toward the glorification of the Triune God.

4

PHILOSOPHY AND HOLY SCRIPTURE

CHRISTIAN philosophy is closely related to Holy Scripture; it is Biblical philosophy. We are indebted to John Calvin for the truth that the Holy Scriptures, as the Word of God, have authority over all of life. Calvin clearly taught that no single sphere of life may be withdrawn from the authority of God's Word, and this truth applies to philosophy.

Reformed philosophy begins with the acknowledgement that the Holy Scripture is the Word of God; it is a Divine Communication of Truth. This fact cannot be denied with impunity. Philosophy must ever take God's Word into consideration; its mere recognition is not sufficient. But in what way must philosophy reckon with Holy Scripture? Biblical philosophy requires something quite different from the haphazard quoting of Bible verses in support of this or that contention. *The quotation of a text offers no proof of the Biblical character of a proposition.*

It must be established once and for all that the Holy Scripture is not a textbook of philosophy, nor for that matter of any other science. The Bible is a revelation of the grace of God. It is a revelation in which the God of the Covenant speaks to the human race in order that humanity can know, and love Jesus Christ. Science, however, is the product of human activity; it is, therefore, fallible and subject to error.

Philosophy and science must pay attention to more than just the Holy Scripture. A philosophical system cannot be constructed from the Bible alone. This fact is generally acknowledged in Reformed circles but it is sometimes ignored, as in the case when the attempt is made to erect a Biblical or religious psychology or anthropology from Biblical data exclusively. We must examine God's works scientifically. We must reflectively contemplate all of created reality and must focus our attention upon the cosmos itself. In it God's wisdom shines forth. However, our examination of the cosmos can only correctly occur by the light of God's Word. "In Thy Light shall we see light."

In its basic conceptions, Christian philosophy must take Holy Scripture into account. In his well-known book, *Calvinisme en de Reformatie van de Wijsbegeerte*, Vollenhoven lists the Biblical data important for Christian philosophy.[1] The direct sovereignty of God over all things is the first and foremost principle. The second principle is that true religion is only possible in the Covenant relationship between God and humanity. The third principle that Holy Scripture teaches is that the fall has corrupted the human

[1] P. 22.

heart, so that it can only be redeemed from sin and death by God who in Christ freely gives His revelation of grace to sinful humanity.[1]

What we have said should be sufficient to permit us to terminate this discussion but we must continue it further since even many scientifically trained Christians sometimes fail to see the necessity of a really Christian philosophy.

The question is often raised, Is not God's Word sufficient? Does not Scripture give us a vision of the totality of created reality? What room is there for a philosophy? Very often by unbelieving philosophers their philosophy is used to replace the Scriptures and to take the place of worship. What need have we of it? Is philosophizing not a dangerous matter? Moreover, you state that the aim of philosophy is to reflect upon the diversity and the totality of the cosmos. Does not theology furnish us with such a view of the cosmos? Are you not attempting to construct a systematic theology by employing a slightly different vocabulary?

To answer such questions it is not enough to point out the fact that Christian thinkers in all centuries have felt the necessity of a Christian system of philosophy. Even capable theologians have sought to develop their own philosophy. In addition to his *Reformed Dogmatics* the famous Dutch theologian Herman Bavinck wrote a *Philosophy of Revelation*.

The following statement of Dr. Abraham Kuyper is of interest at this point: "Contrarily, this again inclined theologians to view philosophy in the strict sense as a hostile phenomenon, and since they themselves did not possess their own Christian philosophy they declared war on all philosophy. Nevertheless, since even in the Christian world it is not possible to live without certain cosmological notions, they filled the gap in their systematic theology with a theology seasoned with philosophy. And this distorted relation can only be terminated if it is seen that philosophy has a completely different task from theology, and if a sharp dis-

---

[1] *Ibid*, p. 21.

tinction is made between Christian and non-Christian philosophy."[1]

Holy Scripture does not make a Christian philosophy superfluous, any more than it makes any special science redundant. God's Word is itself not a science, but it stands above all science, and is the highest norm for every science which seeks truth. The Bible is the divine guide that ought to lead our scientific thought. The guide, however, does not do away with scientific activity, but requires and calls it into existence. The Word of God does not relieve us of the responsibility of examining the great works of God scientifically.

The results of Christian philosophy are not to be found waiting in Scripture. To solve a philosophic problem serious intellectual struggle and study are required. God calls his children to engage in science and philosophy and He is glorified through that philosophy which permits itself to be led by His Word.

Christian philosophy must, however, employ the trowel and the sword. It uses the trowel to achieve more clarity through a scientific examination of God's Wisdom in His works. It uses the trowel to comprehend to a greater extent the truth concerning created reality. And it wields the sword to defeat with its own weapons the spirit of the world which — heavily armed with the implements of science — attacks the Church of Jesus Christ and His Kingdom with ever-increasing strength. It wields the sword to lay bare the falsehoods in which the spirit of the world has enmeshed itself.

Systematic theology can never replace a Christian philosophy as it is only a subdivision of the special science of theology. Its task is to consider the dogma of the Church and to reflect upon its confessions and creeds. It must arrange the revealed truth of God — as comprehended by the Church. Systematics may not appropriate to itself the task of philosophy and engage in an investigation of the created cosmos. Systematics is incompetent to engage in

[1] Abraham Kuyper, *Encyclopaedie* II, p. 568.

science or philosophy, because the dogma of the Church is based only upon the Divine Truth revealed in Scripture. Even though neither science can get along without the other, the fields of investigation of systematics and philosophy are quite distinct. Philosophy is not theology, and vice versa.

The Christian philosophy which seeks to be entirely Biblical must take into consideration the confessions of the Church and can not be indifferent to their theological elaboration. Systematics in turn can labor fruitfully only if it does not derive its presuppositions from pagan philosophy but from Christian philosophy.

5

PHILOSOPHY AND OUR NAIVE EXPERIENCE

THE term *naive experience* usually refers to the experience that we have of concrete reality in our daily life in which we associate with various people and observe a multiplicity of things around us such as plants and animals. In our naive experience we have a naive view of concrete reality. We know how to distinguish a man from an animal and from a plant. We are conscious that family life is something different from Church life. We know that the state possesses other competences than the Church.

We experience the richness and diversity of reality in naive experience. We experience the relations and the coherence through which everything is joined into a magnificent whole. And we are conscious that no single thing is independent of this unity. Nothing exists by itself. Creation is a *totality* in which we are included.

Now what relationship does Christian philosophy bear to naive experience? Does Christian philosophy contradict it, or does the one supplement the other?

Non-Christian philosophy generally sees a contradiction between philosophy and naive experience. The masses who live by naive experience live in a world of illusion and believe reality to be as they see and experience it. Most people never seek to discover true reality and are not concerned with its essence but are content to enjoy a fictitious world which they consider to be the real one. The philosopher knows better. He has learned to see through appearance and knows the essence of the world. He is aware of truth and can distinguish the real from optical illusion, appearance, and fiction. By means of philosophic insight he has acquired a pure vision of reality. It no longer contains any mystery for him. He rules reality with his autonomous reason. Perched upon his pedestal the enlightened philosopher looks down upon the masses and is separated from them by an infinite gulf.

It is no wonder that non-Christian philosophy is so alien to daily life and is so often incompetent to lead and direct it.

The famous system of Immanuel Kant is an example of a philosophy which contradicts our naive experience. Kant believed that it is an open question as to whether or not anything actually exists outside of our mind. And in any case reality outside of our consciousness, *"das Ding an sich"* (the thing in itself), is an unknowable magnitude.

According to Kant the philosopher's task is to demolish to a disordered mass of phenomena the reality which we experience naively. From this mass he must then theoretically construct the real world. The philosopher is aided in this task by our forms of intuition (i.e., time and space), and by our rational forms, (the categories of cause and effect, unity and multiplicity, necessity, and reality, and so on).

According to this Kantian conception, "pure" knowledge can only be acquired with respect to nature or visible reality. And knowledge of anything beyond this is unattainable. Scientific certainty, for example, can never be acquired concerning the existence of God. Man can only conclude that God exists from his own human moral personality, which demands that in the hereafter a "Supreme Being" effectuate a harmony never reached on earth between virtue and happiness. Kant would not be led by Holy Scripture. So he made his own idea of god, who, as the servant of sovereign man, must help him to attain eternal happiness!

Kant held that the philosopher lives in a completely different world from people who live in the concrete world of naive experience, as naive experience deprives the latter of philosophic insight. However, for the Christian philosopher there is no contradiction between philosophy and naive experience. The one supplements the other. The Christian philosopher does not look down upon the masses. The Christian not trained in philosophy does not live in another world. All men live in the same world, and each person, as a part of humanity, has a God-given task to perform.

Philosophy joins forces with naive experience and focuses its attention upon the concrete reality which we experience in our everyday life. The diverse aspects and coherences directly observed in naive experience are subjected to scientific analysis in philosophy. In naive experience the different aspects of reality such as the spatial, organic, psychical, logical, aesthetic and so on, are perceived and discerned as a whole. In philosophy, however, they are separated from each other and are placed in an antithetical relation to the mind and are examined systematically. The things and individualities (for example: family, marriage, school, business) with which we are occupied in naive experience are scientifically inspected in antithetical and analytical thought in order that we can understand their structure.

The explanation that we have given causes the contradiction between philosophy and naive experience to vanish. We do not hold that the former is directed toward the essence of reality and lives in the world of truth while the latter dwells in a world of appearance and fiction.

The scientific view of the created cosmos is not superior to the naive view of everyday experience. In fact philosophy cannot do without naive experience, as it is based upon it. And the naive experience remains always a touchstone of the philosophical truth. A philosopher, in the final analysis, is an ordinary man. He lives as other men and does not eat or sleep philosophically. The only difference between him and other men is that he knows himself to be called to examine the world philosophically by reflecting upon creation in its relation to its origin.

The distinction between naive experience and scientific analysis is that the former places itself concretely within reality, whereas the latter abstracts a distinct aspect of reality and views it in an *antithetical* relation in which a particular aspect is exposed to scientific analysis.

6
The Starting Point and Direction of Philosophy

PHILOSOPHY is scientific reflection over the entire cosmos. Since philosophy itself belongs to the cosmos it must reflect also upon itself. Philosophical thought must be reflective and in critical self-analysis it must answer the question: What is the starting point and the direction of philosophic activity? This question asks, Where can a philosopher find a fixed point from which he can gain a total vision of the cosmos in all its diversity and coherence?

The question of starting point is not a question of scientific method. Where we begin our investigations is of secondary importance. We are now concerned with a primary question which touches the prescientific presuppositions of the scientist. We want to know the point upon which the philosopher can stand in order to view the entire cosmos with the certainty that his observations are true and are not apriori constructions.

Does philosophy proceed from a neutral root? Does it originate in self-sufficient scientific thought? Or does it issue from the religious depths of our existence which can not be neutral? The starting point of philosophy, which Dooyeweerd calls the Archimedean point,[1] proceeds from our religious depths. Anyone who wishes to gain an exact

[1] Archimedes was a Greek physicist who lived about 250 B.C. He reputedly said: "Give me a fixed point and I will move the earth."

view of a landscape must climb a tower from which he can observe the various fields and meadows which constitute it. If he does not gain such a view his perception of the exact position of the fields and of their relations to each other will be distorted. No one can occupy a position outside of himself. Our starting point may not be separate from ourselves, because it must be the starting point of the philosophy in which we are actively engaged. And nobody can naturally go and stand outside himself. Yet an Archimedean point must go above the diversity which is in the cosmos and must transcend it so that we can contemplate it fully. One standing on ground level cannot gain a full view of the landscape.

Such an Archimedean point is to be found only in the heart or the soul of man. Out of the heart, says the Scripture, are the issues of life. The heart is the concentration point, the religious root of our entire human existence. Out of it arise all our deeds, thoughts, feelings and desires. In our heart we give answer to the most profound and ultimate questions, and in our heart our relationship to God is determined. Regeneration, the renewing of the heart by the Holy Spirit, turns us to Christ and redirects the heart from the path of apostasy to God. The heart or soul of man may never be identified with any of our vital functions such as feeling or faith. It is deeper than any vital function, for man transcends in the bond with God all temporal created reality.[1] The heart is the point where the whole

[1]The word heart has various meanings in Scripture. In addition to its literal meaning (a physical organ) and its figurative meaning in an expression such as, "the heart of the sea," the word heart is employed in the following ways.

(1) It signifies the innermost being of man. In this case it is usually contrasted with something external, such as clothes and words. (Joel 2:13, and Jer. 29:13)
(2) It signifies the source of human life. (Jer. 4:18)
(3) It signifies the background of our thoughts. (Ex. 28:10)
(4) The background of all wisdom and reason. (Ps. 90:12)
(5) The background of our words and deeds. (Math. 12:34; 15:19)
(6) The background of our emotional life. (Proverbs 15:13)
(7) And the source of sin. (Gen. 8:21)
(8) It is represented to be the deepest center of our entire temporal

human existence concentrates itself, where man determines his relationship to God. It is not possible to give a scientific conceptual definition of the heart, because as the center of our whole existence, the heart is the deepest (created) presupposition also of our thinking. We can only repeat through faith what God has revealed to us in His Word concerning the center of our life.[1]

The human heart can never be neutral. It loves God or it is hostile to Him. It is renewed or it still lives in apostasy. The heart belongs to the new redeemed humanity or to the world, the totality of unbelievers.

The starting point of Christian philosophy is, therefore, the regenerated heart of the believer. In his heart the believer participates in the Revelation of God in Christ. The Christian is bound in his heart — the center of his life — to the Word of God. Consequently, God's Word occupies a central place in his entire life and must dominate his scientific work. Only in this manner can Christian science serve God and advance the Kingdom of Christ.

The choice of the Archimedean point is not a theoretical deed. It goes beyond science and precedes all scientific activity. It is a religious deed, a choice of position which from its very inception determines the relationship of our philosophy to God. Because of its starting point, philosophy is grounded in religion, in the service of God with all one's heart. Philosophy is not based upon theology or any other special science, nor does it rest upon theoretical thought proclaimed to be sovereign. It rests upon religion and religion spans the entire life of man.

existence. In it the renewing work of the Spirit of God takes place in the believer. (Ps. 51:12)

These different meanings of the word heart illustrate the Biblical doctrine that out of the heart are the issues of life.

[1] F. W. Grosheide writes, in his Commentary on the New Testament, "the heart is the center of all life." Similarly S. Greijdanus calls the heart the innermost, all-dominating center of our existence. He holds that it dominates our thinking, volition, and action to the fullest degree. Also see the work of Dr. F. H. Meyerfeldt: *Het hart in het nieuwe Testament*, p. 196 (Dissertation, Free University 1950).

What we have just said does not apply only to Christian philosophy but it is equally true of philosophy which is non-Christian. The starting point of the latter is also the heart, but a heart which does not participate in the Christ of God. Its starting point is a soul which through unbelief has shut itself off from the Revelation of God in Jesus Christ and is therefore apostate. The apostate heart seeks to find rest and security in any creature which it deifies. It is noteworthy, however, that non-Christian philosophy often refuses to acknowledge its religious starting point. Dooyeweerd never tires of pointing out that by this refusal non-Christian philosophy displays its uncritical character even though it may take great pride in being critical. Non-Christian philosophy is uncritical when it refuses to consider the limits of philosophy honestly.

In spite of the numerous differences between the various systems of non-Christian philosophy, there is one point upon which they are all in agreement. They all claim to choose their point of departure in *pure scientific* thought. For this reason each system claims objectivity in the sense of universal validity independent of the person of the thinker and apart from his heart.

But if one desires to choose his standpoint in scientific thought, then, in order to gain a view of the totality of the cosmos, his thought must first be elevated above all cosmic diversity. To elevate an aspect of reality is essentially to deify it. Non-Christian philosophy begins thus by deifying a created aspect, with this result, that not only the relationships inside the cosmos, but the relationship between cosmos and Creator too is viewed in a wrong light. Therefore non-Christian philosophy is unable to attain truth in all its fulness. This absolutization of scientific thought is in its depths a deed of the human heart. It is an apostate religious deed. The heart that will not seek its repose in Christ seeks it in that which is created (reason) and ends in a lie.

Every philosophy which commences at a point that does not transcend cosmic diversity, but is included within it, we call by the name *immanence-philosophy*, (*immanent* means to dwell within). Human reason belongs to cosmic diversity. Only in his heart does man transcend the diversity of the world. In the heart alone is to be found the real Archimedean point of philosophy.

Dooyeweerd elaborates on this point in his *Encyclopaedie der Rechtswetenschap*. Strictly speaking it is not correct to say that the starting point of philosophy lies in the heart of the *individual* man. The starting point of philosophy is not only anthropological but it is also cosmological. It is a point in which human and cosmic existence concentrate upon the eternal origin of all things. And since the philosopher must participate in this starting point, it can only be the religious community of the human race. However, since the fall and the redemptive work of Christ, a radical irreconcilable antithesis has arisen within this radical religious community. There is a religious antithesis in human life. On the one hand human action strives to achieve the honor and glory of God and is motivated by the Spirit of Christ and God's Word, and on the other hand apostasy obscures the truth. This antithesis is present not only in the heart of every believer, but also in all his works. It appears in all realms of life, in philosophy and in science as well as in all other spheres of human endeavor. Non-Christian immanence-philosophy is religiously determined, in spite of the denial of its adherents. And this religious determination is not individual but communal in nature.

We must still say something about the direction of philosophy. Every one who is active moves toward a goal. And unless it is meaningless philosophy also moves in a direction. Philosophy is religiously determined and therefore it follows one of the two courses which correspond to the two states of the human heart. It is in principle renewed by Christ and then it can lead to God; or it perseveres in apostasy and leads away from Him.

Christian philosophy consciously chooses its direction toward Christ, the Root and Renewer of the entire creation. The Lamb that is slain is worthy to receive the praise and honor and glory of science and philosophy too. Christ renews philosophy as a panegyric to God. Philosophy must point above and beyond itself toward the Origin of all things.

Immanence-philosophy also has a direction and a goal. But because of its starting point it abandons God and Christ. It seeks, for example in the attitude of humanism the honor of sovereign man. Dooyeweerd calls this attitude of humanistic thought, *the ideal of personality*. This ideal of personality is very much in evidence in the philosophy since the Renaissance. Originally modern philosophy sought to achieve the sovereignty of man by following *an ideal of science* (Descartes, Hobbes, and others.). It was thought that man could rule the world by an all-powerful science until the deification of science resulted in his degradation and he became an insignificant atom in the great universe. And this was unbearable to man, so he sought to limit science to the realm of visible nature (Kant) and let man rule unrestrained within the domain of moral freedom. There is a continual conflict in humanism between the *ideal of science* and the *ideal of personality*, a conflict in which first the one and then the other side appears to have the upper hand. And this conflict in immanence-philosophy can never end because the human heart is restless until it finds rest in God.

7

PHILOSOPHY AND THE MEANING-CHARACTER OF REALITY

IN HIS four-volume work, *A New Critique of Theoretical Thought*, Dooyeweerd stresses the *meaning-character* of reality. Everything created possesses meaning or is meaning. In other words the creation is not self-sufficient. Nothing exists by itself or for itself. Everything exists in a coherence with other things. And every aspect of reality points beyond itself toward the other aspects of reality. The creation does not contain any resting point in itself, but it points beyond itself toward the Creator. God has placed all His creatures, including man and societal relationships, in relation to Himself and to each other, thereby endowing creation with *meaning*.

God is the giver of meaning but He is not Himself meaning. He is elevated above all meaning because He alone is self-sufficient. God exists from Himself and for Himself; He alone is Supreme. Everything which is meaning finds its destiny, its final end or goal in Him. "I am the First and the Last," says the Lord Jesus Christ.

The *meaning character* of reality signifies that reality is relative and only God is *Absolute*. All things are related to each other. And as a whole they are related to and dependent upon the Creator and exist for His glory.

Each aspect of reality (number, space, motion, energy, life, feeling, thinking, history, language, society, economy, beauty, law, love) is an *aspect of meaning*. Neither feeling, nor thought, nor any other aspect may be set off by itself. If this isolation is attempted, the coherence of reality is rent, a mere abstraction is retained, and God, the giver of meaning, the origin and the goal of all things, is lost sight of and is no longer praised because of His works.

Every aspect of the cosmos points to the other aspects. And all the aspects have been created together and are sustained by God in an unbreakable *coherence*. Consequently, every aspect and every part of the cosmos is *meaning*. The cosmos in its entirety points beyond itself toward its *fulness of meaning* or *totality of meaning*, which lies in Jesus Christ, to whom all things in heaven and upon the earth are related. Christ is actively engaged in the liberation of God's world from the *meaning-disturbing* effect of sin. Upon His return all things shall be renewed. In the new heaven and upon the new earth the meaning-character of creation will again shine in perfection and the Triune God shall receive the glory.

To anyone acquainted with the Bible it is evident that the preceding section is based upon God's Word. I shall, however, point out one place in particular that teaches that the fulness of meaning of the world's development lies in Jesus Christ. I am referring to the vision which the Apostle John describes in the 5th Chapter of the book of Revelation. In God's hand lies sealed the scroll, the Book of God's eternal decrees which must be effectuated in the world. Yet when the angel asks, Who is worthy to open the book and to loosen its seals? that is to say to effectuate the contents of God's decrees, no one answers the call. Then John began to weep bitterly. For he understood that if the scroll remained shut, then earthly life does not have any meaning. Then the Church has no future, the world will perish and all things will disappear in the eternal night of God's judgment.

John wept until one of the twenty-four elders, a representative of Christ's Church, pointed to the Lion of the tribe of Judah, the Root of David, the Lamb of God in the midst of the throne (He has the power) and in the midst of the four beasts (He is the center of the whole creation) and in the midst of the elders (He is the mediator of His Church). This Lamb is worthy to open the book. As He took it out of God's right hand, the elders broke out in a hymn of joy and were joined by the angels and all creatures present in singing praise to God and the Lamb.

Now sin entered into the world as the great disturber of meaning. The man who is under the power of sin has withdrawn his heart from his Creator, has turned his life's direction away from God, and — living in apostasy — he tries to pull the entire creation down with him. Apostate man has forgotten how to seek the things which are above but he finds no rest in creation. Common grace, the goodness of God over all people, has a restraining influence but it is not enough to renew the heart. Consequently if the sinner does not learn to repent through God's renewing grace in Jesus Christ, if he does not return to God, then he perishes in darkness and does not discover the true meaning of his existence.

God has even included sin in His eternal decree, and He causes it to work for His glory. There is no dualism attached to the final end of God's works, no duality between the fulness of meaning and the disruption of meaning. For even the place of outer darkness — though in a negative way — will give praise to God's holiness and justice throughout all eternity.

Philosophy must ever be concerned with the meaning-character of reality. Philosophy is not a special science which theoretically investigates a specific aspect of the cosmos without regard for other aspects. On the contrary to investigate scientifically the coherence of meaning in the works of God, philosophy seeks to view each aspect of reality in connection with other aspects and in relation to the whole.

Philosophy that is conscious of its true calling answers questions concerned with the "whence" and the "where to" of all things, the questions concerned with the origin of creation and with its *totality* of meaning and meaning-fulfillment. These questions can be truly answered only by a radically Christian philosophy.

It alone subjects itself to the authority of Divine Revelation, in which the Lord reveals to us the meaning of all His works, "Thou, Lord, art worthy to receive the glory and the honor and the power, for thou hast created all things and they exist through thy will and have been created by it."

In these ultimate questions and answers philosophy points beyond itself. And this is the religious apriori of philosophy, its basic idea. Dooyeweerd and Vollenhoven call it the *Cosmonomic-idea*.[1] God, the Sovereign Creator,

---

[1] The question has been raised as to whether it would not be better to speak of the idea of creation instead of the idea of cosmic law. Let us not set up a contradiction that does not exist. We employ the term *"Wetsidee"* or *Cosmonomic-Idea* because it is more precise, and because it includes the idea of creation. The word *cosmonomic-idea* radically severs the very possibility of ascribing sovereignty to any created thing. For the creature aspect that is subject to God's law does not possess any sovereignty proper to itself.

has placed His creation in a *cosmic law order*. By means of it the coherence between the different aspects of things and the relations of reality are determined. (We shall later examine this point in detail.)

Dooyeweerd and Vollenhoven contend that every philosophy is grounded in a certain *Cosmonomic-idea*. Every philosophy has a prescientific conception concerning the origin and the fulfillment of meaning of reality. Philosophy cannot exist without a religious apriori. Non-Christian or immanence philosophy irrevocably *absolutizes* and deifies a part or aspect of the created cosmos. It seeks the origin and the fulfillment of meaning of the cosmos within scientific thought itself. Thus scientific thought about one of the many aspects of the cosmos is elevated above all temporal meaning and honored as divine.

The deification of scientific thought therefore takes on various forms. Whenever scientific thought occupied with the natural aspects of reality is deified, (e.g., number, space, motion, energy and life), various naturalistic systems result which try to explain reality in terms of its natural aspects by applying the method of the natural sciences to all the other aspects, and thus reducing them to natural aspects. However, when the deification of scientific thought occurs with respect to thought concerned with the psychical aspect, a psychologism results which thinks it can explain everything psychologically. Logicism, the deification of logical thought, and historicism, the deification of historical thought, occur in the same manner. A whole list of mutually conflicting systems could be given. They are all erroneous and put us in mind of the Scripture verses, "See, they have rejected the Lord, What wisdom can they then have?"

In order to attain truth — which makes us free — philosophy must refrain from violating the first commandment; it must not erect false gods.

8
THE ANTITHESIS IN PHILOSOPHY

WE HAVE repeatedly referred to immanence or non-Christian philosophy in the preceding section. In its *basic idea*, this unscriptural philosophy rejects the truth of God's Word and is consequently in a direct antithetical opposition to Christian philosophy. Its solutions and its very formation of problems are unacceptable to Christian philosophy. For the manner in which questions are asked and the issues considered determine to a large extent the problems that are to be contemplated. Very often the Christian and the non-Christian philosopher are not in any basic agreement as to the nature of the questions to be discussed. Some questions raised by the non-Christian philosopher are devoid of meaning and others must be posed differently.

The reformation of philosophy is a continual process, and for the continuing of it it is necessary to see clearly the antithesis, so that we can learn to avoid any synthesis of Biblical principles and motives with those derived from non-Christian philosophy. Too often such a synthesis has been made with disastrous consequences to the Christian position in science.

To every Christian who walks according to the Word of God, it should be evident that the line of demarcation dividing humanity does not suddenly disappear in the field of science. The world is divided into a camp of believers (the city of God) and a camp of unbelievers (*civitas terrena*). Science is not neutral with respect to these two opposing camps. It does not exist by itself but is religious in its background. Science arises out of the human heart and every human heart has chosen for or against the Christ. Science is directed to God or away from Him. It is performed in obedience to the Covenant or it rejects God entirely. There is no middle course.

And what we have said of science applies to philosophy as well. If philosophy rejects the light of Scripture, there is no other course open to it but to seek its directive light in man and to try to solve the most basic problems with this false light. Thus in spite of its diverse starting points and different answers regarding the origin and the nature of the cosmos, all immanence philosophy must be rejected by Christian philosophy. The heart that has denied the truth cannot attain it. Fallen man cannot reach God, and Jesus Christ is the Way, the Truth, and the Life.

And, if because of a negative religious choice, one commits an initial error in answering the basic questions, subsequent answers to other questions cannot escape the detrimental influence of the original error. Consequently, this Christian philosophy fundamentally disavows the validity of all synthesis philosophy, and rejects any attempt to unite the basic motives of immanence philosophy with ideas derived from Scripture. In the Christian era such syntheses have not only been harmful to the development of the Church but have equally retarded the development of the Christian life in all spheres. In his work entitled, *Het Calvinisme en de Reformatie der Wijsbegeerte*, p. 110, Vollenhoven treats in detail the attempts that have been made to effectuate such a synthesis.

Among the apologists of the first centuries of the Christian Church, there was a tendency to effectuate a synthesis between Christian and non-Christian thought. Justin Martyr, Tertullian, and others sought points of contact in the philosophy of the Stoics. And others such as Origen, Cyprian, and Augustine tried to unite neo-Platonic and late-Platonic ideas with Christian truths. The struggle to achieve a synthesis was still stronger in Medieval thinking.[1] Up until and including the 13th century, the attempt was made to unite the basic motives of the Old Germanic life with those of the Church Fathers. Anselm of Canterbury, Abelard, Bernard of Clairvaux are representatives of this group. Vollenhoven calls the period subsequent to the 14th century the period of the decline of synthesis. In it the idea of Augustine that philosophy can discover truth only by the

---

[1] See *De Geest der Middeleeuwen* by F. Sassen in, *Europese Geest*, 3rd ed., 1948.

light of Scripture was abandoned. Medieval thought reached its zenith, however, in the conflict between realism and anti-realism — think of such men as Thomas Aquinas, Duns Scotus, and William of Occam. An intrinsic self-sufficiency with respect to Divine revelation is ascribed to philosophy during this period. Revelation was reckoned to the *sphere of grace* and philosophy to the *sphere of nature*, which was considered as the preparatory step to the sphere of grace. The decline of synthesis in this manner was not a gain, as it did not pave the way for the antithesis between Biblical and non-Biblical thought, but substituted for it the false distinction between nature and grace. And in place of a philosophy founded upon God's Word, philosophical systems arose which were still further removed from the light of Holy Scripture. It is not surprising that late Medieval thought paved the way for humanism, which derived its formation from the ideal of ancient pagan philosophy.

In the period of declining synthesis, the union of Biblical and ancient pagan motives continued. The reformation period brought with it the first recognition of the irreconcilable antithesis between Christian and non-Christian thought. It saw that there could be no harmony of thinking between those who recognized God's Word as normative and those who maintained the dogma of the autonomy of human reason. Luther never entirely departed from the Medieval distinction between nature and grace. He openly confessed his bond with Occam (*"Ich bin von Occam's Schule"*).[1] Calvin was the first reformer to break with all synthesis and — though he has not left us a system of philosophy — he cleared the way to a truly Biblical philosophy, because he subjected scientific thought to the norm of Holy Scripture. After Calvin the passion for synthesis again arose within the camp of Christian science. The attempt was made to join such men as Descartes and other representatives of rationalism, who deified reason by making it the Ruler of the total life, and separated it from any limi-

[1] "I am from the school of Occam."

tation. Man's reason was not even limited by the Word of God. Man was considered to be sovereign. People "believed" in the Reason. In reaction some sought comfort in pietism and substituted the individual piety of the human heart for the God of the Covenant who alone is the very Foundation of the life of the believer.

One of the many results of this covetous longing for the "flesh pots of Egypt" was the intrinsic decline of the Church. In the Netherlands it resulted in the joyous acceptance of the pernicious principles of the French Revolution. However, through God's goodness, a reformation of Christian science took place during the last century in the Netherlands. It was Abraham Kuyper who returned to Calvin and in keeping with his spirit, bowed before the absolute authority of the Word of God. With eloquent force Kuyper proclaimed the sovereignty of Christ over all spheres of life, including science. Kuyper's work does not entitle his followers to cease to be vigilant. The fight must be continued. In our own day the urge toward synthesis has in no wise diminished. Think of the fascinating influence exerted upon many by Kierkegaard, by the theology of Karl Barth and Bultmann; by the philosophical movement of the existentialists: Heidegger, Jaspers and Sartre. And consider the post-war trend in many Christian countries, which denies any antithesis in human life and is outspokenly in favor of effectuating a union between Christianity and humanism.

Since we repudiate all synthesis and stress the antithesis between Biblical and non-Biblical philosophy, the question naturally rises as to whether or not there is any value in studying the history of non-Christian thought. Such study is profitable for several reasons. It teaches us where we must not seek the solutions to philosophic problems, and it gives us an exact view of the spiritual movement of our time and its origins in history. Furthermore, it causes us to recognize that non-Christians have discovered distinctions and coherences which actually exist in the rich diversity of God's world. But, and this is what is fatal, non-Christians transform *detailed truth* into a lie by placing it in a larger context composed of false problems and inexact solutions.

Even in Reformed circles conceptual schema and terms often appear in a sense which has originated in non-Christian philosophy (e.g., form and matter, body and soul, substance, subject, object). This constitutes a latent danger and can easily give rise to conflicts in our own camp. Such terms in their original non-Christian or disputable significance arrest the further progress of the reformation of philosophy by leading us into blind alleys, and involving us in antinomies and unnecessary confusion. They deprive Christ of the glory that should be given Him in philosophy.

This brings our preliminary questions to a close. We hope that we have made clearer the necessity of a philosophy which subjects itself to God's Word. We are now in a position to describe the Christian philosophy developed by Dooyeweerd and Vollenhoven.

CHAPTER II

THE THEORY OF COSMIC MODALITIES OR LAW-SPHERES

9

THE MAIN DISTINCTION

WE SHALL follow the same method as Dooyeweerd follows in his four volume work, *A New Critique of Theoretical Thought*. Our first consideration is, therefore, the theory of the modal aspects or modalities of the cosmos (law-spheres).

All philosophy has a religious starting point. Christian philosophy, based upon the regenerate heart of the believer, which is enlightened by the light of the divine revelation of the Word of God, is constructed upon *the distinction between God and the cosmos.*

Scripture begins with the well-known, but pregnant words: "In the beginning God created the heaven and the earth." God is the Almighty Eternal Creator; the cosmos is created and temporal. God is Self-sufficient; the cosmos depends upon its Creator and exists from Him and through Him and therefore possesses the character of meaning. Meaning is the mode of being of all creatures, their very nature or essence, because in "meaning" all created things point out to the Creator, their Origin and Purpose.

The first verse of the Bible expresses a secondary distinction between the heaven and the earth; between what is above and what is below. Heaven is the place where God has established His throne and where since His ascension Christ rules all things. The dead in Christ remain in heaven until His second coming. The earth is the sphere of human action; man must subdue and replenish it in a process of historical development. This is the cultural task of mankind. Since the fall, a conflict is waged on earth between the Kingdom of God and the kingdom of darkness. At His second coming Christ will terminate this period of history, which is marked by imperfection, and after the dead are raised and judgment has taken place, heaven and earth will be united.

As the Creator, God is a Sovereign Ruler. All creation is absolutely dependent upon Him. He has placed it *under law*. This Divine law is not limited to the Ten Commandments. God established many other laws. In Genesis 8:22, God promised Noah and his family that nature would conform to a constant law, "in seed time and harvest, cold and heat, summer and winter, day and night."

When we say that God has placed His entire creation under law, we include under the term "law," all Divine ordinances and norms which have their origin in the Sovereign Will of the Creator and apply to the creation. The entire cosmos is subject to Divine law. All creation must obey its Maker. God is above law and is not subject to it. Law is the expression of His Will. He is the Law-giver.

Calvin employed the expression, *"Deus legibus solutus,"* God is free from the law. Calvin let it be explicitly known that this does not mean that "God stands outside of law," *Deus ex lex*, as William of Occam maintained. Occam thought that God does not hold Himself to the laws which He has established. And the fact that God stands above the law may not be interpreted as arbitrariness in God (as is done by Karl Barth when he speaks of "God's free power"). God holds Himself to His Sovereign laws but only the creation is subject to them.

From this main distinction between the Law-giver and the subjected creature it follows that science, because it belongs to the cosmos, is subject to the law of theoretical thought. It can, therefore, only examine that which belongs to the creation. Law is the *boundary between God and the cosmos*.

No creature can exceed it; all must remain on this side of the boundary. And if this border is violated, an aspect of the cosmos is deified. Science ought to examine the entire cosmos and penetrate to the outer limits and then it ought to stop and resist every speculation.

God Himself is never the object of investigation. Christian theology examines the revelation of God's Word. Since the fall this revelation has become revelation of grace and so entered into the cosmos. It belongs to the creation and possesses like all other things an historical aspect, a beginning, a development, and an end. The Bible belongs to temporal things, but this does not imply that the truth revealed in Holy Scripture is transitory.

The thesis that the law is the boundary between God and the cosmos is repeatedly misunderstood and is sometimes rejected on the ground that since God is infinite and unlimited, He cannot have any boundary. Such an argument is mere quibbling. We confess the Scriptural doctrine that God is Omnipotent and Eternal and can in nowise be subjected to limits. Yet on the basis of the same Word of God we also confess that the creation is not God. The creation remains eternally distinct from its Maker just because it is governed and sustained by the Omnipotence of God.

Anyone who after serious consideration reaches the conclusion that he must reject the thesis that the law is the boundary between God and the cosmos, abandons the very foundation of Christianity, and no matter what theory he then seeks to develop, it cannot claim to be Christian. When we say that the law is the boundary between God and the cosmos, we simply mean that it distinguishes the Creator from the creation. A creature can never exceed his creaturehood. He is always subject to divine law and cannot traverse this boundary. Divine law does not restrict the Creator; His infinity transcends all limits. And in the second place this boundary must never be thought of as spatial. Even in creation there is a good deal that exceeds the spatial. (See our later treatment of the cosmic law order.) Moreover we are not implying that the distinction we have made exhausts the difference between God and the creation, but it is of primary importance to philosophy.

In examining the various philosophical systems we must ask, do they recognize the boundary between God and the Cosmos and fully take into account the consequences of this recognition? All non-Biblical philosophy can be classified according to the answer that it gives to this primary question. Vollenhoven developed the following system of classification.

There are philosophers who deny and philosophers who affirm the existence of a boundary between God and the cosmos. We call the former monists and the latter dualists. This main division does not tell us all we wish to know. It makes a difference whether or not a monist denies the existence of God or the existence of the world. If he does not wish to deny the existence of either the world or God, then as a monist, he must either place God in the cosmos or resolve the cosmos in God. Consequently, there are four kinds of monism.

1. Atheism denies the existence of God and retains only the world.

2. A-cosmism denies the existence of the cosmos.

3. Pan-cosmism subordinates God to the world and places Him in the creation.

4. Pantheism resolves the world in God.

Dualists also differ among themselves. Anyone who does not honor the boundary as God has prescribed it in His Word either places the line of demarcation too high or too low. In the first instance a part of Divine Being is ascribed to the world of created things, and in the second something created is deified. There are, as clearly appears, two types of dualism: *partial cosmism* which places a part of Divine Being within the cosmos, (e.g., Modernism which denies the Deity of the Son and the Holy Spirit), and *partial theism* which places a portion of the cosmos in God by drawing the boundary line between God and the cosmos through the cosmos. The cosmos is divided into a higher and a lower sphere. That higher part is elevated above the lower one and is deified. God must share His Sovereignty with a portion of creation. Partial theism has found adherents among Christians in all ages. The Roman Catholic doctrine of the worship of Mary (Mariolatry), and of transubstantiation (the change of the essence of the bread and wine in communion), and the Lutheran doctrine of the deification of Christ's human nature during His ascension are partial theistic, as is the idea that the soul of man is a divine element which is higher than the body. The idea that reason belongs to a higher order, since God is absolute reason, is also an expression of partial theism. And the error of antinomianism, which places the Christian above the law, is a further example of its influence.

All of these trends and theories do not do justice to the sovereignty of God, who is the Only and Real One. Christian philosophy may not unite with any such view. It must for the sake of truth avoid synthesis and bear in mind the antithesis between Christian and non-Christian thought.

This Christian philosophy does not wish to define its viewpoint as theism. The conception, that theism is the correct middle way between pantheism and deism, is very well known, but there are serious objections to this traditional formula.

The terms deism and pantheism are not sufficient to describe the many views which do not recognize or which incorrectly comprehend the boundary between God and the cosmos. Moreover truth is not achieved by steering a middle course between two errors. And from a philosophical point of view the term theism is inadequate to indicate the philosophical conception which is based on the Bible.

10

THE COSMIC LAW ORDER

THE Christian philosopher must start with the revealed truth that the Sovereign Creator has placed His entire creation under law. The term *cosmic law order* expresses the fact that everything created is subject to the laws of God. We speak of a *law order* because we recognize a *multiplicity* of divine laws established by the Creator in a specific regular order. Every part of creation belongs to several law-spheres. Therefore, everything exhibits as many aspects as there are law-spheres.

When Reformed philosophy speaks of a *law-sphere* it intends to express the fact that various types of laws can be distinguished. Not all laws are of the same nature. A law of logic is of a different sort from a juridical law; and the law of gravity is different from the law of metabolism or reproduction. A law of beauty cannot be compared with a law of faith. Now all laws of one specific sort, taken together, form a law-sphere.

Correlative to the term "law-sphere" is the term *"meaning-aspect"* or, for shortness' sake, only: aspect. There are as many meaning-aspects as there are *law-spheres*. If someone speaks about the size of a thing, he contemplates it from a different perspective than if he were to discuss its price, age or aesthetic value. The various meaning-aspects of a thing arise because a thing belongs to all the law-spheres, or otherwise expressed, because each thing is traversed by all law-spheres. There is a specific meaning-aspect of creation correlative to each law-sphere. We can distinguish 14 law-spheres and thus 14 meaning-aspects in creation. (Other terms which this philosophy employs for meaning-aspects or law-spheres are: aspects and modalities. The word aspect is readily understood, but the term modality has the additional connotation that all law-spheres are particular revelations of a deeper basic religious unity, namely of the human heart which participates in the radical religious communion of the human race.)

Prof. Dooyeweerd uses the term "ontical apriori" to designate law-sphere, modality, or aspect. A law-sphere is apriori as a constant foundational structure of empirical reality. Law-spheres, modalities, or aspects form the foundation upon which are enacted all changing phenomena in reality. And, as such, they possess an ontical character, and are not as Kant affirmed, grounded in subjective consciousness but in the created temporal order of reality.

The cosmic law order is not an order of separate laws.

It is an order of law-spheres, an order of various sorts of laws: mathematical laws, laws of motion, biotic laws, laws of thought, laws of beauty, and so on. The cosmic law order is withdrawn from human arbitrariness; it is determined by God, who from the very beginning subjected His creation to His laws. This law order is not invented by science but is only systematically discovered by it. Even the man of naive experience is aware of various sorts of conformity to law. He knows, for example, that the law of gravity, as a "law of nature," is qualitatively distinct from the law of supply and demand. He knows that the aesthetical law of harmony is specifically different from the norm of faith of Holy Scripture. No one can change these laws. They are unchangeable in time but not because they are eternal. It is not accurate to speak of eternal laws. They are unchangeable because the cosmic law order is the *sine qua non*, the basic possibility of all temporal change.

God has established His laws over created things in a cosmic order. According to their different aspects created things belong to the different law-spheres and are traversed by them. The laws valid in one sphere are of the same sort; the laws of another sphere are different in nature from the laws in other spheres.

Laws exist to be obeyed, and all creatures are *subject* to them or under their control. The term "subject," expressing here submissiveness to the law, is not to be identified with our ego, person, or analytical function. A stone, for example, is *subject* to the physical law of gravity. And in addition to being subject to the laws valid for a stone, an animal is subject to the biological laws of metabolism and reproduction and to the psychical laws of feeling. And, in addition to being subject to physical, biological and psychical laws, man is also subject to laws of thought, language, history, and so on.

Every creature, as a creature, is subjected to God, the Creator of all. We have already named different sorts of laws which belong to different law-spheres. The law of gravity belongs to another sphere than the analytical laws which apply to human thinking. The laws pertaining to reproduction, circulation and digestion are of an entirely different nature or modality from the cultural laws of history or the laws of love pertaining to ethical life.

We must now examine the law-spheres in more detail and clarify the comments that we have made. In naive experience man lives among sensorily perceivable concrete things. Naive thought is enriched and deepened in science. Science abstracts specific aspects from concrete reality and isolates them. Biology, as a science, is concerned with the vital functions of men, animals, and plants. When biology examines a horse, for example, it may be concerned with its conformation, vital functions, and derivation, but it is indifferent to its commercial value and to whether it is a saddle or a work horse. Biology does not examine a concrete horse which plows a field but it abstracts a specific aspect from a concrete horse. It abstracts the biotic aspect (bios means life) and investigates a horse only insofar as it obeys and is subject to the laws of the biotic law-sphere, established by God for the organic life of men, animals, and plants.

This illustration demonstrates that the various sciences: mathematics, physics, biology, psychology, logic, history, linguistics, sociology, economics, aesthetics, jurisprudence, ethics and theology do not occupy themselves with the full reality of concrete things as they are naively experienced. The sciences investigate the different aspects of creation, the different law-spheres which traverse cosmic reality. Every law-sphere possesses its own complex of laws. All creatures in the aspect corresponding to a particular law-sphere are subject to the laws of this sphere. A man, an animal, a plant and a stone are equally subject to the law of gravity, a law of the physical law-sphere. A man stumbles to the ground just as readily as a stone falls. However, only man can receive an injury from his fall and feel the ensuing pain. He alone is a *subject* in the biotic and psychical law-spheres, hence, his wound and pain. A stone does not function as a subject in the biotic and psychical law-spheres.

Animals and men, however, are subject to both biological and psychical laws. A plant is a biotic thing; it possesses a subject function in the biotic law-sphere, but it does not feel pain and therefore does not function as a subject in the psychical sphere.

Notice that there are law-spheres in which a specific thing does not function as a *subject* but then as an *object*. A plant, for example, does not possess a psychical subject function; nevertheless, as the object of our sensory perception, it has a psychical function, as an *object*. Subsequently we shall discuss *object-functions* in more detail. For the present it is sufficient to note that the reality of a thing does not prematurely cease in any particular law-sphere. In principle every creature functions in every modality or law-sphere, either as subject or partly as object and partly as subject.

Not only are the various sciences concerned with the various modalities, but everyone experiences them in his daily life and directly comprehends the difference between a legal fact, a crime for example, and an act of love. Everyone is immediately aware of the difference between an economic act, such as the purchase of a book, and an act of thought, such as the thoughtful assimilation of the book's contents. Science does not create the law-spheres. God has endowed creation with these various aspects of meaning. God has inserted all things in law-spheres and has orderly criss-crossed the cosmos with modalities.

The various modalities are not first distinguished by science. Non-scientific thought is also aware of them. No one ever confuses a number with a circle or attributes feeling or reason to a stone. No one seeks the beauty of a picture in the canvas upon which it is painted or desires the church to regulate traffic.

All aspects of reality are intuitively encountered in naive experience. In philosophy this encounter is deepened to a theoretical insight into the various law-spheres. Philosophy reflectively analyzes and separates the law-spheres and seeks to explain them systematically.

Conclusively we can state: *the law-spheres are God-arranged complexes of laws correlative to the many by God created aspects of cosmic reality, to which laws all creatures have to obey.*

11
The Cosmic Law Order (Cont.)

Every creature is, as subject, subjected to the laws which God has established for its existence. Insofar as they are subject to God, that means to His law, all creatures are alike. And in this respect it is indifferent whether or not the creatures in question are plants, animals, men, tools, art objects, families, factories, or churches.

Numbers are not things but only functions of things; they are as subjects, subjected to the laws of one modality. Numbers obey arithmetical or numerical laws. Spatial figures such as a line or a circle are not things either, but are subjected to the laws of two modalities, the laws of the numerical and of the spatial spheres. A physical thing such as a stone is, as subject, subjected to the laws of motion. And a plant, as subject, is controlled by the laws of the biotic sphere. An animal in addition, is controlled by the psychical laws of feeling. Besides all the laws just mentioned, man is, as subject, subjected to the laws of the additional modalities: to the laws of thought, history, language, society, economy, aesthetics, and to juridical, ethical, and pistical law (the law of faith).

Every creature, insofar as it is not an object, (we will elaborate upon this directly) is classified in relation to the highest law-sphere in which it functions as subject. A stone is a physical thing, a plant a biotic thing, and an animal a psychical thing. However, it would be just as incorrect to call a number an arithmetical thing, and a spatial figure a spatial thing, as it would be to consider beauty and patience as things. Numbers and spatial figures are not logical constructions or the products of human thought which exist only in our thought. God has created all things with a numerical and spatial aspect.

It is also incorrect — although for other reasons — to call man a pistical thing. Man is the sole creature that cannot be characterized by any specific temporal function. In his heart he concentrates all temporal functions into a spiritual point, his ego, his self.

For the sake of completeness it is already mentioned here: there are things which we do not classify according to the highest modality in which they function as subject but which we classify according to the last modality in which they function as object. All things which are formed through human activity, such as tools and art objects, are classified according to their object functions and can be called *objective* things because their existence is determined by an object-function. For example, to classify a painting according to the last sphere in which it functions as subject is to misunderstand its real character, which is to be found in the aesthetical aspect. We shall treat this point in more detail, in a later chapter concerning the structure of temporal things.

Now if the reader has digested the preceding he will be in a position to understand that a distinction must be made between the *law-side* and the *subject-side* of every law-sphere. The law-side and the subject-side stand in an unbreakable correlative coherence. The one points toward the other. Laws would be meaningless without subjects which obey them; and there could be no subjects without laws to determine their existence and function. Not to be under law would be to be as God. Recall the lying words of the serpent in paradise: "Do not be bothered about God's law; elevate yourself above it and you will be as God." But to be like God is unattainable to a creature. Even in apostasy from God, creatures remain subject to His law without which there would be no sin, judgment, or punishment.

Furthermore, the correlation, the mutual connection between law and subject, implies that one can not be reduced to the other. A law is never subject and a subject may never be elevated to a law. A person who disregards the Word of God, that has to rule our whole life, and considers himself to be his own law, opposes the divine law-order and places in his thinking — of course not really — the subject on the law-side. He sins against the first commandment of the decalogue by constructing other gods.[1]

The cosmic law-order has its origin in the Sovereign Will of the Almighty Creator and is composed of a series of law-spheres which do not arbitrarily intermingle but which have been placed with their laws and subjects in a specific order.

How can philosophy discover the order of the law-spheres? How can we scientifically establish that the sphere of number precedes the sphere of space or that the biotic sphere precedes the psychical, and not vice versa? The cosmic order can be established if we notice an increasing complicatedness in the order of the various law-spheres. The more complicated follow the less complicated so that the simplest sphere is the first and the most complicated is the last.

To determine the sequence of the modalities, it is therefore necessary to conduct a logical analysis to determine exactly which are more and which are less complicated. Let me give here an example.

The numerical sphere is the first, since it is the simplest. It is only concerned with the *numerable,* as a specific aspect of things. The numerable is expressed in numbers. The people of a large group are not only numerable. They also occupy a certain place in space, are living, and possess certain feelings; they think, speak, and have an aesthetic,

---

[1]This is entirely different from what Paul said of the heathen in Romans 2:14. When Paul said the heathen are a law unto themselves, the apostle refers to the remnant of law of God which originally had been written in the human heart and is still present among the heathen. However, we are referring to those who live in the delusion of autonomy or self-determination.

ethical and faith function. In other words they possess functions in all modalities. Now we can abstract or withdraw various *aspects* from the members of the group. But if we think away their faith, nationality, language, ideas, feelings, motion and spatiality, we still retain their number. And if we remove their number too, there is no aspect or function, there is totally nothing that remains. It is impossible to think away their number and retain their spatiality, motion, or any other aspect. To speak of a group of people without number indicates metaphorically its immense size.

The second modality, the spatial, is more complicated. It presupposes the numerical aspect. Space does not exist without multiplicity. We can always indicate a certain number of points on a line or divide the line into a number of segments. Space presupposes also a number of dimensions.

The third modality presupposes the preceding modalities. A physical thing, such as a stone, is not only subject to the laws of motion, heat, gravity and so on, but it occupies space and is numerable.

With respect to the later law-spheres, it is not difficult to see that the linguistical sphere of the language precedes the social sphere. Without a spoken or a sign language, without symbols, social intercourse would not be possible. The ability of man to express his thoughts in sensory signs and symbols makes social intercourse possible. Thus the social modality presupposes the linguistical, and the cosmic order cannot be reversed.

We shall try to make this clear by one additional example. We will show that the aesthetic law-sphere must necessarily follow the economic modality, and not vice versa. The economic modality is distinguished by *saving* and *thrift*. Things are economic objects only if they are not present in an unlimited supply and are not accessible to everyone. The free air, for instance, is not an economic object. To be an economic object a thing must be scarce so that its possession is valued. Moreover, if an economic undertaking is to be remunerative, then it must be as thrifty as possible. Well then, everyone who possesses an insight into what is beautiful and harmonious must directly agree that only that is aesthetic which arouses in us a feeling of harmony and is devoid of redundancy and excessiveness. All frills and unnecessary trimming diminish the beauty of an art work. Thus it is evident that the aesthetic sphere rests upon the economic. Beauty presupposes economy.

We are now ready to present a diagram of the modal aspects, but before doing so it must be stated that Dooyeweerd and Vollenhoven emphasize the fact that they do not wish their system to be considered closed nor unchangeable. They both wish to allow for the possibility that in the future it may be necessary to add other modalities.

DIAGRAM OF THE LAW-SPHERES

Boundary between God and Cosmos

	pistical sphere (faith)
	ethical sphere (love)
	juridical sphere (judgment)
	aesthetic sphere (harmony)
	economic sphere (saving)
A	social sphere (social intercourse)
	linguistic sphere (symbolical meaning)
	historical sphere (cultural development)
	analytical sphere (thought)
	psychical sphere (feeling) **B**
	biotic sphere (life) **C**
	physical sphere (energy) **D**
	kinematic sphere (motion)
	spatial sphere (space)
	arithmetical sphere (number)

This system of law-spheres is not brand new. In the foreword to the third volume of his work, *A New Critique of Theoretical Thought,* Dooyeweerd writes: "This philosophy is not entirely new in its starting point. It builds upon the foundation of the ages. Thinkers of all periods have distinguished various aspects, even though they did not call them law-spheres. A critical history of philosophy must show the extent to which previous thinkers correctly comprehended the diversity of the cosmic law order and it must show their errors, and misinterpretations."

The explanation of the Schema given is as follows. The uppermost thick horizontal line represents the boundary between God and the cosmos. Everything above this boundary is God and everything underneath is the cosmos, which is subject to God's law. This is of course no spatial division, but a law division. For God is above all His creatures and with His divine power He also dwells in His creation; but as Law-Giver He is only above His laws and never under them.

The horizontal compartments represent the law-spheres which traverse concrete reality in a cosmic order. A man is vertically portrayed by the vertical line A. The smaller vertical columns are schematical representations of an animal (B), a plant (C), and a physical thing (D). The lowest law-sphere is the least complicated and the highest the most complicated. The latter presuppose all earlier spheres.

12

Sphere-Sovereignty

THE principle that each sphere is sovereign was developed by Abraham Kuyper. Kuyper maintained that the sovereignty of each sphere is a normative structural principle to guide us in the construction of such relationships of human society as the church and school. Kuyper defended this position against those who had lost sight of the principal difference between the church, the state, the school, science, and industry. Kuyper and his followers tenaciously contended that each sphere possesses its own laws independently of the other spheres. Each sphere of life has received from God its own peculiar nature. The competences of one sphere may not be transferred or appropriated by any other sphere. A government, for example, is instituted by God to exercise and maintain justice on the basis of the sword. However, it is not competent to interfere with the internal questions of science or the affairs of the church. And except in certain instances, such as neglect, it does not have the right to relieve parents of the responsibility of educating their own children. The church, likewise, does not have a voice in the affairs of the state nor a calling to discuss and decide scientific matters.

Many benefits have accrued from the struggle conducted by Kuyper and others. In Holland and abroad this principle has not been forgotten. It is still employed in various activities, in the spheres of science, education, politics, industry, and social movements. The principle of sphere-sovereignty is used to oppose political principles which seek to mix the political scene with ecclesiastical views and to relieve parents of their responsibility for their children's health. It opposes socialization of industry, a state-controlled radio, and it would restrict church controversy to the church.

We accept the principle of the sovereignty of each sphere as a Biblical principle which Christian philosophy must take into account. It can hardly be doubted that this principle is derived from Scripture. There are no particular texts which literally enunciate it, but it runs as a continuous line throughout the Bible. The Bible teaches us that God created all things according to their nature. And in Israel the offices of a prophet, a priest, and a king were sharply delineated. Moreover, when the Lord was on earth He refused to act as a legal judge, and the apostles did not involve themselves officially in the affairs of the state or in the problems of the existing social order. They proclaimed the Word of God and nothing else. The Bible contains basic principles for human society but it does not give the church the task of establishing norms for the internal sphere of the family, state, and economic life.

This philosophy has seen that the sovereignty of the family, industry, state, church, and so on, can be maintained only if we proceed from the sovereignty of each law-sphere. One law-sphere can not be reduced to the other. Each aspect of cosmic reality possesses its own peculiar meaning and laws. And the laws of one aspect do not apply in the same way to the other aspects. A number and a spatial-magnitude, (e.g., a line) are different magnitudes, each possessing its own nature. Number can not be reduced to space, nor can space be derived from number. If such a reduction is attempted an ensuing confusion results from which there is no escape. The same is true of all the other law-spheres. Feeling is essentially different from thinking, and thinking is different from speaking. Social intercourse is other than jurisprudence and love is different from faith. To each of these spheres, God gives specific laws, whose validity does not exceed the limits of the specific law-sphere in question. This is directly evident if we notice, for example, that the law of gravity is valid for physical things and for the physical aspect of all other things whose character is determined by another law-sphere. But it is not valid for our psychical life. (A sensation of pain, and a feeling of desire cannot fall to the ground.) Organic laws, valid for the biotic modality, (e.g., laws of digestion and reproduction), are not valid for concepts of the logical modality. Laws which intrinsically dominate the formation of language are of another nature than the laws of the state. An aesthetic law may not be identified with a social law; an economic law may not be confused with an ecclesiastical creed which is the norm of our faith.

We speak of sovereignty because in the final analysis all norms and laws valid for creation derive their validity from the Sovereign God. The sovereignty of the cosmic laws and norms is a derivative sovereignty; it must be distinguished from the original sovereignty of God. It is **not** absolute. It is a relative sovereignty because of the limits of each particular sphere. Within the borders of a particular modality, only the laws pertaining to that sphere are valid; the laws of other spheres do not apply. If the sovereignty of each sphere is overlooked, confusion and tyranny follow. The attempt to enforce the laws and norms of one sphere in another sphere results in the enslavement rather than in the liberation of life. And this very thing is done when the attempt is made to reduce feeling to thinking, or faith to history. In the latter case it is thought that the Christian faith can only be understood as a mere historical phenomenon of culture, which is coming up one time and afterwards disappears.

The principle of sphere-sovereignty may not be understood as ascribing a certain self-sufficiency to the law-spheres. To do so would not only be guilty of deifying a creature, but it would also make deep clefts between the various spheres and thereby deprive them of their meaning. The creation is in no way self-sufficient. It does not rest in itself but either moves toward the Creator and His Christ or falls away from Him. The law-spheres are aspects of meaning. They point beyond their modal meaning toward other spheres, and in the renewed human heart are directed toward Christ and the Triune God, the Origin of all things. In the foreword to the third volume of the Dutch edition of *A New Critique of Theoretical Thought*, Dooyeweerd pertinently writes, "Anyone who criticizes this Christian Philosophy for possessing a passion for originality does not know what he is saying. Christian philosophy does not have a passion for originality but for the Origin. It drives thought restlessly beyond supposed resting points and points it toward Jesus Christ, its real Origin."

We must also repudiate the contention that is sometimes made in objection to this principle of sovereignty, namely, that the reality of life is divided into compartments, because of a multiplicity of self-sufficient law-spheres. This is not true. Together with the principle of the sovereignty of each sphere, Reformed philosophy recognizes the coherence of the law-spheres. And the boundaries of the spheres are not clefts. It is impossible for one sphere to exist apart from the other. All law-spheres hang together inseparably. Each sphere points to every other sphere. Psychical life, for example, does not exist apart from organic life. Moreover, physical things presuppose space and number, and language without thought is unthinkable, yes, more than that, unreal.

God's creation is a great and rich whole; it is a cosmos in the full sense, an ornament with a rich diversity of meaning and in that diversity many coherences which preserve its unity. However, if we commence to reflect *scientifically* over creation, we must first separate the law-spheres from each other by theoretical abstraction. And in this way we must exchange cosmic continuity for logical discontinuity. This separation occurs only in thought. In reality the continuity continues to exist. As a matter of fact, our thought itself remains enclosed within the cosmic coherence and can never exceed it in self-sufficiency.

We have already said that misjudgment with respect to the sovereignty of each sphere always results in confusion and leads to contradictions in thought. In philosophy, such contradictions are called antinomies, which literally means "a contradiction between laws."[1]

Mathematicians, for example, become involved in such contradictions, if they do not acknowledge numbers to be created by God but consider them solely as the product of human thought. Additional antinomies arise if historians consider history as an aspect of organic life and twist all facts into the framework of the dogma of evolution. Moreover, further antinomies spring into existence if the attempt is made to explain law, ethics, social intercourse,

---

[1] Dooyeweerd considers that an antinomy occurs in science alone. He says, "Law in its foundational sense of cosmic law order of the modal law-spheres can not be antinomical. Nor can the laws of the different temporal modalities contradict each other. All theoretical antinomies arise in theoretical thought, involving itself in self-contradictions when it makes theoretical judgments. It forms then an erroneous conception of the coherence in the modal diversity of the cosmos and contradictions thus appear to arise between the various laws."

and faith, psychologically. Additional antinomies result if in Neo-Kantian fashion these modalities are considered solely as the product of analytical thought. Such antinomies result when the sovereignty, the independence and *irreducibleness* of the different modalities are denied. In that case the difficulties can only become unraveled by returning with one's heart and thought to the obedience to the divine revelation in Scripture and creation.

Real antinomies do not exist in the cosmic law order. "In due time God made each thing good." Even sin did not destroy the divine law order. Antinomies are always evidence of the fact that the sovereignty of a modality has been scientifically violated. They can be avoided if a thinker is willing to accept the cosmic world order and acknowledge creation as the first principle and guide to his reason. As pain is the sign of danger in organic life, antinomies inform us that we have exceeded the proper limits of the cosmic modalities.

Christian philosophy has developed the *principium exclusae antinomiae*, the principle which excludes antinomies. If a scientist is confronted by two mutually contradictory thoughts, he can be certain that he has violated a modal boundary and has disregarded the principle of sphere-sovereignty. The cosmos is a unity because it has been created. And because it is this unity which is the object of scientific reflection, the scientist can never be confronted by intrinsic contradictions. Such contradictions can be avoided if a scientist strictly observes the laws applicable in his particular field of investigation.

We must, in conclusion, distinguish an antinomy from the many truths revealed in Scripture which transcend our understanding. We call them mysteries. The truth that God's decree over mankind includes sin, while the sinner himself is still responsible for his deeds, is beyond our comprehension, but it is not an antinomy. An antinomy would arise if it were simultaneously affirmed that God's decree includes sin and also that the sin of man is not included in His decree.

13

Cosmic Time

A careful examination of our schematization of the cosmic modalities will disclose that there is no modality of time. That is no error, for time is not one of the modalities which traverse reality. Time does not allow itself to be enclosed in any one aspect of the cosmos, but all the aspects of cosmic reality are enclosed in universal time.[1] Why is it impossible that time should be one of the cosmic modalities? Well, in that case only a modal *part* of creation should be temporal. The modalities which precede the so-called "time-modality" should be then *pre-temporal* or *timeless*. And all the law-spheres following the "time-modality" should only be *founded* in time, although their own reality should be *super-temporal*. However this is a dangerous error, because the Holy Scripture clearly teaches us, that the total creation has been subjected to the great and mysterious Cosmic Time as a divine order for all creatures in heaven and earth. There is no pre-temporal nor super-temporal created reality.

Time and space are often placed next to each other as two equivalent magnitudes on the same level. Our world is frequently referred to in general discourse as being temporal and spatial. This is a popular expression of an unbiblical philosophical theory.

The philosopher Immanuel Kant placed time and space next to each other as forms of perception. Time and space for Kant are not creatures of God but are ordering-forms of our perception and as such are the necessary prerequisite for all sensory experience. The act of perception assigns the raw material of sensation, coming towards us from outside, a place in space and in time. Time and space are not real magnitudes which exist apart from a perceptive subject, but they are only conditions of our perception,

---

[1] Who will be informed at large about the problem of the time can read my Dutch book: *"Tijd en eeuwigheid"* (Time and Eternity). J. H. Kok N. V. Kampen, 1953.

cadres in which we arrange things.[1] Now since perception is a psychical activity, Kant actually reduces space and time to the psychical modality and as a result he misconstrues the true nature and structure of the cosmos.

Space is the second modality in the cosmic law order; it is but one of the many aspects in which concrete things function. A house, for example, is not only spatial, but it is also beautiful or ugly; it has an aesthetic function. A thing has aspects which exceed the spatial and cannot be reduced to it. Moreover, time and space cannot be placed on the same level. Time is not equivalent to space. Time cannot form a separate modality or be reduced to any particular modality. All modalities, all aspects of things, from the first (number) to the last (faith) are subject to time. God has included the whole of creation in time. "In the *beginning* God created the heaven and the earth" (Genesis 1:1). Cosmic time began when God began the work of creation. "All flesh is grass, and all the goodliness thereof is as the flower of the field. The grass withereth, the flower fadeth; but the word of our God shall stand forever" (Isaiah 40:6, 8).

"Of old hast thou laid the foundation of the earth; and the heavens are the work of thy hands. They shall perish, but thou shalt endure; yea, all of them shall wax old like a garment; as a vesture shalt thou change them, and they shall be changed; but thou art the same and thy years shall have no end" (Ps. 102:25-27).

The cosmos is temporal in all its aspects. Time runs through all the modalities so that we can speak of cosmic time. This is not only revealed to us by God in His Word, but everyone can also see it and understand that time is an intrinsic element in all that exists.

We have already stated that creation is fulfilled in Christ and all things are related to Him. Not only are all things created by Him, but He has redeemed them and rules them.

---

[1] According to Kant, space and time are distinguished only by the fact that the latter is the perceptive form of the internal *"Sinn,"* sensory function, whereas the former is the perceptive form of the external sense-organ.

Everything in the world would lose its meaning, if it were not related to Christ, because He shall bring creation to its completion. Now in cosmic time, which was ordered by God in the beginning, this *fulness of meaning* is diversified, unfolded and divided. And this variegation of the fulness of meaning is not due to sin but to the unfolding of the manifold wisdom of God. This unfolding is grounded in the order of creation and graciously maintained in re-creation in spite of sin and its curse.

Sin is not the cause of the various modalities, nor has its presence abolished any modality. Dooyeweerd compares the dispersement of the modalities within cosmic time with the dispersement of light in a spectrum when a ray of light passes through a prism. The prism represents time. An unbroken ray strikes the prism on the side facing the source of light and passes through to the other side, where it appears as a broken collection of colors. In a similar fashion cosmic time encompasses all of creation. The cosmic law order is a cosmic temporal order. Within the unchangeable temporal order, anchored in God's creative will and redemptive grace, are included all temporal law-spheres or modalities which, in turn, include all temporal things and social relationships. *Cosmic time encompasses all of creation and expresses itself in each modality in a unique manner.* No single modality is timeless. No aspect of reality transcends time; the super temporal is not to be found within any law-sphere. *Cosmic time expresses itself in each law-sphere in a manner determined by the peculiar character of the sphere.*

In the arithmetical or numerical sphere, time expresses itself in *succession*, in the sequence of numbers. The number 2 is earlier in order than the number 4. And this order is its positional value, its greatness or smallness.

In the spatial sphere time expresses itself in spatial *synchronization*. Two circles which touch each other are simultaneous in space, just like two things, or two persons or two families. In the kinematic sphere time is the *duration of motion*. In the physical sphere we encounter time as the *duration of working energy* as the time-distance between cause and effect. The mechanism of a clock is adjusted in accordance with the daily rotation of the earth upon its axis. Therefore the clock is a measuring-instrument of the earthly physical time. And in the biotic sphere time appears as *organic development,* as the growth of the organism. In the psychical sphere, it is revealed in the *feeling of duration* which exists in connection with psychical tension. One who waits for something with great inner tension has the feeling that five minutes lasts forever.

And in the analytical sphere we must take into account what is *logically earlier and later* in the order of thought, the so called prius and posterius. A conclusion is logically later than the premises upon which it rests.

History has *periods;* and time possesses *symbolical significance* in language, (e.g., a pause between two sentences, the different tenses of the verb). In the social sphere we ascribe *priority* to the one person above another. In the economic sphere time appears for example in the phenomenon of *rent.* Rent rests upon the ascription of a higher value to present serviceable goods than to future goods. Economic time is also enclosed in the fact, that the value of things ordinarily diminishes, when they become old and threadbare. With antique objects it is just the other way round. And in the aesthetic sphere we encounter *aesthetic duration,* i.e., the time in which a novel is finished or the rhythm in music. We encounter a *time of validity* or enforcement in the juridical sphere. A legal penalty is usually not imposed with respect to acts committed before a certain prohibitive law is enacted. In the moral (ethical) sphere of love we encounter time in what we call *"suitable time"* for making a request or performing an act of love. And in the life of faith, time reveals itself in the religious "ups and downs" of the life of the believer.

Cosmic time expresses itself in all spheres. Even the function of faith possesses a temporal character since faith has to show its genuineness in the perseverance of saints.

Cosmic time penetrates the entire creation and expresses itself in each modality according to its *law* and *subject side.*

The former, the law side, is the unchangeable *temporal order* in which the modalities and concrete things are enclosed. The latter, the subject side, reveals itself as a *duration* which has its own peculiar character in each law-sphere. Philosophy theoretically separates and analyzes these subjective modal *duration-moments*, but in reality they form a unified cosmic continuity which penetrates all the law-spheres. Thus within the *temporal diversity of meaning*, there is *a coherence of meaning* of everything temporal. And this coherence is related to Christ, who, since His incarnation Himself in the time, reigns over His temporal world and leads it toward its final destination: to serve God in perfection, throughout all eternity, for ever and ever.

This view of time is of great importance for the Christian life. It enables us to see that man — the only creature that can consciously experience cosmic duration — can concentrate his temporal existence in a center in which he transcends the *diversity* of time, namely in his deepest point of being, his religious ego. This religious center is, as God's Word teaches us, the heart of man.

Here arises the question whether the human heart itself is temporal or not.

In former days Prof. Dooyeweerd learned that the human heart was characterized by super-temporality. In the deepest center of his existence man would concentrate all temporal functions in a point, that is no longer temporal. In our heart, our deepest Self, we would not be subjected to the cosmic temporal order. If our heart were subject to temporality, we would be unable to concentrate the various modal forms of time in the unity of cosmic time; man would not possess an idea of eternity; we would not have the possibility to relate in religious self-concentration our temporal life to God, the eternal firm Ground of all things. Therefore man in his heart necessarily transcends the cosmic time-order.

However, it was not Dooyeweerd's opinion that the human heart was flatly eternal. For the Holy Scripture clearly says that only God is eternal, exalted above all temporality. And man as creature never becomes divine— not in this life nor hereafter. Dooyeweerd solved this question in this manner — he appealed to a scholastic distinction, which posited an intervening condition between time and eternity. This state is designated by the term *aevum* and is considered to be a created eternity. He himself wrote: "I believe this term is acceptable since it arose in a Christian system which felt the need of a distinction between the super-temporal in a created sense and eternity in the sense of the being of God."

Some years ago I published my book "Time and Eternity" (*Tijd en eeuwigheid*) and in that work I disputed in detail not only the idea of aevum, but also the contention of the so-called super-temporality of the human heart.

It is my positive conviction, that there is no intervening condition between time and eternity, no aevum, no created eternity. This idea is a fiction, speculative, antinomous. The Bible teaches that all creatures are totally temporal, men not excluded. If it were true, that man would be temporal in his modal functions, in his corporal life, but super-temporal in his heart, where he concentrates all his functions in the center of his existence, his ego, then there would be a deep cleft inside the man himself. Therefore I reject fully the idea of human super-temporality.[1]

Nevertheless it is true, that man by concentrating his functional life in all its diversity in his religious heart, at the same time also concentrates in his inmost being all the modal time-forms in an experience of the unity of the cosmic time. Then he experiences time in its religious character, i.e., in its relation to the Eternal God as Creator and Redeemer.

So I wish to speak about *the religious time* as the time of

[1] In his later works Prof. Dooyeweerd no longer mentions the word "aevum" nor the term "super-temporal" in relation to the human inmost Self. It appears that now he fully agrees with the thought of the temporality of the human heart. However he emphasizes — and that is true — that man in his heart, in the deepest root of his being, has the relation to the things that transcend the time, namely the things of God, which are eternal.

the human heart. In this manner I am in harmony with the Word of God. For the Bible speaks in various texts about time in a religious sense. Since the Fall mankind lives in the time of apostasy. This time became in Jesus Christ for sinners the time of grace, "for it is time to seek the Lord" (Hosea 10:12). We all know the expression of Christ: "but ye cannot discern the signs of the times" (Matthew 16:3). In Mark 1:15 we read: "the time is fulfilled and the kingdom of God is at hand." In Galatians 4:4 it says: "When the fulness of the time came, God sent forth his Son."

We can multiply these testimonies from the Scripture. Everyone can find them in abundance. But we terminate them by remembering of the prayer of Moses: "so teach us to number our days, that we may get us an heart of wisdom" (Psalm 90:12).

So the human heart lives on the border of two worlds. On the one hand, it shares fully in temporal life, and on the other, it concentrates its own temporal existence upon eternal things which are not seen. Through Christ the believer has fellowship with God in his heart.

The human heart is apostate by nature and if it persists in unbelief and disobedience, the man outside of Christ loses his life in temporal things. However, if the heart is renewed by grace and is directed in Christ toward the God of the Covenant, then the believer rejoices while living in this temporal world and is happy in the promise of God that whoever acts according to His Will shall inherit life everlasting.

Our view of time enables us to understand that everything temporal is in a state of unrest. There is no resting point to be found in temporal things. Everything temporal is restless: possessing meaning as its mode of being, it points toward Christ, the Alpha and Omega. Moreover, we may not and we cannot make faith a resting point. To elevate faith above the temporal would rob it of its meaning. If the heart of man seeks its rest in faith and not in God through faith, it seeks its repose in man and makes man an idol. Such a course ends in deception. An idol is nothing. Faith as such is not a resting point, but through faith, the child of God rests in the Eternal Father of our Lord Jesus Christ, who says in His Word, "There is rest for the people of God."

14

Transcendent and Transcendental

To understand this philosophy we must acquire an exact knowledge of the meaning of the terms "transcendent" and "transcendental." It is not sufficient to analyze these terms philologically or linguistically. Both are derived from a Latin word which means to overstep, climb over, or cross over. The difference in suffixes does not suffice to signify the difference in meaning. We must, therefore, examine the scientific usage of these terms. For centuries the word transcendent has been employed in theology. Reformed theology has always made the distinction between the transcendence and the immanence of God. The former signifies the fact that God is above His creation and is not absorbed in it. The latter term signifies that the omnipotent power of God fills the entire creation, "For whither shall I go from thy Spirit, or whither shall I flee from thy presence?"

The word "transcendental" has always been used to denote a philosophical conception. Kant frequently used it to signify everything which is a prerequisite for and belongs to the universally valid conditions of human knowledge. This Christian philosophy broadens the meaning of both terms. The term "transcendent" denotes more than it had in theology, and the word "transcendental" is not limited to the prerequisites of knowledge.

Under "transcendent" Reformed philosophy understands everything which lies on the other side of the cosmic temporal border, everything which exceeds the temporal limit and duration of cosmic time. God, the creator of the temporal world order, is transcendent in an absolute sense. He is not enclosed in the temporal order. Even in His immanence, in His indwelling in the world, God the Father is not subject to the cosmic law order. However we cannot say this of our Lord Jesus Christ, who took upon Himself since His conception by the Holy Spirit the very nature of man. Not only in the time of His humiliation, but also now in the time of His exaltation He is still subjected to temporality, sitting as the King of ages at the right hand of God. Therefore He remains, according to His human nature, related to the human race and to temporal reality. "We have" — says the Heidelberg Catechism — "our flesh in heaven as a certain security." This is the reason that the Bible speaks of the future of our Lord, but never of the future of God.

In one sense even man transcends the boundary of cosmic time, namely, in his temporal heart, the religious concentration point of all his functions. Nevertheless the heart of man — though in itself subjected to the cosmic time-order — is transcendent in this sense, that man has in his religious-temporal heart the relation to the things that are eternal. In his heart man directs himself in obedience to Scripture toward the true origin of all things. Or, in apostasy, he seeks this origin in an idol. In both ways he has a relation to God.

By "transcendental" we understand that which — enclosed in cosmic time — is a necessary prerequisite for temporal existence, to make possible the concrete reality. Transcendental does not itself belong to concrete things, but it belongs to what is general and what exceeds the variable *individuality of things*. "*Transcendental*" lies in and behind concrete things. It refers to what is at the foundation of reality as the necessary prerequisite of temporal existence.

Cosmic time in the first place is transcendental. It is the prerequisite and foundation of all cosmic reality. All reality in the cosmos is included within time, nothing excepted.

The temporal law-spheres, the modal functions as cosmic aspects are also transcendental. They are prerequisites for the possibility of the existence of concrete reality. And in the third place, the structures of individuality of things and relationships also belong to the transcendental. For as the products of human work are produced in accordance with certain structural principles, there are also individual principles of construction, according to God's will for the particular nature of societal relationships and products of culture. These *structures of individuality,* which have a character of law, lie at the basis of the concrete reality which we experience daily. We shall say more about this later on.

The following schema will help to clarify what we mean.

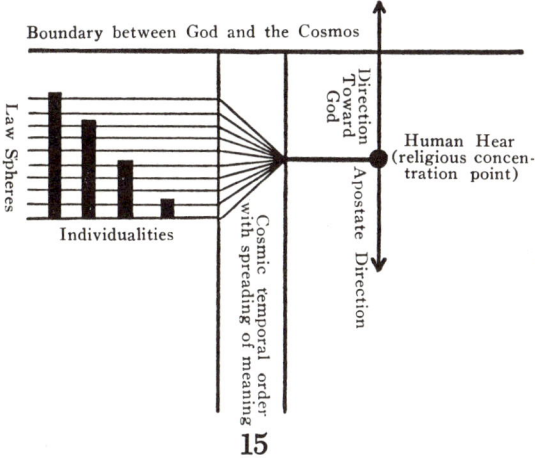

15

THE ARCHITECTONIC STRUCTURE OF THE COSMIC MODALITIES

WE have considered the sequence of the cosmic modalities, their individual sovereignty, and the manner in which cosmic time expresses itself in the various aspects of reality. We can now examine the coherence of the law-spheres in more detail. The existence of such a coherence can readily be surmised, if we consider the fact that cosmic time permeates each modality.

Therefore we have now to consider more exactly the character of this coherence.

The law-spheres or modalities of meaning are aspects

of the same created cosmos. And these aspects of reality are not disconnected from each other but within cosmic time they constitute an *architectonic structure*. From the first modality, the numerical, to the last modality of faith, there is an ever-increasing complication. If we pass from the lowest to the highest sphere, both the law side and subject side of each modality progressively display a greater degree of complexity.

The spheres which are earlier in the temporal order possess a simpler modal structure than those which are later. The progressively greater complicatedness of every modality subsequent to the numerical, is due to the fact that each later modality has as its foundation the modalities which precede it in the cosmic order. The later a modality is in the cosmic temporal order, the more complicated and broader is the foundation upon which it rests.

For example, the second modality, the spatial sphere, is based upon the sphere of number. Every spatial figure presupposes number. A line can be divided into a *number* of segments, and a rectangle into a *number* of sections, and so on. The physical modality, in contrast, has three spheres as its foundation, namely the spheres of number, space and motion. A stone, for example, not only can move and has inside its atoms a continuous movement of particles, but also occupies space and besides it has a numerical function. And the biotic sphere, the organic vital aspect of reality, is based upon four spheres. This progression continues so that the last modality has as its foundation all the other spheres. The *pistical* sphere or the sphere of faith is the most complicated sphere. It presupposes all other cosmic modalities.

If in scientific thought we focus our attention on a particular modality, such as the historical, the spheres preceding it in the temporal order serve as its foundation. And we call these spheres the *substratum* of the historical modality. We call the modalities which follow the historical modality, its *superstratum*. If we begin with a modality which is early in the temporal order, the number of modalities belonging to its superstratum will exceed that of its substratum. And if we start with one of the later modalities, the number of spheres belonging to its substratum increases in direct proportion to the decrease in the number of spheres belonging to its superstratum. Each modality has a different number of substrata and a different *number of superstrata* spheres, but the sum of the spheres contained in its superstratum and substratum is the same for every modality.

There are two border spheres in the order of cosmic aspects. The first, the modality of number, does not have any substrata spheres. And the last, the modality of faith, does not have any superstrata spheres.

The numerical law sphere does not possess a modal foundation. This does not mean that it hangs in the air. The numerical sphere, like all other aspects, is embedded in cosmic time. It occupies a place within the temporal structure that lies transcendentally deeper than any modal foundation. And as a part of creation it rests in the omnipotent and omnipresent power of God, which sustains all things.

The sphere of faith does not have a superstratum. This does not mean that it is windowless and without perspective. The pistical modality does not have any further modal vision; it has no meaning-fulfillment in a higher sphere. Yet, through faith, as a member of the body of Christ, the renewed heart of the believer has a vision of Christ, the Head of the New Covenant. Through Christ the church, not a particular church on earth, but the unity of all believers in all ages, this church is directed to God, the Origin of all things. The heart of the unbeliever, in contrast, is directed toward idols. His apostate faith functions in a direction which leads away from God toward sovereign man.

The cosmic modalities are anchored in cosmic time and can be contemplated from two points of view. We can consider the foundation of a particular sphere. When a particular sphere is late in the cosmic order and we seek to determine which spheres precede by examining its foundation, we have followed what we can now call the *foundational* direction.

We can also view the cosmic modalities from a second perspective by concentrating our attention on those modalities which occur later in the cosmic law order. We can try to ascertain the purpose of a particular sphere, to see what it is that completes or fulfils its meaning. We can thus raise the question as to what follows an earlier aspect. From this perspective, we contemplate the aspects of reality from the point of view of their *end*. When viewed through the eyes of faith the whole cosmos is seen as the redeemed creation of God. We can call this last direction, the *transcendental direction*.

The coherence of the law-spheres is still more intensive than we have hitherto seen. *The structure of each particular modality is the expression of the temporal coherence of all modalities.* And this fact enables us to gain a clearer insight into the manner in which a particular modality is based upon the modalities preceding it. It aids us also to understand what is meant by the statement that a modality reflects its subsequent modalities. The phrase *"thought-economy"* or economy of thought, for example, expresses the fact that something in the logical modality points toward the economical modality. And the phrase *"logical domination"* indicates that the logical modality *anticipates* the historical. The expression *"logical multiplicity"* points from the logical sphere back to that of number.

Our language contains many compound expressions which express the coherence between the different modalities. Instances of such expressions are vital motion, spatial image, the joy of faith, feeling of beauty, and so on. In such expressions one component *qualifies* the entire expression, as belonging to the same modality by which that component itself is characterized. In the expression thought-economy, which means that in scientific thinking the chain of logical reasoning is unhampered by superfluous links, thought is the qualifying term. It indicates that the entire expression belongs to the logical modality. And the word "economy" signifies that there is a connection between the logical and the economical modalities, arising in the analytical sphere and pointing to the economic one. The reverse is possible too. But then arises another notion.

In the expression *vital motion,* vital is the qualifying component. Vital motion belongs to the biotic sphere. The term motion signifies that the biotic sphere coheres with the kinematic.

In both of these examples, the qualifying component happened to be first in the expression. In some instances the qualifying component is the second part of the expression. The expression spatial feeling, for example, is qualified by feeling. Philosophical analysis is required to determine in each concrete case which part qualifies the whole expression.

It is evident from these examples that both the later and the earlier modalities are bound together into an unbreakable coherence. The connections between the earlier and later spheres do not resolve one modality into another and deprive it of its distinctive character. Thought-economy remains logical in nature; thought is not an economical action.

Each modality has its own irreducible kernel or nuclear moment. And the nuclear moment of one modality cannot be reduced to that of another. The nuclear moment of a law-sphere endows the law-sphere with its own particular meaning and causes each modality to be distinct from every other modality. *The nuclear moment of every modality guarantees each sphere its own internal sovereignty.*

Within the structure of each modality, many *modal moments* are grouped around the nuclear moment. And these modal moments guarantee the coherence of each modality with the remaining earlier and later spheres. Some modal moments point forward toward later modalities and some point back to earlier modalities. Those which point forward are called *anticipatory* moments and those which point backward are called *retrospective* or *analogical* moments.

Logical domination is an anticipatory moment of the logical sphere; it points forward to the historical sphere, because the historical function of man is characterized by cultural development or formation and mastery. In the psychical sphere spatial-feeling is a retrospective moment, as it points back to the spatial modality. Spatial feeling is, in other words, a spatial analogy in the psychical sphere.

How can we determine whether or not we are dealing with an anticipation or with an analogy? If we take *thought-economy*, for example, we see immediately that thought-economy expresses a relation between the logical and the economical modalities. The question is: are we dealing with an economic analogy or logical anticipation? In other words: what is the qualifying constituent of the expression? Is thought-economy a logical or an economical phenomenon? It is the former, since the economist, the industrial leader and the bank director, as such, are not concerned with thought-economy. Thought-economy is the preoccupation of the scientist and theorist. Consequently, it is a logical anticipation of the economical sphere and not vice versa.

We must stress the fact that anticipating moments enrich and open the nuclear moment of a modality, whereas analogical moments point back toward its foundation. And from this we can see that *thought-economy* must be an anticipatory moment. We can think without being economical in thought. Thought-economy is a scientific enrichment of naive thought; it is therefore a logical anticipation of the economical sphere. And on the other hand in view of the fact that thought is not possible without a multiplicity of concepts, logical multiplicity must be an analogical moment, an analogical or retrospective moment which points back to the foundation of the logical modality in the numerical modality.

The anticipations and analogies of the various modalities form an architectonic structure. These anticipatory and analogical moments constitute an inner coherence between the various modalities, so that each is indissolubly

THE THEORY OF COSMIC MODALITIES

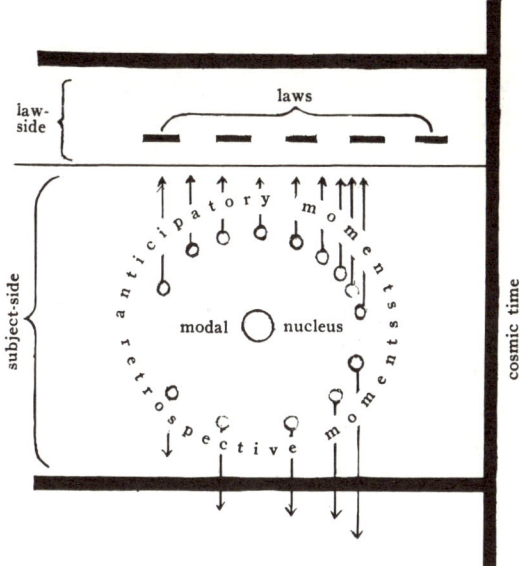

Diagram of the psychical law-sphere

connected with every other. No single aspect of reality exists apart from the remaining aspects. Each sphere occupies a different place in the cosmic order, and has its own nuclear moment. Each following sphere in the cosmic temporal order has one less anticipation and one more analogy than the preceding sphere.

We must again notice the peculiarity of both border spheres. As the least complicated modality the numerical sphere does not possess any modal foundation and therefore lacks any analogical moments. The pistical sphere does not possess a modal superstratum; so it lacks any anticipatory moments. But created in the image of God and renewed in the image of Christ, man can enrich his transcendental outlook by transcending the boundary of time through his faith. His heart is the transcendent concentration point of all temporal functions, and from it he can direct his glance toward Him, through whom and unto whom are all things.

16

The Modalities Separately Considered

The modalities of the cosmos lie in the grip of cosmic time. They are mutually intertwined and interwoven through the complicated network of anticipations and retrospections or analogies. And as we have seen, the analogical and anticipatory moments of a modality cannot abolish its internal sovereignty, because they cannot change the character of its nuclear moment. The nuclear moment of every modality impresses the character of the modality upon the moments which are grouped around it. Each anticipatory and retrospective moment is qualified by the nuclear moment of the sphere to which it belongs.

It is therefore of primary importance that we have a correct insight into the nuclear moment of each aspect of reality. Consequently, we shall now briefly discuss the individual modalities.

A. *The Numerical Modality*

The first sphere in the temporal order is that of number. What is the meaning (*Sinn*) of the numerical sphere, what is its nuclear moment? Dooyeweerd called this nuclear moment *discrete quantity*, or literally, the distinct amount. Numbers are quantities which are mutually distinct from each other. Two is more than one and four more than three, and so on. The transition from one number to another is not gradual, but it is always a leap, the bridging of a distance. The addition of fractional numbers can make this distance very small. Yet even between the number 1-99/100 and the number two, there still remains a certain distance, a *discreteness*, a sharply delineated boundary. We never find essential continuity in numbers.

Around the nuclear moment of number we find only anticipating moments which point forward to later modalities. We do not find retrocipatory moments, since the numerical sphere does not possess a modal foundation. Consequently, the numerical nuclear moment is the least complicated of the nuclear moments.

The numerical modality is the foundation of all other modalities. There is nothing in the world in which number does not play a role. Space has a certain number of dimensions and movement traverses a distance which can be expressed in numbers. Moreover, a living organism possesses a number of organs; feeling arises from several sensations and thought is only possible through a multiplicity of concepts, etc.

Like every modality, the numerical law-sphere has a law side and a subject side. Numbers belong to the subject side. The numbers 1, 2, 3, 4, and so on, are subject to laws which God has established for the world of numbers. Two times two is always four. Numbers cannot deviate from these Divine laws. A person engaged in mathematical calculation can commit errors, but this is something entirely different. His faulty calculation is a mistake in thought and an offense of the knowing subject.

Cosmic time expresses itself in this sphere in the sequence of numbers.

B. *The Spatial Modality*

Space has its modal *origin* in the second aspect of reality. That is to say all that is spatial is here original. Every concrete space like atmosphere or outer-space has its modal origin in this modality, though both mentioned spaces have a physical qualification. The same is true about spaces with a qualification from other modalities, like feeling-space or thinking-space. The nuclear moment of space consists in extension. And *extension* is essentially different from distinct quantity. In the numerical sphere an unbridgeable distance always remained between numbers. The spatial modality, in contrast, confronts us with pure continuity. Space therefore is *continuous extension*.

A plane is equally extended in all horizontal directions;

it reveals no gap or boundary line where two-dimensional space would come to an end. Three-dimensional space, space which displays length, breadth, and height is continuously extended in all horizontal and vertical directions and within the cosmos, it does not encounter a terminating boundary.

The spatial law-sphere contains a numerical analogy which refers to the nuclear moment of the numerical sphere. Numbers are presupposed in everything spatial. The spatial magnitude of things is expressed in numbers.

Many anticipations exist in this modality. A movement is possible only on a spatial foundation. Organic life cannot function without space: life-space. And all the following law-spheres — the psychical, the logical, historical, and so on — are founded or based upon the spatial sphere.

A legal order or injunction applies, for example, to a given territory; its sphere of validity is a spatial analogy inside the juridical modality. And the notion of a cultural area is a spatial analogy which occurs in the historical aspect.

Things are subjected to spatial laws in their spatial *subject-function*. Every *thing* is subject to the unbreakable law that two spatial things cannot occupy the same space at the same time. An imperialistic state may try to deprive another state of its territory and may succeed in expelling it from its homeland. This offense however is not spatially qualified and thus does not violate any spatial law.

Cosmic time expresses itself in the spatial modality in *simultaneity*. Two things can be present next to each other in space at the same time.

The science which investigates the first two law-spheres is mathematics. Mathematics is actually a composite name for different sciences, such as algebra and geometry.

C. *The Kinematic Modality*

In his first project of the modal law-spheres Prof. Dooyeweerd placed as third sphere after the modalities of number and space the physical modality qualified by motion. But afterwards he changed this conception. About that he himself says in his book "A New Critique of Theoretical Thought" Vol. II, page 98: ". . . in the first (Dutch) edition of this work I tried to reduce the original sense of movement to the meaning-kernel of the modal aspect which is the specific field of physics. But it appeared later on that this attempt could not satisfy the demands of an exact analysis and must lead philosophical thought into inner antinomies."

Scientifically it is not allowed to identify movement and energy. Naturally, in the concrete reality we every day experience, both go together. But they are not the same. Between both is an essential difference, which can clearly be seen in the fact, that a uniform movement without any reference to a causing force is a meaningful matter in a kinematic modality, but not in the physical sphere. For *physical* movement is always related to energy, to cause and effect, to a potential or actual force. The science about motion, kinematics, on the contrary can deal with all sorts of motions, their peculiarities and laws, without any reference to a causing and working energy.

This is the reason that philosophically we have to distinguish a separate modality of motion, the kinematic modality, which precedes in cosmic time-order the physical law-sphere, for all physical movements caused by energy are founded in motion as such.

In the kinematic modality motion presents itself in its modal nucleus-kernel of *continuous flowing*. Here cosmic time expresses itself in the *succession of moments*. The science of kinematics, which is a branch of pure mathematics, examines the laws to which motions have to obey.

It is clear that this law-sphere of motion possesses two analogies. First the analogy of space in the sense of *flowing space* or flowing extension, which occurs in the modal kinematic sphere, but is founded in the spatial aspect. The moments of flowing space form a series of moving moments, while the simultaneity of positions, points or figures in the spatial sphere is a statical matter. The *direction* of a movement in flowing space is also a spatial analogy referring to the spatial dimensionality. In the second place: in the kinematic aspect exists a numerical analogy, because not only several movements but also the successive moments of one motion are countable.

After this brief analysis of the first three modal law-spheres it has to be observed, that in those three modalities there is not yet concrete reality in the sense of individual things. For numbers, spaces and motions are not things. People sometimes call them "abstract" matters. But that is not a good appointment, because the word "abstract" always applies to products of the human analytical cogitative function. Indeed, numbers, spaces and movements are concrete; existing in reality, but not like "things." They are only *qualities* of things, qualities of all existing reality.

D. *The Physical Modality*

The second sphere is static and fixed in its continuous extension. The third sphere is the origin of motion. This is the source of all that is movable, while the physical modality is characterized by *energy*. In this physical aspect of reality movement appears too; however not motion as such, but motion in its physical sense, namely movement caused by energy. For energy is here the meaning-kernel, the nuclear-moment. Energy is the essence of all physical reality, revealing itself in chemical substances and their reactions, in light and sound, in electricity and also in energy of the atom, liberated in a technical process. Fields of gravitation, electro-magnetical fields, quanta, photons, electrons, neutrons, protons, and so on are real physical events, in their movements, spatiality and countability founded on the three former law-spheres.

All physical reality is variable and changeable in character and varies from moment to moment.

Since every form of energy presupposes motion, space and number, the physical modality possesses three analogies, the kinematic, the spatial and the numerical. It also possesses a profusion of anticipations. The process of growth in organic life is possible only because the physical modality anticipates the biotic modality. Or stated from a different perspective, growth in organic life is a physical analogy that occurs in the biotic modality. The logical moment of thought indicates the presence of a mutual connection between the logical and physical modality (thinking energy). And these examples could be multiplied to include all post-physical modalities. They all have an energetic character, since the physical modality is a part of their modal foundation or substratum.

The law of gravity is a simple example of a physical law. All things are subject to it, in their physical subject-function.

Cosmic time expresses itself in the physical modality in the physical duration of working energy. Physics, chemistry, and related natural sciences investigate this aspect.

The world and life view which is commonly known as materialism deifies the physical modality. The Christian believes that the human heart can find rest only in Christ. The materialist seeks to anchor his heart in matter. He disavows the sovereignty of the post-physical modalities and would reduce all existence to force and matter. He seeks to solve every problem in the world by subsuming it under the magic formula of physical reaction.

This physical sphere is the first modality with reality of individual *things*. For all lifeless things are characterized by the physical aspect of reality.

E. *The Biotic Modality*

The nuclear moment of the biotic modality is *life*. All living things, whether plants, animals or man have a subject-function in the *biotic* modality. The so-called inanimate things of nature are qualified by the physical modality, since it is the last modality in which they have a subject-function. A plant, in contrast to an inanimate thing, functions as subject also in the biotic modality; and since the biotic modality is the last modality in which it has a subject function, a plant is biotically *qualified*.

The biotic modality is frequently described by the word "organic," since all creatures which possess a biotic subject-function have organs and organs distinguish biotic things from physical things. Physical things are composed of parts which display an intrinsic homogenity, but organs are parts which display an inner heterogenity. Their constitutive vital elements are not replaceable, since every element has its own proper place and function in the totality of organs. The different organs in the total organism are not exchangeable, even though they display a relative self-sufficiency with respect to the total organism. As a part, an organ is qualified by the same modality which determines the character of the whole. The organs of a plant are biotically qualified and the organs of an animal are psychically qualified.

It should be noted in passing that the term "organic" is preferred by many instead of the term biotic. The term organic often serves the purpose of indicating that numerous structures are not mechanical. When used in this sense it is a rejection of *energetism* which seeks to give a physical explanation of the full richness of the whole reality. However, in spite of good intentions it is necessary to exercise caution in using the term "organic." If one understands it to mean that *everything* that is not mechanical is organic, then one is in danger of reducing the post-biotic modalities to the biotic. Biologism and vitalism fall into this error and they exert a near magical influence on many.

The relation of the whole to its parts presupposes number and is a numerical analogy in the biotic sphere. The concept of vital space is a spatial analogy; the concept of vital motion, a kinematic analogy, and the vital strength a physical analogy. In addition to its analogies, the biotic modality has a number of anticipatory connections with post-biotic spheres. Sentiment and emotion, thought, historical development, language, and so on, would not be possible without the substratum of organic life.

In their biotic subject-functions, all living creatures are

subject to biotical laws (e.g., laws of growth, respiration, metabolism, reproduction, heredity, and so on.)

Cosmic time expresses itself in the form of organic development, which is implicit in the progress of growth.

The science of biology studies the biotic aspect of plants, animals, and man. Insofar as it investigates the dynamic of living things, it is physiology; and insofar as it investigates their static forms, it is morphology.

F. *The Psychical Modality*

The psychical modality is based upon the so-called "natural" aspects of reality which precede it. Naturalistic philosophy recognizes the existence of only these natural aspects. Consequently, it absolutizes them as the "real" reality and has the tendency to explain all things according to the method of natural science.

This naturalistic approach does not go unchallenged, even within the camp of *immanence-philosophy*. In opposition to the universal application of the natural scientific method, some advocated a second method, the method of the spiritual sciences. We do not agree with this distinction, because each science has its own method, but we can appreciate the fact that the advocates of the former distinction have at least seen that reality is not exhausted in its natural aspects. They have recognized that post-biotic reality is essentially different from the physical and biotic aspects.

Nevertheless, from our standpoint we must reject the positive answers given by immanence philosophy to the question, What is the nature of post-biotic reality? Each answer absolutizes an aspect or modality. One may absolutize the psychical and fall into psychologism. Another may absolutize the analytical (logicism) and a third the historical (historicism), but all succumb to the error of *functionalism*: the view that one modal function is the origin of the others. Only Christian philosophy can avoid this error. It alone knows the true religious center of the cosmos, which transcends all temporal modal functions. Therefore, only

Christian transcendent philosophy can distinguish the post-biotic spheres according to their own nature without being compelled to reduce them to one modality; or as Kant, to two, namely, the analytical and the ethical.

The psychical is the first post-biotic modality. Its nuclear moment is *feeling*. The psychical modality is a separate aspect of reality. It is not identical with the biotic or the analytic. Every living thing does not possess feeling, nor does every living creature which does possess it have a subjective analytical function. A plant lacks feeling and therefore is biotically qualified. An animal has feeling; it receives sensory impressions through its sense organs and is therefore psychically qualified. But it is not able *to think*. What sometimes appears to be the result of thought in animals is an habituation to certain actions which follow specific sensory impressions. It is always an instinctive psychical reaction, even though in the case of highly developed animals it is possible to ascertain a certain spontaneity which can be called intelligence. This form of intelligence is in no way analytical or logical in character. The analytical must be sharply distinguished from the psychical, and we must guard against making the psychical aspect the receptacle of everything not included in the natural aspects of reality.

The psychical is limited to feeling and perception. To it belong all the sensory impressions that man and animals receive through their sense organs (i.e., via sight, taste, hearing, and so on.) The psychical modality contains a biotical analogy, since sense organs make it possible for us to have feelings.

The biotical, physical, kinematic, spatial and numerical modalities constitute the substratum of the psychical modality. Consequently, the psychical modality contains biotical, physical, kinematic, spatial, and numerical analogies. Emotion, for example, is as an affective movement a kinematic analogy; the feeling of space is a spatial analogy; and the multiplicity of sensory impressions refers to the numerical sphere.

Logical feeling, historical feeling and the feeling of legality are psychical anticipations. Only man and animals have a psychical subject-function by which they are subject to the laws which God imposes upon sensory and affective life. Pain and anxiety, joy and sorrow, and sensible impressions are all dependent upon a conformity to psychical law.

Time expresses itself in the psychical modality as a feeling of duration. Minutes passed in anxiety seem very long, while hours of pleasure and happiness pass quickly.

Empirical psychology is the science which studies the psychical sphere. There is, however, a general confusion concerning the scope of this science, a confusion which arises from a lack of insight into the nuclear moment of this sphere. August Messer, for example, ascribed to the psychical modality, words, concepts, judgments, volitional acts, and desires, self-consciousness, and even the human Ego, the religious concentration-point of all our functions. He practically considered all human post-biotic functions as being psychical. And even in Christian circles this same error is often committed.[1]

The term psychological is often incorrectly or inappropriately employed when used loosely in a non-scientific manner. A *psychological* reaction is sometimes spoken of when a *psychical* reaction is meant. And it is sometimes said that the psychological construction of a novel is good. Such usage of the term is wrong. The portrayal of the characters in a novel is not a scientific matter and also involves more than their affective life. Instead of referring to the "psycho-

[1] J. H. Bavinck, in his *Inleiding in de Zielkunde*, treats representations, concepts, thought, self-consciousness, personality and the ego, in a similar manner. Our contention is that the psychical modality is one of the fifteen modalities. It has been inserted in the cosmic order by God and it possesses its own sovereignty and meaning. If our view is correct the tendency to identify psychology with anthropology, the science which studies the structure of the human individuality, must be emphatically rejected. Such an identification necessarily leads to a psychologism, which by absolutizing the psychical aspect of reality is unable to maintain the transcendent character of the human heart and is unable to acknowledge that the latter is created in the image of God. While psychology is one of the many sciences, there is anthropology as a totality-science a part of philosophy.

logical" structure of a novel, it would be more exact to say that an author has a fair knowledge of human nature.

G. *The Analytical Modality*

The analytical sphere follows the psychical. In the cosmic temporal order, thought is subsequent to feeling and not vice versa. Creatures exist which possess a psychical subject-function and lack an analytical cogitative function, but no thinking creature lacks feeling. This indicates that thought is modally based upon the psychical aspect. Moreover, thinking and knowing are always necessarily based upon psychical perceptions.

The nuclear moment of this sphere is cogitative analysis, the observation of diversity. Not only science engages in cogitative analysis. The latter is also found in naive experience. In effecting a synthesis of meaning, science systematically engages in analytical and antithetical cogitative activity. Science unites or synthesizes the analytical function with the particular modality it seeks to investigate. (This will be treated in our discussion of epistemology.) Cogitative analysis is not restricted to science, but outside science this analysis is un-theoretical, un-antithetical and un-systematic.

A person occupied in naive experience does not think scientifically, but he does engage in cogitative analysis. And he does come into contact with the world without employing analysis and synthesis in a scientific sense. The man of naive experience lives without theoretical abstraction. In its stead he employs the subject-object relation. A person forms concepts through analysis and synthesis and then joins them together to form judgments and arguments. This process occurs primarily in naive thought and not only in science.

Feeling is an analogy of thought. This is readily seen from the fact that every idea is colored by a specific emotion, and naive thought forms ideas which are still statically bound to sensory impressions. One idea can arouse within us a joyous attitude and another a serious one. Such feelings possess a particular stormy intensity. But no single idea is psychically neutral. The analytical is also based upon the biotic. An injury to the brain can disturb the cogitative function.

The analytical modality contains physical, kinematic, spatial, and numerical analogies too. The notion of progress from one idea to another, the movement of thought, is a kinematic analogy. The notion of room to think and the notion of a multiplicity of concepts are, respectively, spatial and numerical analogies, while the notion of thinking-force is a physical analogy.

The analytical modality also contains numerous anticipations. The moment of logical domination anticipates the historical aspect and the moment of thought-economy anticipates the economic sphere. The moment of harmony in thought anticipates the aesthetic sphere, and the moment of logical evidence anticipates the juridical modality. The love of knowledge, the platonic eros, anticipates the ethical sphere, and the logical certainty, for example in mathematical axioms, anticipates the sphere of faith.

Previously we indicated that every modality has a law side and a subject side. The *active-subject* and *passive-object,* that is: all about which man in naive experience forms himself concepts and judgments, belong both to the subject side of the analytical modality. Man is the only creature who is subject in the analytical modality. No other creature possesses an analytical subject-function.

The laws of thought or the principles which govern our thought belong to the law side of the analytical modality. We ordinarily differentiate four laws of thought which comprise the analytical norm.

1. The first is the *principium identitatis* or the principle of analytical identity. It affirms that in an analysis, the analyzable element remains identical with itself. This identity is not ontical. It is concerned solely with identity in thought. We must not confuse logical concepts if we are to attain clarity and truth in our thinking. Consequently, we may not employ the same concept in different senses. The

principle of identity is generally formulated by the expression A is A. Vollenhoven correctly objects that this formulation does not make it clear that the identity here intended is analytical and not ontical. This formulation does not make it evident that the analytical law is a rule or norm, which can be transgressed. For this reason Vollenhoven gives a trial formulation in these words: "distinguish the analyzable A (whatever this may be) as the analyzable A from all the remainder, that is analyzable and that therefore is non-A, because in the totality that is analyzable, only A is A." It can readily be seen that this formulation vitiates the above-mentioned objections.

In connection with the fact that the principle of identity is not concerned with ontical, but with analytical identity, (identity in thought) Vollenhoven, following Leibniz, would rather speak of the *principium identitatis indiscernibilium,* the principle of the identity of the indiscernible. This principle of identity formulates the positive side of the analytical norm.

2. The second principle is the *principium excludendae contradictionis,* the principle of non-contradiction, which formulates the negative side of the analytical norm. Ordinarily the following formula is used. A is not equal to non-A. This principle can be formulated in a fuller manner if we follow the course indicated in our formulation of the *principium identitatis.* The principle of non-contradiction can be stated as follows: distinguish the analyzable A that alone is identical with itself, from the remaining analyzable non-A, with which A is not identical.

As a matter of fact the *principium identitatis indiscernibilium* and the *principium excludendae contradictionis* are really one principle. Vollenhoven states them in a single formula: "no matter what it is, correctly distinguish the analyzable." The first principle develops the analytical norm positively and the second negatively. The positive development of the principle of identity is an analytical analogy which points back to the arithmetical law that one is equal to one. The negative development of the *principium con-*

tradictionis anticipates the linguistical modality, as the latter is concerned with *contradiction*. This anticipation implies that the *principium contradictionis* is normative for thought as related to language. An idea which contradicts a true idea is false. This principle does not contradict the existence of contradiction. It only says that contradiction may not exist without violating truth.

3. The *principium exclusi tertii*, the principle of excluded middle, means that when we divide a specific group of phenomena into two classes, A and non-A, then it follows that a phenomenon which does not belong to A, must belong to non-A. There can be no third possibility.

From what we have said we can conclude:

(a) That the principle of excluded middle is not an independent law of thought but is a consequence of the *principium contradictionis*. As such, however, it has validity and must be recognized as a rule for our thought.

(b) The principle of excluded middle is only valid in a limited sphere. It is in force only where thought is placed before a dilemma, an either/or. There are a number of cases in which our choice is not limited to two and then the law of excluded middle is not valid. If two people, for example, not related to each other in any way are accused of the same crime, a demonstration of the innocence of A does not prove the guilt of B. The guilty party may be a third unknown person. And if one proves that a toothache is not an analytical matter, it does not follow that it is a biotic phenomenon, it may be physical, or something else.

4. The *principium rationis sufficientis*, the principle of sufficient reason, involves the fact that a result of thought, i.e., a conclusion, can only lay claim to truth if it rests upon a sufficient ground in that which is knowable. If such a basis is lacking, we are not dealing with truth but with fantasy and speculation.

We must however remark that this fourth rule of thought is not to be elevated to be an analytical norm. For a norm must be valid for the entire analytical life. That is not the case with this rule. The validity of the principle of sufficient reason on the contrary is limited exclusively to the results of thought in their relation to the knowable.

After this constructive and critical examination of the law side of the analytical modality, there is reason to ask whether the law of thought is one or many. Strictly speaking, the principle of sufficient reason is not a law of thought, because it is only valid for the *result* of thought. And the *principium exclusi tertii* is only a specific application of the *principium contradictionis*, which, in turn, is the negative formulation of the *principium identitatis*.

Ergo: there is but one analytical norm which can be stated thus: distinguish the analyzable correctly.

To this we must still add one thing. We have already noted that the *principium identitatis* points back to the numerical sphere, and the *principium contradictionis* anticipates the linguistical. In addition the analytical norm anticipates and points back to other spheres. The idea of motion or the movement of analytical activity is a kinematic analogy; the notion of force or power in thought is a physical analogy. The *formation* of concepts and judgments anticipates the historical modality. The love of truth anticipates the ethical modality and logical certainty anticipates the modality of faith. A complete formulation of the one analytical norm would have to include all analogies and anticipations.

The analytical modality is the first modality in the cosmic order whose laws are normative in character. A law of thought is a norm to which we ought to subject our thinking. The person who transgresses a law of thought thinks improperly and is guilty of error. In the pre-analytical sphere there is no question of a norm or obligation. However, we do not mean that the pre-analytical spheres are completely free from norms. When a pre-analytical thing appears as an object in a post-psychical modality, it is subject to the norms applicable in the normative modalities. Analytical norms not only apply to men in their subjective analytical function; they are also valid for the *analytical object*, the object of human thought. Things which are subject merely in the psychical, biotic, physical, kinematic, spatial and numerical modalities are not free to disobey the laws of the psychical and pre-psychical spheres.

Man alone is *subject* in the analytical modality and in all post-analytical spheres. And since the laws of the post-analytical spheres are normative in character, and since man is free, he can disobey these laws. The post-psychical spheres are normative spheres. God has given man the freedom of choice, and man is responsible for his conduct in the normative modalities.

There is a basic difference between normative and pre-analytical or non-normative modalities. Things which are subject to the laws of the latter are controlled directly by them. These God-given laws are concretely applied in these spheres. Anything which has a subject function in the physical modality, for example, is directly subject to the law of gravity, even if it is unaware of the existence of this law. All physical reality obeys the law of gravity independently of man, as man did not positively form it from a normative principle to a concrete rule.

The laws of the normative modalities, in contrast, are not directly applied by God. God has placed certain *principles* within the structure of the normative spheres, but man must discover and acknowledge their existence. And the knowledge that man has of these normative principles must not be equated with the principles themselves. Normative principles demand also human *forming* and development. They must be concretely applied by man. It is *human work* which renders them concrete and positive, applied to every case separately.

Love, for example, is a normative principle, but the principle of love does not itself tell us what is demanded in a concrete instance. It does not always afford parents an immediate solution to the concrete problems which arise in rearing children. Moreover, a legal code, although normative, does not relieve the judge of the task of reaching a verdict and in case of guilt making up the measure of penalty.

Similarly the formulation of analytical laws of thought and the formulation of what is true in a concrete instance, in a specific situation, is the result of the *specification* of logical principles. And as a matter of course human subjectivity plays a role in such specification.

Cosmic time expresses itself here in being *logically prior and logically posterior*. A conclusion is logically later than the grounds upon which it rests.

Logic is the science which investigates the analytical modality. It is a division of epistemology and as a special science it rests upon a philosophical basis. It is therefore incorrect to speak of a formal logic, if by formal we intend to imply that the philosophical basis of logic is of such a nature that the same logical system can be neutrally employed by all philosophical trends. Logicism is a form of non-Christian philosophy which absolutizes the analytical modality and makes logic the foundation, origin, and goal of the cosmos. By its denial of the sovereignty of each modality, logicism tries to reduce all aspects of reality to the analytical aspect, thereby barring the way which leads to a full comprehension of the richness of the handiwork of God.

H. *The Historical Modality*

The analytical modality is followed by the historical sphere and thus belongs to the substratum of the latter. This order cannot be reversed. History is formed by people, who have an active subject function in the analytical modality. History is made by thinking people who are capable of performing free responsible deeds which are the result of free rational judgment and choice. Animals do not form history. Animal life, as such, does not display any historical development. Bees make their honeycombs now the same way as they did 2000 years before. Animal life is concerning animal forming static. The historical development of human culture is dynamic.

The historical modality precedes the sphere of language, society, economy, etc., as all post-historical spheres contain the moment of *formation*. In the linguistical sphere we encounter the formation of language; in the social we encounter societal forms. The *moment of formation* has its modal origin in the historical sphere. And this fact enables us to determine the position of the historical modality.

What is meant by the term historical? What is the *nuclear moment* of history? In scientific circles there has been a great deal of misunderstanding and confusion on this point. It is frequently affirmed that everything is history because it comes and goes, and changes and shifts its position. The element of change and alteration is very often, although incorrectly, proclaimed to be the essence of history.

We deem this contention to be incorrect because change does not originate in the historical but in the kinematic modality. No history is formed at the North Pole where there are no people, yet all sorts of change and shifting occur there in nature. To consider everything as history is to view history as a tremendous all-absorbing stream which gushes forth and never comes to rest; a stream in which men and things momentarily rise to the surface, only to sink again into the past.

Nevertheless, there is a truth at the foundation of the conception that everything is history. The view that history is the totality of human life in all its forms and relationships is not wholly in error. Each thing and each action, every form of life, every event, and every societal relationship has an historical *aspect* which breaks the stationariness of static existence and the monotonous cycle of natural things, thereby giving to human existence the form of linear development.

The view under discussion loses sight of the character of the non-historical aspects and erroneously reduces them to the historical. The norms of law, morality, faith, for example, are sought in history, with the unavoidable result that all norms are destroyed and all certainty is engulfed in historical relativity. To consider everything as history is to extend the historical perspective illegitimately so that the sovereignty of each modality is misconstrued. The historical modality is absolutized and is virtually deified. Man withdraws his heart from God and forgets that history is one created aspect of the cosmos. To absolutize it is to make history an idol. The deification of history is historicism, an error which in recent times has poisoned a great deal of modern non-Christian science.

What then is history? The answer often given is that history is everything which occurred in the past. A single example will suffice to show that this is not sufficient.

That I put on my coat last evening is a fact that belongs to the past, but in itself is not a fact of historical significance. The passing of an automobile is a fact, but it is not history in the full sense. It does not possess any historical formational influence. But the fact that on January 7, 1937, the royal carriage transported the Dutch Prince and Princess to be united in marriage is an historical event. Why? Not because there were many spectators. Historical events can occur in solitude. The marriage of the Princess, however, is an historical fact of primary importance since it influenced the continuation of the dynasty of the House of Orange and the life of the Dutch nation. Thus one element which constitutes history is that of *forming* or *formation*. In our example we can detect the forming of a dynasty and of a folk.[1]

Dooyeweerd defines the nuclear moment of the historical

---

[1] The facts portrayed in our illustration have only a partial significance for the formation of history. We do not wish to imply that human actions can be divided into events occurring in history and contributing to its development, and into events which are outside of history. Man lives and acts upon the earth in all temporal functions. He can never render any of his temporal functions inactive. Our illustrations were only employed to show that some events have a *direct formational* influence on the process of historical development, whereas the influence of others is often indirect. For anyone interested in the subject, K. J. Popma has written a splendid book based upon a Christian philosophy of history, *Calvinistische Geschiedenisbeschouwing*, T. Wever, Franeker, 1945.

aspect as "*The controlled formation of a given aptitude, structure, or situation to be something which it otherwise would not have been. It is the normative free realization of a thing in the process of culture.*"[1]

By controlled formation we intend to convey the idea that every individual does not form history to the same degree. History is primarily formed by the *possessors* of *historical power*. Those called to extend and to develop culture within a certain *societal relationship* belong to this class of people. Leaders in our national life, our schools, churches, economy, and science lead the process of historical development, and help civilization proceed to further unfolding.

The fact that we speak of leaders indicates that strictly speaking no single person is outside of the process of historical development. Leaders have followers. Leaders possess power in societal relationships, in which many other people, in subjection to the powers placed over them, co-operate in the formation of history. No single person lives by himself. One who is not called by God to be a leader follows the direction given by others. And a leader in one *societal relationship* may be a follower in another.

Every person has his own place in the process of the development of culture. Everyone is called to engage in the formation of civilization in various ways. Everyone possesses an historical subject-function. A baker forms bread from meal. A farmer forms land from unplowed fields, a mother forms children's clothes, and a teacher forms his pupils.

All these human activities have an historical aspect as they are based upon the historical modality. But the above mentioned activities are not purely historical. Each thing, deed, and societal relationship functions in every modality and is not prematurely shut off or arrested in any particular sphere.

These just mentioned actions in which formation is in

[1] *Wijsbegeerte der Wetsidee*, 11, p. 143. Also compare Dooyeweerd, *Recht en Historie*, p. 32ff.

evidence are grounded in the historical aspect but they are not *qualified* by it. Their *determining* or *end-function* lies in a higher sphere. We shall subsequently discuss this point in detail when we treat the structure of individuality of things and societal relationships.

We must point out that the historical calling to form history is a Divine calling. It is primarily given to the human race as a whole and to the individual person who is a member of various societal relationships. The historical calling is a Divine one (Genesis 1:28: Subdue the earth and have dominion over it). And in the final analysis it rests upon the creation of man in the image of God (Gen. 1:26: Let us make man in Our Image). The fact that man is created with an historical subject-function is due to his being created in the image of God. And in the Covenant that God instituted with the human race, humanity received the kingly office which entitled it to rule and form created reality. In separating the cultural task from religion, the mystic not only falsifies Revelation but he deprives the Lord of the honor which ought to be paid Him in the formation of culture. The mystic would abandon the cultural aspect of reality to the *civitas terrena*, to the powers of this world. But the Kingdom of God has also an historical aspect. It develops in an historical manner and is brought about by applying Christian principles in the exercise of historical power.[1] The mystic ignores this power of Christ in the world and actually he seeks to withdraw himself from the Kingdom of God.

Up until now we have chiefly spoken of the subjective process of historical formation. We have discussed the subject-side of the historical modality but we have not yet considered its correlative law side. The subjective process of historical formation occurs according to normative principles to which the formers of history are subject. The call *to dominate* and *to form* the natural aspects of reality, which is actualized in technique, is an historical normative

---

[1] Dooyeweerd. *A New Critique of Theoretical Thought*, Vol. II.

principle. Another is the principle of *continuity*, i.e., the uninterrupted progress of cultural development. The *former* of history ought to join with the past; no one can radically sever himself from it and make a completely new beginning. No one can create something entirely new. God alone has this power but even He does not deal with fallen humanity in a discontinuous manner. In every moment of history the number of ways leading to the future are limited so that the former of history must select between the existing possibilities.

A third principle is the so-called *integration-norm* which insures the actualization or completion of that which God has placed in the cosmos as merely potential. It insures the fact that the richness inherent in creation will develop or unfold.

The principle of integration is coupled with the principles of *differentiation* and *individualization,* which insure the *unfolding* of the individual tendency of nations, societal relationships, and persons. In the historical modality, as a normative sphere, these principles require *positivization* or *specification*. In other words they must be concretely applied in all human relationships which have an historical aspect. It is not possible to determine beforehand or in general what ought to be developed in a particular societal relationship. The leaders of a societal relationship possess historical power and they must formulate the concrete requirements of culture for their own societal relationship; but their power is not arbitrary. They ought to act in accordance with normative historical principles and must subject themselves to the Divine world order. But since the historical sphere is normative, violations of historical norms are possible, and leaders may fail to act normatively. Reaction, for example, is an anti-normative deed or attitude. Reactionaries praise the "good old days" and would roll back the progress of cultural development. Reactionaries arise in every field and oppose each new norm. Revolution is also anti-normative. The revolutionary intentionally breaks with the historical past and disavows the continuity of history. The revolutionist dares to make a new beginning, e.g., Hitler's Third Reich.

We can now answer the old controversial question as to whether or not history is normative. If history is conceived of as the subjective process of historical development, then it is evident that no factual moment of the subjective process which belongs to the historical past can be a norm for our conduct today. Anyone who elevates the subject to a norm falls into a subjectivism and misunderstands the divine order of creation. However, if the term history includes the entire historical modality then it is normative, as cultural development is ruled by historical norms.

Before we proceed to the next modality let us note a few analogies and anticipations. The moment of historical *development* is an analogy of the vital development found in the biotic sphere. The *sphere* of culture is a spatial analogy. And the *power* of the leader who forms history depends upon the psychical influence that he has upon his followers, (psychical analogy). It is evident that development-planning is a logical analogy, while historical-movement is a kinematic one. The historical sphere anticipates the linguistic in cultural symbols, through which the historically significant is distinguished from the historically insignificant. (Statues and memorials are examples of expressions of historically significant events.) Historical development takes place in an historical process in which nations associate with each other and this free association anticipates the social modality. Civilized nations live together. Primitive peoples and cultures are isolated from each other. Their culture is closed. Historical development *opens or unfolds a* culture.

Cosmic time expresses itself in the *periods of history* which are delineated by the predominance of certain important cultural motives. And although separated from each other, one period exerts an influence upon the other. The past contains the present, and the present the future. The Christian calendar bears witness to the fact that the most important point in history is marked by the Incarnation of the Word.

The historical modality is investigated by the science of history; the latter labors fruitfully only if it recognizes its limits and acknowledges that there are other modalities which transcend the historical and cannot be reduced to it.

I. *The Linguistic Modality*

The linguistic sphere of language or symbolic signs follows the historical modality, in which all formation originates. Since we can observe the formation of language even among primitive peoples, the linguistical sphere must follow the historical and not vice versa. The historical modality is a part of the modal substratum of language.

We are using here the concept of language in the broadest sense. It is not restricted to diverse spoken languages but includes all sorts of gesticulative language and every other manner in which ideas are expressed in symbols and sensory signs, such as books, letters, numbers, musical notes, flags, and statues.

The nuclear moment of language is *symbolic signification*. Every phenomenon in the world in which symbolic signification plays a role is in some way or other related to the linguistic aspect. The sacraments, for example, are signs; they are linguistic analogies in the modality of faith.

We have already noted that the formation of language is an historical analogy, consequently the pre-historical spheres necessarily belong to the substratum upon which all symbolic signification rests.

Economy of language (thriftiness with words) and linguistic harmony are examples of anticipations in the linguistic sphere.

The linguistic sphere is a normative modality. Only the principles of language are given. These principles must be specified and positivized in order to become concrete linguistic norms. Consequently the norms of grammar are the results of human work and can be violated by every creature possessing a *subjective* linguistic function.

Cosmic time expresses itself in the *symbolic significance of temporal moments* (pauses, semi-colons, and commas). And the science of linguistics investigates this sphere.

J. *The Social Modality*

We can speak of a social modality because temporal reality has also a social aspect. Man is the only creature that possesses a *subjective* social function; he alone has a subject-function in all the normative modalities. In animal life there is collective activity (symbiosis, living together), and an instinctive feeling of belonging together, but no instance of veritable social intercourse. A social subject-function necessarily presupposes as its foundation the linguistical, historical, and analytical modalities. Animals appear only as objects in human social life.

Social *intercourse* is the nuclear moment of the social modality. The word social is not to be thought of as primarily referring to or being restricted to labor unions and related matters. The social modality covers a much broader terrain. The expression, "the social question," refers to a problem of labor. Such problems have a social aspect, but the juridical and economical aspect play a more dominant role in labor disputes. This is, in fact, substantiated by the very notion of a just wage. Every organization, of what nature it may be, has a social aspect, though the social sphere is broader than the terrain of human organizations. A social aspect exists wherever man comes into contact with other creatures.

The linguistic modality is a part of the modal foundation of the social sphere. Consequently the social modality contains a linguistic analogy. Every social action, such as a handshake and salute, is necessarily based upon a symbolic foundation. If we greet someone with a kiss or by the removal of our hat, this action is symbolic and signifies or conveys a meaning. The social modality anticipates the economical. The requirements of custom among primitive peoples are greater in number than in an opened society or culture. The relative simplicity of social forms in opened cultures anticipates the economical modality. For it is not true to mean that primitive peoples — sometimes called: nature peoples — would be characterized by a total lack of culture. No, primitive societies have also a primitive culture. That means, that the culture of primitive peoples is strongly and statically bound to the lower, the "nature-aspects" of reality. Their culture is still closed, because the anticipatory moments of their cultural life have not yet been opened. The disclosing of these anticipatory moments only occurs when a primitive society is taken into partnership with civilized peoples. Then the social forms of that former primitive people become simplified. See chapter 17.

The social modality also anticipates the aesthetic and ethical modalities. When social intercourse is marred by hatred, not only is the harmony of life destroyed but social and ethical norms are trampled under foot.

Cosmic time appears for example in our permitting older persons to enter a room first and in the obligation that we have to be polite in our conduct against other people. Sociology is the science which investigates the social modality.

K. *The Economic Modality*

The nuclear moment of the economic modality consists in the *saving of calculated values*. Or stated more simply, it consists in thrift, because of the fact that things have value, unless they are available to everyone in an unlimited quantity. Air for example, is free, because its supply is unlimited. The nuclear moment of the economical sphere combines the principle of *saving* with the moment of *parsimony* of serviceable goods. In the economic modality the value of one commodity is measured by the value of another. Money is the *measure of value* employed in economic transactions of an advanced society.

Since the value of commodities is determined by human intercourse, the economic modality is based primarily upon the social modality. The expression of value in price symbols is a linguistic analogy. And the fact that we speak of the *formation* of prices is an historical analogy.

The economic modality anticipates all the modalities which follow it. The moment of weighing and balance is present in all post-economic spheres. Concerning the aesthetic modality: in a work of art the artist balances the contrasts in order to get an harmonious object. In the juridical sphere occurs the balancing of rights against each other. In the ethical sphere the moment of weighing is present in the idea of economy in charity. The economic modality rests upon the analytical modality, and therefore its laws, as in all post-analytical spheres, are normative in character; they do not operate as a natural necessity, but they must be formed by the *positivization* of the principle of saving. An example of a law of economy is the law of supply and demand which determines the prices on the free market.

The laws of the economic modality are norms. They can be violated, for example, by extravagance, dishonest competition, and usury.

During the middle ages, economic life could not *unfold* according to its own character, as it was governed by the Church. The Church forbade the taking of rent, condemned competition, and formulated its own theory of a just price. The Renaissance emancipated economic life from Church control.

Cosmic time expresses itself in the economic modality e.g., in the phenomenon of *rent*. Rent is inseverably connected with time as it assigns a greater value to the present possession of goods than it does to the possession of future goods. A temporal factor is also present in money. One possessing money has an indefinite quantity of future goods at his disposal.

Up until now we have examined only the modal structure of the economic modality. However, like all other modalities, it appears in its own peculiar form in the various *societal relationships*. Consequently, we can distinguish various types of economy, e.g., political economy, family economy, business economy, and so on.

The economic aspect is systematically investigated by the science of economics.

L. *The Aesthetic Modality*

The nuclear moment of the aesthetic modality is *harmony* or *beautiful proportion*. Superfluity in a highly developed or primitive work of art detracts essentially from the beauty of the art-object. And this principle is an economic analogy in the sphere of aesthetics which indicates that the aesthetic modality rests upon the economic.

Since the artist expresses his aesthetic conception in color, sound, words, and pictures the aesthetic modality points back to the linguistic sphere of symbolic signification. Beauty is present in natural things in a way different from a work of art. The beauty of things of nature is given. The beauty of art objects is *formed*. Things of nature function, as objects, in the aesthetic modality; their beauty is objectively given. The beauty of art on the contrary is not given but it is formed by the artist. And this element of formation is an historical analogy.

The aesthetic modality precedes the juridical. Jurisprudence includes a harmonization of interests in the sense of rendering each his due.

Aesthetic laws are norms which must be rendered positive by human specification and which ought not to be violated. Their violation gives rise to disharmony and dissonance. The style of an art object (e.g., Gothic or Renaissance) is an historical analogy. A specific style is always joined with a specific historical period. And if we should today build churches in Roman style, or write a book in the literary style of the 17th century, we would be repeating the past and would be reactionaries. We would be guilty of opposing the positive aesthetic norms of the present time.

Beauty also has its duration, its own expression of cosmic time. The aesthetic temporal order is different in principle from the historical. If this is forgotten in an historical novel, then moments arise which are aesthetically empty, even though they may be filled with an exact historical description of events. Cosmic time has as many expressions in the aesthetic modality as there are sorts of beauty and art. Beauty-time in music e.g., is another one, namely *rhythm,* than in the art of painting. In the latter time expresses itself in the *harmonious simultaneity* of the parts of the picture.

The science of aesthetics scientifically examines the aesthetic modality. And it is deplorable that almost nothing has been done in this field from a truly Christian point of view. Only a few attempts have been made to construct an aesthetics based upon Christian principles. And if a radically Christian aesthetics is ever to be developed, then such concepts as form and matter, essence and appearance, spirit and matter cannot be of assistance. For, at the most, they can only lead to an aesthetical view that is based upon a synthesis philosophy.

If the norms of aesthetics are employed in order to judge things which are not aesthetically qualified, then the error of aestheticism results. A sermon, for example, has an aesthetic aspect but it must not be primarily evaluated according to norms of aesthetics. It must be judged primarily by the Holy Scripture, the norm of faith.

M. *The Juridical Modality*

The peculiar character of law, in the juridical sense of the term, is expressed by the term, *retribution.* Retribution is not to be exclusively thought of as punishment. This term "retribution" is used here in the pregnant sense of an irreducible *well-balanced harmonization of a multiplicity of individual and social interests.* Prof. Dooyeweerd adds here: "This mode (of balancing) implies a standard of proportionality regulating the legal interpretation of social facts and their factual social consequences in order to maintain the juridical balance by a just reaction...." Vol. II, page 129. Three analogies are present in this definition. Harmonization points back to the aesthetical. Well-balanced refers to the economic. To be well-balanced is to be free from all excess and to prevent one interest from encroaching upon another. And the multiplicity of interests is a social analogy. There are many different interests in society. However, the main distinction is that between the interests of *authoritative societal relationships* and those of *free societal relations*.[1]

Injustices arise when one interest illegitimately replaces another. Injustice must be repaid. Harmony must be restored and the unlawful interest must be curbed so that the suppressed interest can again assume its proper place. The government of the state has the power to establish law. Do not misunderstand this point. We must guard against all forms of totalitarianism, and be careful not to succumb to the notion that law derives its origin and validity from the state. This is the error which led to such detestable results in Nazi Germany. It is the error of all totalitarianism, which makes an idol of the state. Christian philosophy is radically opposed to absolute individualism. And it is equally opposed to a totalitarian state.

God Himself has established different structures for society. Within the juridical law-sphere these structures possess their own individual internal juridical spheres or spheres of right which have their own independent validity. An internal structural diversity is present in juridical life. State-law, family-law, associational-law, and church-law are independent legal structures. And with the exception of family-law, which has the biotical foundation of consanguinity, the other structures have their foundation in the

---

[1] An *authoritative societal relationship* is a form of society where members are joined together by authority, e.g., the family, the state, and the church. The members of a *free societal relation*, in contrast, are coordinated, e.g., in the relation of friendship, and in the relation between buyer and seller.

historical modality. They have developed and unfolded historically in the development of culture.

This does not imply that law is only an historical phenomenon. Historicism tries to reduce law to history. But even though most structures of law have an historical foundation, law transcends history and has its own *sovereignty which cannot be reduced to any other modality*.

We have digressed slightly from our treatment of the theory of modalities to consider the theory of the *structures of individuality* of human society. Modal juridical theory, however, is concerned with all sorts of law. All juridical structures: family-law, state-law, church-law, have a modal juridical function, even though they are different in their inner nature: they are all essentially juridical (standardization misinterprets their peculiar character, and in practice leads to unbearable tyranny). Church-law, for example, is not just conventionally referred to as law, but it possesses a juridical character to the fullest degree. Its character is expressed by the term "retribution," but retribution employed to acquire a well-balanced harmonization of internal ecclesiastical interests. The civil government has no authority in this sphere.

The formation of juridical norms is the task of the proper organs of authority. The government correctly determines the laws of the state, but parents properly determine the laws applicable in the internal relations of the family.

Whether considered individually or collectively, only man can be a juridical subject. Other created things can be a juridical object (e.g., a house can be the object in a law suit). We shall consider this point later on.

Time has also a function in this juridical sphere. We speak of a *juridical duration of validity*. A contract is made for a certain time and a law can lose its validity by repeal. Delay in the fulfillment of contractual duties has certain legal consequences and through superannuation rights are acquired or lost. Jurisprudence is the science which investigates the juridical modality.

N. *The Ethical Modality*

Love in its temporal relations, as parental love, child love, love for one's country, and companionship, is the nuclear moment of the ethical modality. This temporal love must be distinguished from *the religious fulness of love.* The latter is revealed by Christ as the fulfillment of the law. It is the love to God and the neighbor that the Holy Spirit places in the hearts of believers. In 1 Corinthians 13, the Apostle Paul speaks of this religious love in Christ which is also the fulfillment of justice, beauty, and wisdom and which has to be the deepest motive of all functional activity by a believer. It is not love in the modal sense.

Moral love is a temporal modality. It is a mere segment of the love which is directed to the service of God and one's neighbor. As a temporal modality, moral love can not be reduced to any other modality. Love is essentially different from law, but even though different, law and love do not exclude one another, and are not contradictory.

The view of Emil Brunner is diametrically opposed to this view. Brunner believes that law belongs to the sphere of worldly ordinances. Law is a loveless rule. A Christian intrinsically participates in the terrain of grace, and is thus emancipated from all worldly ordinances. A Christian must love according to Christ's commandment of love. Christ's commandment is a commandment of the moment and not a universal rule. It tells us what we must do in a specific concrete situation. We cannot agree with Brunner as we do not believe that love and law are contradictory.

The ethical modality rests upon the juridical and does not contradict it. Rather the ethical modality contains a juridical analogy. The very principle of love signifies a proportionate amount of self love and of love for one's neighbor. And the idea of proportionate amount includes the notion of retribution. Love also possesses a social analogy. We must love our neighbor in our intercourse with him in all the social relationships in which God has placed us.

Love in modal sense may not be identified with the pistical function. Scripture distinguishes between love and faith. The former is directed by the latter. For faith is of all functions the directive one. And it is clear, that faith presupposes love. Believing always occurs on the base of loving, because everyone is faithful to whom he loves. This principle of love must be rendered positive in the many relationships which men sustain to one another. The positivization of the principle of love must take place in the case of Christians, under the direction of their faith in the Word and the Law of God. The Ten Commandments, as a part of Divine revelation, do not constitute a "moral law," in the sense of a moral norm. The Ten Commandments are a norm of faith; they influence moral norms through the faith of Christians. The faith of Christians is able to render the principle of love positive in the ethical sphere (e.g., it influences parental love, child love and all other kinds of love in this way, that the parents have to love their children and the children their parents for God's sake).

Ethics is a science and as such it investigates the ethical modality. Ethics does not establish ethical norms. It merely investigates them. In this respect ethics is similar to the science of jurisprudence. For the latter investigates the juridical modality but does not establish juridical norms. Ethics is not a science dealing with the totality of all human actions and dispositions, but only with those relationships that are based on temporal love. The science of ethics is not a part of theology nor of philosophy, but an independent science, investigating the moral law-sphere with all its analogies, anticipations and individualities.

O. *The Pistical Modality or the Sphere of Faith*

The last modality in time-order is that of faith. The modality of faith is a border-function, as it does not contain any modal anticipations. In this respect it is similar to the numerical sphere which as the first modality does not contain any modal analogies. Number is the simplest function and faith is the most complicated, with a maximum of analogies.

To understand this sphere correctly we must notice three things.

1. Faith may not be identified with religion. For faith is only one of the many functional expressions of life. God is not to be served only in our faith-life but in our entire life. God is to be served in our thought, and in the social, historical and economical spheres. *Religion is the service of God with all the vital functions* which proceed from our heart. The foundation of religion is the Covenant of God, and the latter is not related only to our worship of God but it includes our whole existence. "Whether you eat or drink, or whatsoever you do, do all to glory of God," 1 Corinthians 10:31. The demands of the Covenant require grateful obedience to God in all spheres. The promise of God embraces our entire existence and because of the curse of the Covenant the grace of the Lord is completely withdrawn from those who have departed from Him.

The care which a God-fearing mother exercises in taking care of her family is also a part of religion. And a God-fearing man engaged in his daily vocation in a factory or an office is thereby serving God. No matter where performed human work is religious, but office work or factory work are not acts of worship. They are not the same as attending church, engaging in prayer, or partaking of the sacraments. If faith is identified with religion then life is secularized and the largest part of it is withdrawn from the service of God.

A correct conception of the relationship between faith and religion does not divorce the one from the other. In our catechism we confess that good works must be performed through faith, which directs our service of God with all our heart.

2. Faith is a temporal function possessed by everyone in

the cosmos. The unbeliever exercises faith to the same degree as does the believer. This point was forceably enunciated by Abraham Kuyper.[1] An unbeliever is not a person who lacks a *pistical* function. Such a view is compatible with the Roman Catholic notion of a *donum superadditum*, according to which faith is a gift of grace that can be joined to nature, and as a gift faith can also be absent. Such a position is erroneous. An unbeliever is not a person lacking faith but is someone whose faith is mistakenly directed. The faith of the non-Christian is not directed to the One True God who has revealed Himself in Jesus Christ, but it is directed toward an idol. An atheist, for example, believes that God does not exist. In apostasy from God an atheist also possesses the certainty of faith and this "unbelieving" faith is the *directing function* of his life. It withdraws his whole life from God and causes him to devote his life to the service of the things that are beneath.

3. As a temporal function faith is not only distinct from the other functions, but it is also not the same as the heart. The heart is the religious center out of which all functions proceed. For this reason Scripture says that we believe with the heart in order to be justified.

If one understands what has been said, he can comprehend what is meant by the *border-character* of faith. The *border* or *boundary* character of faith means that the function of faith always points beyond and above itself to that which is the transcendent firm foundation of faith. By pointing beyond itself faith points beyond everything temporal. Apostate faith also points beyond itself toward a supposedly firm foundation. Apostate faith seeks its fixed ground in an idol which it finds in the cosmos. It erects and absolutizes a created idol by seeking to project a part of creation above the cosmos. The border-character of faith, its border-position between time and eternity, is thus characterized by a reaching out toward its own super-temporal

---

[1] See *"Encyclopaedie der Heilige Godgeleerdheid,"* 1909, Part 11, p. 86.

foundation. To see the coherence between faith and the firm foundation of faith, compare Hebrews 11:1.

The border-character of faith is also proper to all the analogies included in the modality of faith. Pistical adoration, for example, is a pistical analogy of moral love. Faith does not exist without adoration, without a cult. Adoration and love are what distinguish faith from magic. Magic does not seek to adore the "supernatural" but it seeks to dominate and rule it. The pistical-adoration of the cult obviously shares in the border character of faith. Adoration is either directed toward the true God or toward a false god. Man adores Him in whom he trusts and honors whatever he acknowledges as the foundation of all existence. In addition to the moral analogy the joyous faith consists in an inner joy that accompanies the certainty which is experienced when a person trusts the promises of God.

The joyous faith is joy in God and it is a happiness that extends beyond all temporal things.

The knowledge of faith is an analytical analogy, and sacrifice is an economical one.

Dooyeweerd defines the nuclear moment of the temporal function of faith as, *"the transcendental certainty which we possess in time concerning the firm foundation of all things."* It is the certainty which is grasped in the heart of our existence by means of a revelation from the Origin.

Faith is transcendental certainty, a certainty which points beyond itself. It is the certainty that we have concerning what we believe to be the foundation of our life and the basis of all things. In other words, it answers the question: Where lies the deepest foundation of our life, the divine ground of all things, upholding all things by the word of his power? (Heb. 1:3). And such a question can only be answered by a revelation from the Origin. Consequently, all men are prompted by their faith to appeal to a revelation. Men either believe in and trust the Bible as the revelation of God or they believe in a supposed revelation of their idol. That revelation grips man in the heart of his existence and touches the center of his life impressing its stamp upon his entire being. Those who seek final certainty in the Incarnate Word accept Christian revelation. The faith of a Christian enables him to accept the Bible as the Word of God. Therein he finds the last certainty about Him, who is the First and the Last, the Beginning and the End.

We have indicated that the modality of faith possesses a maximum number of analogies but does not possess any anticipations. And we have cited ethical, psychical, economical and analytical analogies. The following discussion should suffice to show that there are many additional analogies.

We encounter the notion of forming also in the modality of faith. Ecclesiastical forms and the formation of the confessions therefore are historical analogies. And when the Church expresses the content of its faith in its confessions, it employs symbols. Consequently, the linguistical and the historical modalities both constitute a part of the modal substratum of the modality of faith. Furthermore, since the communion of the saints includes social intercourse with those who love the same Redeemer, it is a social analogy. There is also a connection between faith and the aesthetical aspect. The certainty of faith endows life with harmony and balance, and doubt creates disharmony and unbalance.

Man alone has faith. He alone is a subject in the modality of faith. And in a way this pistical subjectivity is a part of the image of God in man. This does not imply that God has faith in the human significance of this word. But this is here the analogy, the image, that God Himself is Certainty. He is the Faithful One. A child of God has faith in God and thus possesses certainty. Only man can have a pistical subject-function. Other creatures can appear only as an object in the modality of faith. A church building, for instance, is pistically characterized, but it does naturally not function as a pistical subject. It only has a pistical object-function. We shall discuss this point in greater detail, in our subsequent treatment of *the structure of the object.*

Insofar as it is normative, Divine revelation — as well in the Bible as in all the works and deeds of God — is the norm of the modality of faith. Our faith is subject to the revealed Will of God. We ought to put our trust and faith in Divine authority and not in the authority of men. When belief based upon authority is disqualified, the authority of God is exchanged for the authority of man and man believes in man.

The revelation of God, brought to fulfillment in the Lord Jesus Christ, the Incarnate Word, is the normative principle of faith. Divine revelation ought to be believed. We ought to accept and place our trust in it, because God, who has spoken in His Word and is still speaking in His works and deeds, is Truth and cannot lie. The ground of faith does not lie in man but in God. When we accept God's Word by our faith it leads all other functions. And by giving them a transcendental direction, it causes them to transcend temporality. For example, when motivated by faith, our love in temporal relationships is not only directed toward our neighbor, but it includes an element which is directed toward God.

The fact that faith causes other functions to look beyond or transcend the temporal may also be seen when a former of history is motivated by the Christian faith. Such a person will form history in order to advance the Kingdom of God. He will try to create and to employ historical power in order to give concrete actuality to Christian principles. And thus he becomes a co-worker with God, and endeavors to bring God's Kingdom on earth, looking forward to the day of the completion of the Kingdom of God, in which He may be all in all.

The pistical norm must also be rendered positive. One of the ways in which this occurs is through the confessions which formulate the faith of the Church. But all positive rules of faith, made by men, and even the confession, remain always appealable to the Word of God, the highest and only Norm of faith.

Faith is the last temporal function. Cosmic time expresses itself here in the operation of the subjective work of grace in the life of the believers. One does not only increase in the knowledge and grace of Jesus Christ, but this grace can also decrease. So a Christian has his different times of faith. And when the poverty of this time is ended, faith will be replaced by sight, and we shall behold Him face to face.

Theology is the science which examines this modality. Theology is a special science, and, as such, it ought not to constitute itself as a rival of philosophy. A Christian theology ought to derive its philosophical presuppositions from Christian philosophy. And whenever Christian philosophy enters the sphere of theology, it ought to permit itself to be led by theology, and to avail itself of the fruits of theological labor. Theology, however, must fully recognize the fact that it is not called to give solutions to philosophical and psychological problems. If it attempts to do so, then theology exceeds its limits, and engages in activities for which it is not competent.

Theology can exceed its proper limits in additional ways. Within the church there are those who would grant a directive or leading function to theology. Such people argue that since the church is concerned with the Word of God, and since theology supplies the correct interpretation of God's Word, theology is therefore competent to direct the life of the church. This argument seriously violates the principle of the perspicuity of the Holy Scripture, which in protestant circles — at least — is a fundamental article of faith.

Theologians, as other scientists, must learn that the task of science is secondary. Science ought to aid life, but it ought not to dominate. Theologians must learn that theology is no longer the "queen of the sciences." And as theology — like all sciences — is a subjective human work, it never can be a norm of faith and life.

17
The Opening or Unfolding Process

This brings our discussion of the individual modalities to a close. We have discussed each modality separately, but we stressed the fact that no modality exists in isolation. There are no separate theoretically abstract modalities. In reality each modality is connected with every other modality. Each sphere points toward and interacts with all the others. All the modalities are interwoven to form a cosmos which displays the manifold wisdom of God.

The modalities do not constitute a static unity in their *coherence* and *interwovenness*. They do not constitute an immobile mass, but they form a dynamic whole in which there is a constant movement, a *meaningful enrichment* and *unfolding*, which we shall henceforth call the *unfolding* or *opening process*. The term *"unfolding"* or *"opening"* process designates the fact that under certain conditions, the anticipatory moments of a particular modality *unfold* in such a way that its meaning (*Sinn*) is enriched. It is also possible for the anticipatory moments of a particular modality to be *shut off or closed*, in which case, only its analogical moments function. The coherence of a modality between its nuclear-moment and its modal analogies is called its *primary structure*. Dooyeweerd speaks about this primary structure of a cosmic aspect: "The modal structure of a law-sphere is primarily expressed in the continuous coherence of its nuclear moment and retrocipations (analogies). . . . The modal retrocipations are *inseparable* from the modal nuclei of all the law-spheres, so that, in general, *modal meaning cannot express itself outside of the retrocipatory coherence of meaning*" (Vol. II, p. 181). And if the anticipatory moments of a particular modality are closed we speak of this modality as functioning in a *static* and *restrictive* manner. But if its anticipatory moments are opened, then this modality is *enriched* and we speak of it as possessing an *expansive function*.

Perhaps, an illustration will help. Both men and animals

possess a psychical *subject-function*. The psychical function is the last subject-function that animals possess. An animal is not a subject in a higher modality. It does not think, talk, believe or form history. In contrast to animals, man functions as subject in all the post-psychical modalities. Human subjective feeling, in other words, is anticipatory in character (e.g., it points forward to human *subjective* cogitative action, and so on). These *anticipations* are lacking in animal life, because animals do not have any *subjectivity* in the post-psychical modalities. An animal, for example, cannot think analytically. It can be an object but it cannot be a subject in the logical modality. And this accounts for the difference between human and animal pain. If an animal feels pain, then this feeling is statically bound to pre-psychical reality, to the sensory organism. The feeling of pain in animal life is included in what we mean by a restrictive function. Since an animal is psychically qualified and lacks all higher subject-functions, the animal feeling of pain cannot be *expanded* or *enriched*. It can only be differentiated in relation to a greater differentiation in its vital organs.

Whenever the psychical anticipatory moments of man are opened, human pain is an opened feeling. A man who feels a pain can give a thoughtful reflective explanation of it and can investigate its cause and speak of it to others. Moreover, when a man is struck unlawfully, he may feel the ensuing pain as an injustice. As a matter of fact injustice unaccompanied by bodily pain, or even a lack of love, may itself prove painful to a sensitive person. And a child of God may view pain as a beneficial chastisement from God and may be led by it to repentance and new obedience. In other words man's feeling of pain functions in an *opened expansive manner*. It is not statically connected to the modal substratum of the psychical modality but it reaches out into all post-psychical spheres.

Incidentally this illustrates that man bears God's image in all his functions, even in those that he shares with other creatures. The psychical subject-function of man is a feature of the image of God, because through its opened anticipatory moments, it differs essentially from the psychical function of animal life.

When is a modality opened or expanded? This is the answer: if an anticipatory moment of a lower modality points toward a function which becomes its *leading* or *directive* function, then it can be said that this anticipatory moment is *opened* or *expanded*.

Consider the following two examples. We can speak of a logical feeling or a feeling whose anticipation of the analytical modality is opened. The psychical subject-function of man becomes a logical feeling when the analytical function gains ascendency or guidance over feeling. The function of feeling is thus enriched or expanded. Secondly, when love directs or leads law, the ethical anticipatory moment of the juridical modality is opened. If law is not directed by love this juridical function is closed and is statically bound to the modal substratum of the juridical modality. When the juridical function is thus closed the principle of an eye for an eye and a tooth for a tooth is in force. The Lord commanded us to love our enemies. In the final analysis our faith directs or leads the *expansion* or *opening* process of the normative modalities. But this statement does not explain everything we wish to know. For the entire life of primitive peoples is closed in character. It is statically bound to its natural substratum. And yet the function of faith is not lacking there and is also the leading function of primitive peoples. We are confronted by the fact that even though the expansion process of the normative anticipatory spheres can be completely absent among primitive peoples yet the pistical function appears even to play a greater role among primitives than in a differentiated society. As long as life among primitive peoples retains its closed character, scientific thought, historical consciousness, a differentiated economy, an enriched idea of law, and the opened principles of love for one's neighbor are not present. However, when through various factors, a primitive people is brought into contact with historical cultural nations, then they gradually develop an opened culture. The normative anticipatory spheres develop under the leadership of faith, but the *historical modality is the basis of the expansion or opening process*. It is, as Dooyeweerd says, the cornerstone of the normative dynamic of meaning.

Opened historical development, namely historical development which is a part of world history, is not found in a primitive cultural situation. Primitive cultures have many individual characteristics, nevertheless a uniform tradition dominates each successive generation. The past is rigidly followed. Each generation is shackled to an iron tradition, which is jealously guarded by those in possession of power.

Non-Christians have often stated that this primitive cultural situation is the original state of mankind, or the beginning of the history of humanity. Since we believe the Word of God, our viewpoint is quite different. A primitive culture is the result of apostasy from God; it is a consequence of His curse. God confused and scattered the nations of the earth at the tower of Babel. Consequently, they were isolated from historical intercourse and gradually degenerated. In addition they lost contact with the Divine Revelation which originally was directed to the whole human race. In the first chapter of the Epistle to the Romans, the Apostle Paul states repeatedly that God has given the nations over to themselves.

By his deification of natural forces, primitive man exercises his function of faith in such a way that the normative modalities are statically bound to their natural substratum.

When a primitive culture is no longer isolated, it expands and unfolds its culture under the leadership of faith. (One of the secondary tasks of Christian missions is to direct and aid this expansion.) The expansion-process can take one of two possible religious directions. A culture can expand positively or negatively. From the Christian point of view, positive religious expansion is directed by faith in the true God, whereas negative expansion is directed by a faith which is apostate from God.

Positive religious expansion occurs when — through the primary opening of the heart by the Holy Spirit — the function of faith is opened to Divine revelation. In this expansion the life of man, which was restrictively bound to deified nature, is emancipated from it and freed from superstitious fear. The whole life is directed toward Christ and man is thus brought into the service of God with all his heart.

Negative religious expansion takes place under the leadership of apostate faith. The positive expansion of a culture advances the Kingdom of God; negative expansion advances the *civitas terrena*, the kingdom of darkness. When the latter occurs, the function of faith detaches itself from its static union with the gods of nature. But, instead of placing its faith in the true God, a negatively religious expanded culture deifies the normative functions of human personality. A primitive culture deifies the lower modalities and a negatively religious expanded culture deifies the higher normative modalities. In the former, the sun, moon, and the stars are worshiped. In the latter, gods are made in the image of man and man becomes conscious of himself and of his freedom. The life of a primitive man is completely absorbed in his tribe. In an expanded culture, however, the individual acquires personality and develops an independent character and the normative modalities are opened under the direction of faith. (Faith may be exercised negatively or positively.) Non-Christian science and philosophy are the fruit of a negatively religious expanded culture.

In the life and world view of modern humanism, a conflict exists between faith in the ideal of science (the deification of the analytical modality), and faith in the ideal of personality, (the deification of the free, unrestrained personality in one of the post-analytical spheres.) This struggle takes place within the camp of the *civitas terrena*, the kingdom of darkness. A Christian is a citizen of the Kingdom of God; he must relentlessly oppose both sides. Christian philosophy is religious thinking from and toward Him, who is the Origin of all creatures. It can never cease to wage war against the kingdom of darkness.

Thus the expansion process can be negative or positive; it

can occur individually, in the development of a child to an adult (without necessarily ceasing at any specific age); and collectively, in the transformation of a primitive people to a cultured people. And it also occurs in the further unfolding of the latter in the differentiated life of societal relationships.

18

The Universality of Each Sphere

We have examined the cosmic principle of the sovereignty of each modality and have seen that the various spheres are mutually irreducible since each possesses in its modal structure a peculiar nuclear moment.

The laws of one modality are not valid in another modality. Any attempt to reduce one modality to another, or to transfer the laws of one sphere to another sphere, unavoidably results in antinomies or unsolvable contradictions.

The antinomies of Zeno, the Eleatic philosopher, afford us an example of such contradictions. Zeno logically demonstrated that Achilles, a marathon runner, can never overtake a turtle if it is given a head start. To overtake it, Achilles must arrive at the point at which the turtle was when he began to run. However, when he arrives at this point, the turtle will have gone farther. And again, before Achilles can overtake the turtle, he must repeat the process of arriving where the turtle was, and so on, ad infinitum. The turtle can never be caught; theoretically Achilles always remains behind it.

Nothing seems to be wrong with the reasoning employed here. But of course in reality the situation is different. If an automobile could not overtake a perambulator, the automobile industry would never have arisen. The error which Zeno commits is that he does not recognize the sovereignty of the modality of motion. His antinomies arose because he tried to reduce the function of motion to the spatial modality. The motion of running is *mathematicized* to an infinite series of progressively smaller static spatial distances.

Zeno makes the same fundamental mistake in his proof that a flying arrow is always at rest. The antinomies of Zeno were caused by his philosophical system in which he denied motion and reduced all modalities to the spatial. A similar reduction is inevitably made by every form of immanence-philosophy. It is required by every philosophical system that is based upon a primary deification of one of the various functions or modalities. Psychologism, for example, deifies the psychical aspect and thus tries to reduce all modal differences to feeling. It considers thought, speech, and faith to be forms of individual or group feelings. Faith, for example, is reduced to a feeling of certainty or trust. Antinomies also arise here. The experience of one person is different from that of another. And two people are often affected differently by the same feeling.

The same type of *reduction-acrobatics* is demanded by all other -isms, such as, historicism, logicism, biologism, materialism, socialism, and ethicism. Consequently, immanence-philosophy does not display a gradual development. One philosopher after the other upsets the system of his predecessor. One extreme evokes another. But the reality of life does not permit itself to be dominated theoretically by one specific function.

The principle of sphere-sovereignty challenges the very existence of all sorts of immanence-philosophy and it furnishes the Christian thinker with a key by which he can unlock the treasures of creation. Immanence-philosophy cannot accept the principle of sphere-sovereignty as long as it retains its idea of totality and tries to squeeze the fulness of creation into the cadre of a deified modality.

In spite of our radical rejection of the -isms which we have just mentioned, they all rest upon an element of truth, and their reduction-acrobatic is in a certain sense successful. The history of non-Christian philosophy is not just a history of errors. It would be absurd to claim that philosophy began at the Free University of Amsterdam in 1926, the year that Dooyeweerd and Vollenhoven became professors and started to develop their system of Christian philosophy.

It may appear difficult to understand how the extremes which we reject in principle have been able to advance philosophic thought and have given us theoretical insight into conditions which had previously been unknown. But all such difficulties are removed by the principle of the *universality of every sphere*, which is the counterpart of the principle of sphere-sovereignty.

The universality of every sphere means that in its full coherence all of temporal reality is expressed within the boundaries of every modality. Each function reflects the entire cosmos. But each image is different; no two are alike. Each image reflected is determined by the peculiar nature of the sphere in which it arises. Therefore it is meaningful to speak of the *world* of feeling, the *world* of numbers, the *world* of beauty, and so on.

The principle of the universality of every sphere is easily understood if we remember that every modality contains anticipations and analogies which point to every other modality. The totality formed by the nuclear moment, anticipations, and analogies is an image or reflection of the entire cosmos. The nuclear moment, anticipations, and analogies are different in each case. And this difference is not merely due to quantity but to quality. Anticipations, analogies and nuclear moments differ because of the modality in which they appear. For example: the psychical analogy in the modality of faith, namely a joyful faith is a matter radically different from the psychical analogy in the ethical sphere, namely an impulsive love or love-passion, because the meaning-kernel of each sphere puts its stamp on all the anticipations and analogies belonging to that modality.

The universality of every sphere makes it possible for the various systems of immanence-philosophy to reduce the various modalities to a single function, with a degree of credibility. No single modality is totally different from the other modalities. Every modality contains moments which point toward all other modalities. Each function is unbreakably connected with all other functions. And this fact is the power behind every -ism; it makes the deification of a single modality possible. Falsehood rests upon truth!

Consequently, it is quite natural that each system of immanence-philosophy evokes another system, and that the history of philosophy is not ruled by a single -ism. Philosophy can only develop continuously if it respects the created order of the cosmos.

Historicism, for example, is based on the deification of history. It tries to reduce all the aspects of reality to a historical phenomenon by contemplating only that moment in every modality which anticipatorily or analogously points toward the historical modality. It reduces feeling to historical feeling; thought to historical thought; and faith, to the history of religion. Historicism disavows the moments which point to any function other than the historical. And because of this denial, no single immanence system can be fully satisfying. The disavowed moments lead to antinomies and thereby demand recognition. Faith, for example, is no longer certainty, if the absolute character of the Christian religion is undermined and all faith and religions are historically relative.

The history of philosophy demonstrates that after a particular -ism develops to a certain degree, the expansion process of the modalities is arrested. Historicism has advanced the science of history and has uncovered a great deal of historical material, but it has also led to a crisis in humanistic science. And the latter cannot be solved in the right way by accepting another one-sided view. Such liberation carries with it the seeds of new bondage. Science needs the light of God's Word and of Scriptural thinking to be truly free. That alone can aid us in the discovery of the principles by which God has made every thing beautiful in its time.

19
The Object

As we have seen, each modality contains a law side and a subject side. The laws of the analytical and post-analytical modalities are norms or rules of conduct which ought to be obeyed by the subjects in all their deeds and behaviour. A norm is given in the normative modality as a principle which must be worked out and given a concrete positive form in a specific instance by the authorities of that terrain of life.

Correlative to the law side of a modality is its subject side. All creatures that are subject to the laws of a modality belong to its subject side. With this distinction in mind we are now in a position to state what we mean by *objects*, which have received from God their own specific place in His creation.

Subject and object are not identical. Nevertheless, the object belongs to the subject side of a modality and never to its law side. In every modality, except the numerical we can distinguish three elements, law, subject, and object. (See schema on this page.)

Before we can define what we mean by "object" we must pause a moment to consider the tremendous confusion existing in science and in everyday speech concerning the terms object and objective.

Since Kant the so called critical immanence-philosophy identifies the "object" with the field of investigation or "*Gegenstand*," upon which scientific thought is focused. Thinking man is called the subject and that which is thought about, is called the "object." This view forgets, however, that *everything* created is subject to the laws of God, and is thus a *subject*.

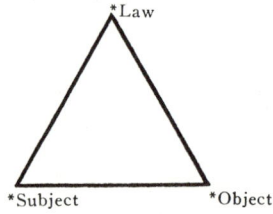

And it also overlooks the fact that objects also exist outside of the analytical sphere. Such objects are not affected by human thought. A brooding bird sitting upon its nest is, as a living animal, psychically characterized, but its nest is a *psychical object* and as such not a subject. A nest does not brood; it is only a subject in the first four modalities, subjected to the laws of energy, motion, space and number.

To identify the object with the field of investigation is to misconstrue the subject-object relation. The subject-object relation is entirely different from the theoretical epistemological relation between the scientist and his field of investigation. This is obvious if we remember that the law side of a modality belongs also to the field of investigation which is scientifically examined. But laws and norms can never become objects.

Another confusion concerning the concept of the object holds that the term *"object"* should be used to designate the external world, the world outside of myself as "subject." This notion conceives of my fellowmen and even of God as objects. It eradicates in this respect the boundary between God and the world. Objects are only to be found in creation.

All too often the word "objective" is used in the sense of universally valid. Something is then "objective" if everyone agrees to it. An "objective communication" is considered to be free from subjective impressions and judgments, and is thought only to report objective facts.

This sense of "universally valid" would identify object with a law or norm. And this contradicts our thesis that the "object" never belongs to the law side of a modality.

We also encounter this confusion between object and law wherever, in Christian circles, the question is raised as to whether or not the *preaching of the Word*[1] must be subjective or objective.

Some maintain that it must be "subjective" and "experiential." The preacher must display his own experience

---

[1] This expression is incorrect. It gives the impression that the Word of God is an object of the human activity of preaching. Preaching is not service *of* the Word of God, but a service *to* the Word.

or that of others. Apparently, some would rather hear "a sermon" about Christians than about Christ. Subjective mysticism (often found in Fundamentalism) is in direct opposition to the Word of God. It characteristically pays more honor to pious men than to Holy Scripture. Very often this type of mysticism neglects the sacraments and overestimates the office of a minister. It usually indulges in psychological preaching. It is greatly concerned with what took place in the soul of Abraham, David, or Peter and it gives a great deal of prominence to psychological self-analysis.

In contrast, some believe that preaching must be "objective." They rightly contend that the Scripture must be proclaimed free from all "subjective" augmentation, but the description "objective" is not correct here.

And a third group find the latter conception too cold and holds that preaching ought to be subjective and objective. It ought not to be one-sided but steer a middle course and strike a happy medium. The exposition of Scripture must be augmented by the proclamation of what the Holy Spirit does "to the soul."

By calling God's Word objective, even this latter usage of the term identifies the object with law. This is meant well, but the Holy Scripture is not objective; it is "normative." We ought to subject ourselves to the Word of God. We are not subject to an object, since *an object is itself subject to law.* Anyone who calls the Holy Scripture objective, unconsciously detracts from its divine authority and paves the way for the spread of all forms of subjectivism.

In this critical Christian philosophy *an object is the recurrence of an earlier function in a later modality.* This recurrence is not a mere repetition. When an earlier function recurs in a later modality it has a new modal meaning. And the subject-function which recurs in a later modality *as an object-function* is subject to the laws of the modality in which it functions as object. That is to say, the object is relegated to the subject side of the sphere in which it functions as object.

That which is *objectivized* or rendered an object does not have an active subject-function in the modality in which it recurs as object. But it does have a passive object-function which is related to a subject in the modality in which it is an object.

Perhaps a few illustrations will clarify what we mean. Since it does not have a modal substratum the numerical sphere does not have any objects. The spatial modality is the first sphere in which objects arise. A point in the spatial sphere is an *objectivization* of number. A point only exists in spatial figures such as a line, a triangle, a cube, or a circle. A point is qualified by the spatial modality, but it does not occupy space and does not have a subject-function in the spatial aspect. A point is an object; it is the recurrence of number in the spatial modality, for a point is not measurable, only countable.

In the third modality, the sphere of motion, we not only encounter points as numerical objectivizations, but we also encounter spatial objectivizations. The trajectory of a bullet, for example, is itself not in motion; it does not have a subject-function in the kinematic modality, but it is only meaningful to speak of a trajectory in connection with a thing that moves along this path.

Now a plant cannot live without a regular movement of chemical elements: water and carbohydrates, which have their highest subject-function in the physical sphere. These chemical elements have, with relation to plants, an object-function in the biotic modality. Chemical elements, as such, do not possess life; they are therefore necessarily related to plants which are biotic subjects. Also the wall, along which climbing-plants grow, is in this respect functioning as a biotic object.

A bird's nest is a psychical object. Plants eaten by animals are also psychical objects. And things which we perceive are the objects of our psychical perception.

An object-function can be either *opened* or *closed*. To know the time it is necessary to look at a clock. If no one looks at it then the clock does not have an opened psychical object-function. Its psychical object-function remains closed and its physical subject-function alone is in action. The same we encounter in the empty bird's nest. During the bird's absence the psychical object-function of the nest is closed.

Perhaps a few more examples will further clarify what we mean. The pre-analytically qualified creatures are analytical objects in the analytical modality. The highest subject-function of a mammal is psychical. However, if I form a concept of a mammal, then it becomes an analytical object. An animal does not cogitate but it can be the object of my subjective cogitative activity.

Moreover, the horse ridden by Napoleon during his retreat from Russia had an object-function in the historical modal aspect. For, as an object it was related to the historical subject-function of the Emperor.

The paper upon which are printed the letters and sentences of a book is an object in the linguistical sphere. The furniture of a house is an object in the social sphere as it is used in the human social intercourse. Economical objects are things to which we ascribe value, things which can be bought and sold for a certain price. A picture is an aesthetical object, an object of aesthetic appreciation. A piece of ground whose ownership is the question of a law suit, is a juridical object. A wedding ring or love letter, are objects in the ethical modality.

And finally there are pistical objects, objects in the aspect of faith. A sacrament, baptism or holy supper, lacks a subjective function of faith; it does not believe, but since it is used by believers who function actively as pistical subjects, it possesses in the sphere of faith only a pistical object-function. This is in force for the visible signs of the sacrament; they are objects of faith. But insofar as the sacraments are seals, then they belong to the law side of the sphere of faith because they serve to seal the Word of God. That which establishes the pistical norm must itself be a norm. For it is the Lord Himself, who strengthens His promises by means of the sacraments. The church building used for public worship is also a pistical object.

It follows from what is said, that man as *such* can not be *objectivized* or made into an object. Human existence is not characterized by a specific temporal function. Man transcends the modal horizon in his heart, in religious self-concentration. Certain *aspects* of human life, however, can be objectivized. When I observe someone running, the pre-psychical functions of man are *psychically objectified* in the act of seeing. The *objectifying* of man, as such — for example, in slavery, in which man is reduced to an economical object — is forbidden by the sixth commandment, which commands us to respect man as the image of God.

It is, therefore, incorrect in principle to speak of people as being *objects* of missions or evangelization. Man ought to subject himself to the Word of God in his function of faith. And the Word of God is addressed to him as a pistical subject and not as an object.

We can only speak of an object if an *earlier* function recurs in a *later* function in a new modal sense and there as an object has been placed in relation to a subject. A later function can never be repeated in an earlier. Objectivization takes place in a transcendental direction, from the substratum toward the superstratum. Consequently, all objects of faith share in the particular border-character peculiar to the modality of faith. Objects of faith point beyond themselves toward Him who is the Foundation of our existence. A church steeple points heavenward. And the symbols of the sacraments point toward Christ, whose blood was shed for the remission of our sins.

Anyone who has carefully followed the preceding argument should now be able to understand the unavoidable confusion which results if the object is identified with law. No one is subject to a church building. But the subject-object relation of the congregation to its own church building is in its entirety subject to the norm of faith in the Word of God. Therefore, since the Divine Word is a norm, it can never be made a pistical object. Unadulterated preaching shares in this normative character and in consequence is neither objective nor subjective. The proclaimed Word must be subjectively *believed*. The desire for subjective or objective preaching is not merely a question of accent or nuance; it arises from an erroneous view of the Word of God. Objectivism and subjectivism are not merely extremes which can be avoided by following a middle course. They are positive errors and violation of the first commandment. Both the subjectivist and the objectivist seek religious certainty in creation instead of in the Creator.

Objectivism seeks its final certainty in the deified object; it makes the object to be law by shifting it from the subject side to the law side. Objectivism is in evidence in the Roman Catholic Church, which unites the operations of grace with the mere use of the sacraments. However, according to our interpretation of the Bible, grace is imparted only by the Holy Spirit and never directly by the symbols of the sacraments as objects of faith.

Subjectivism is in even more error. By its denial of the object-functions, it completely denies one of the diversities which God has created in the cosmos. Subjectivism seeks its solidity in the subject, which being dissatisfied with its subordinate position, illegitimately assumes the position of law and ascribes sovereignty to itself. Within the church subjectivism seeks its final ground in the piety of the individual heart, in experience, and in inner qualities. It desires that experience and subjective piety be preached. And in keeping with its denial of the object, subjectivism depreciates the holy sacraments.

Subjectivism is also present wherever the deification of non-human subjectivity occurs, as for instance, in the deifying of science, beauty, money, the state or nation, or anything else. For these matters are also subjective magnitudes which being subject to the laws of God cannot themselves be identified with law. Subjectivism is not individualistic per se, but can be collective and universal in character, as in national socialism. Recall Hitler's slogan, "You are nothing; the folk is everything!"

Both objectivism and subjectivism forget the absolutely normative character of God's Word. Both errors lose sight of the fact that God's Word is the power of God (I Cor. 1:18) and the Holy Spirit works through the instrumentality of the preaching of the Word. By seeking divine power in the subject or in the object, both subjectivism and objectivism detract from the work which God performs through His Word and Spirit.

Anyone who rejects these errors in principle can rest in the God of the Covenant through faith. God has created both a subject and an object, and He wishes to be glorified through all temporal relations. "Whether therefore ye eat, or drink, or whatever ye do, do all to the glory of God" (I Cor. 10:31).

What I have said in this section concerning the object is up until now the same as in previous editions of this book.

Dooyeweerd's work, *Encyclopaedie der Rechtswetenschap* (Encyclopedia of Jurisprudence) necessitates, however, that I expand and revise the standpoint of the earlier editions.

In the first place it must be pointed out that we can experience the *universality* of temporal reality because of the cosmic subject-object relation within the structure of the modal aspects. Because of this subject-object relation, naive experience does not present us with an *abstract picture* of reality in which the latter is restricted to one or more theoretically isolated aspects. The subject-object relation enables us to grasp reality in all of its temporal aspects, including those which are *super-subjective.* The super-subjective aspects of a physical thing are those which transcend the physical modality. In the case of a plant they are those above the biotic, and in the case of an animal, they are those aspects above the psychical. Our naive experience is in nowise restricted to the numerical, spatial, kinematic, physical and biotic aspects of a flower; it includes also the object-aspects of that flower, which are correlative with the human subject. We can form a logical concept of a flower, estimate its price, respect it as the property of someone else, and we can believe that it is created by God, and so on.

The second main point that we must consider is what immanence-philosophy calls the *doctrine of secondary qualities*. With respect to natural phenomena, it is customary to distinguish between primary and secondary qualities. The former are qualities which are numerical, spatial, kinematic, physical, and chemical in character. It is assumed that these primary qualities possess an *objective* existence, thereby meaning that they are inherent in the things of nature. Secondary qualities, on the other hand, are — according to the accepted psychological and philosophical view — the sensory (psychical) qualities of color, sound, smell, and taste. Consequently, they must be sharply distinguished from primary qualities. For whereas primary qualities are inherent in the things of nature, secondary qualities are not. They do not exist in the phenomena of nature, but are merely ascribed to things by our *subjective perception*. Naive experience is deceptive and childish since it thinks that a rose is really red. The scientist, however, knows better; he has unmasked naive appearance and in science has grasped the true reality.

This view is completely erroneous. It distorts and limits the connection between subject and object. The scientist does not investigate reality as an object. He is concerned with *aspects* of reality as *"Gegenstand,"* or fields of investigation. (See the subsequent section on epistemology.)

Moreover, the so-called primary qualities are not *objective* but are *subjective* in nature. Natural things function subjectively in the first four modal aspects of reality. And the so-called secondary qualities are not subjective but are objective. The things of nature appear as objects in the psychical aspect of perception. The color, sound, smell, and taste of things are not properties which we ascribe to them — if such were the case, how could we distinguish a really perceived thing from an image in a dream? — They are real *objective-psychical* qualities of temporal reality.

And finally it must be noted that a special science can

not furnish us knowledge of reality in its concrete *fulness*; it only gives us an insight into a specific *aspect* of reality. The full reality is grasped in naive experience which is, therefore, not deceptive but trustworthy.

Now we must correct a statement previously made in this section to the effect that a later function cannot return as an object in an earlier. That statement, that a later function cannot return as object in an earlier modality, has been asserted by Vollenhoven and he refuses to follow his colleague Dooyeweerd in the correction which I am about to mention now.

Let us consider the perception of a flower. The psychically qualified action of perception is related to the objective and psychical image of perception of the flower. We are here concerned with a psychical, sensory subject-object relation.

The question is: Which aspects of the flower are objectivized in its sensorily perceived image? Only its earlier pre-psychical qualities, its subjective numerical, spatial, kinematic, physical, and biotic functions and nothing more? According to our earlier view, the answer would be affirmative, but a closer examination reveals that this view cannot be maintained as it would jeopardize the universality of each sphere. And the objective perceived images of things would no longer contain their full *all-sided* reality. They would be denatured to an incomplete abstract complex of some of their temporal functions.

Our previously defended position is not only inconsistent with the system but it is in opposition to naive experience, too. The super-psychical objective qualities of the flower, which are normative in character, are anticipatorily expressed in the sensorily perceived image of the flower. We see in a flower also its *objective logical* characteristics by which we directly distinguish it from other things. We see its objective historical qualities, that it is cultivated with great care and has a cultural function. In the sensorily perceived image of the flower we can anticipatorily perceive all its normative qualities in an objective sense, namely, in a psychical subject-object relation.

When we view a flower as the property of our neighbor, we recognize its objective juridical character. Similarly we recognize its objective-pistical character when we view it as created by God.

In the sensorily perceived image of the flower, we must distinguish between its objective pre-psychical and super-psychical qualities. The former are *objective* analogies and the latter *objective* anticipations. The objective analogies moreover are merely *given* in the perceived image and are accessible to anyone who can see. The objective anticipations in contrast belong only to the *opened* enriched perceived image. They can be observed only by those whose subjective psychical function has been opened under the direction of the normative functions. A small child, for example, does not notice the objective juridical quality of a thing; another person's property affords him the same degree of pleasure as do his toys. Our earlier definition of the object needs to be revised: an object is as well the analogous recurrence in a new modal sense of an earlier function in a later sphere, as the anticipatory recurrence of a later function in an earlier sphere.

Finally notice that both the object and subject have an *individual* existence in contrast to law, which is always universal.

20

The Problem of Sin

Our position up until this point has made it evident that the confession of the fall occupies an important place in Christian philosophy. We have pointed out that philosophy issues from the human heart and is directed by a religious choice which we make in the religious concentration point of our existence. Our whole life is directed by a religious choice. We can follow two courses, the one leads toward and the other away from God. The latter direction is apostate as it seeks to deify an aspect of creation and to engage all of life in the service of the "civitas terrena," the kingdom of darkness. Consequently, any philosophy which is not built upon the Holy Scripture as revelation of God, sharply opposes Christian science, for the latter seeks to advance the Kingdom of God, in obedience to the Word of God.

In this section we shall deal with the problem of sin and we shall pay particular attention to the relationship between sin and the theory of modalities.

What is the position of sin in the cosmos? Does it lurk only in *temporal functions* or is it rooted in the human *heart*, in the religious concentration point of life? Does sin belong only to the subject side of the modal aspects? And did the fall cause the loss of any functions of human life? Is sin active in all modalities?

A correct knowledge of sin depends upon a pure knowledge of God by faith; and since our purpose is to construct a Christian philosophy, we are compelled to answer such questions by appealing to Divine Revelation, because real knowledge of sin is not possible without true knowledge of God. Unless we appeal to the Word of God we cannot arrive at a solution which strikes the roots of the problem and we are in danger of falling into a moralism.

In the Bible we read of an historical fall and from this we can ascertain that sin entered the world because man withdrew his *heart* from the God of the Covenant. Instead of believing the life-giving commandment of God, man put his trust in the false word of Satan. And from that moment the human heart became corrupt, inclined to all evil, and unable to perform any good.

Secondly, we read in the Bible that Adam represented the entire human race. He was the first head of the Covenant. When he fell, man fell (original sin). All mankind which descends from Adam sinned in him and shares in his guilt and corruption.

In view of these data we acknowledge that sin has a deeper foundation than the temporal functions. Sin lies in the very depths of our existence, in our religious center.

Christ expressed this when He said, "For out of the heart comes forth evil thoughts, murder, adultery, false witness, blasphemy." (Matt. 15:19)

The sinner has withdrawn his heart from God, the Fastground of our life. But, as a creature, man cannot live without certainty. Therefore, he seeks certainty in a part of creation. The direction of the apostate human heart has been radically changed. Before the fall the heart was directed toward God but now it is directed toward idols.[1]

The sinful state of the human heart cannot avoid exerting an influence upon the temporal functions which proceed from it. The modal aspects cannot be free from sin. However, this raises the question as to whether sin appears on the law side or on the subject side of the modalities. For the Bible-believing Christian, Romans 7 affords the answer: "Is the law sin? God forbid. So that the law is holy and the commandment holy and righteous and good." The Apostle's statement concerning the Old Testamentary law is equally applicable to all the laws and ordinances of God. In spite of the fall, God's laws remain valid and do not lack perfection.[2] Imperfection lies in the person who is subject to God's laws, which he violates by replacing them with laws which he himself has made.

Basically sin is the turning away of the *heart* of man from the *central meaning* of the Divine Law, the service of God with his entire heart and power. Sin in its *functional form* is the subjective violation of the temporal laws that

---

[1] Pelagius denied this truth and disavowed original sin by holding that evil was external to the nature of man. Sin is the result of an alien influence exerted upon man, and as a bad habit can be broken. A similar position is taken by those who maintain the freedom of the will in a religious sense (Semi-pelagians, Remonstrants, and Humanists).

[2] In the later middle ages, however, the doctrine that sin lies on the law side so that God is its author is adhered to by the followers of the nominalist, William of Occam. Occam had propounded the God-dishonoring theory that God is an arbitrary God who does not restrict Himself to His laws. According to Occam God can elect also those who are outside of Christ. And His absolute power enables Him to compel man to hate Christ. Occam's followers concluded that sin occurs because God, by substituting every now and then new laws for old ones, confuses man so that he must sin.

God has given to His creation. Sin has therefore a dual aspect. It is an expression of the apostate human heart which moves away from God toward idols. And it is also expressed in the subjective violation of modal laws.

The second aspect of sin is not connected with the antithesis which, in accordance with divine predestination, divides mankind into two camps. This antithesis is not connected with the violation of modal laws but it pertains to the *direction* taken by the human heart. The entire life of the unbeliever is directed toward the *left,* whereas, the life of the Christian is directed toward the *right.* In spite of what may be an otherwise exemplary life the non-Christian follows a course which leads from God, whereas a Christian in spite of many trespasses follows a path toward Him. The heart of a Christian is renewed by the Holy Spirit.

We must notice that as well in the life directed toward God (to the right) as in the life directed away from *Him* (to the left), there are those who keep and those who violate the modal laws. A pagan mother, for example, who lovingly takes care of her child, obeys the temporal norm of love and keeps in this respect the ethical law. A person who does not serve God can still excel in logic by obeying the functional laws of the analytical sphere.

Thus, even though non-Christians are unable to perform any truly good act in a religious sense, because they don't possess a contact of faith with Christ, yet they are in a position to perform all sorts of so-called "civil" good deeds. Christians, on the other hand, even though their hearts have been renewed, can still violate functional laws: David was capable of falling into a grievous sin. And a Christian, by being unduly conservative, can oppose the historical norm of cultural development. He can commit errors in thinking, have·bad manners, wrong his fellow-man, live as a spendthrift, and doubt his faith.

If the reader has been in agreement with our position up to this point, then he will readily understand that sin, in its aspect of modal disobedience, is not restricted to one modality. For example, it is not limited to the pistical sphere but is present in many others as well. Sin in the ethical sphere is disobedience to the norm of love; in the social it is the violation of social norms by considering only oneself; in the historical it is the opposition to the norm of culture which opposition is found in conservatism, reaction, and revolution. Although, in essence, sin is the transgression of the law of God, yet there are many different types of sin. Sin is not restricted to the sphere of religion, in the strict sense, but its power permeates the entire human life in all its relations and relationships. The sinner is guilty before God; he distorts all cosmic relations and brings disharmony in all the coherences or relationships which God has instituted and ordained in His world.

Oppositions arise in human life because of disobedience to the laws of the normative modalities. And such opposites as justice and injustice, love and hate, beauty and ugliness are grounded in the principle of logical contradiction. In his *Encyclopaedie der Rechtswetenschap*, Dooyeweerd calls these opposites, "*contradictory oppositions.*" They are distinct from the oppositions which arise in the non-normative pre-analytical modal aspects, such as: sickness and health, emotion and lack of emotion, joy and sorrow, and so on. The latter are called *polar oppositions*. The distinction between *contradictory* and *polar* oppositions is that the former must be viewed as sin for they are in contradiction to law, whereas the latter do not violate law. The latter obey the modal laws in both poles. Those who are sick and those who are healthy are both equally obedient to biotic laws; the one group with and the other without organic disorders.

Both of the aforementioned oppositions are distinct from the antinomies or theoretical contradictions which arise when the scientist disregards the modal boundaries of the law-spheres and confuses the laws of one sphere with those of another so that a conflict seems to exist. An antinomy only exists in science, never in reality; it is a sin of scientific thought.

In spite of the extensive influence of sin, fallen man has not *lost* any single temporal function. Man has not even lost his pistical function. Even unbelief is not equivalent to the loss of faith. Unbelief is merely to believe a lie rather than the truth; it is apostate faith. Reformed theology taught this same truth by maintaining that the sinner retains the image of God, even though this image is now corrupted by sin.

The problem remains as to whether or not sin arises *in all modalities*. Can the laws of all spheres be transgressed? Since sin is subjective disobedience to law, in order to answer this question, we must commence by examining what we mean here by the term "created subjects."

The Bible clearly teaches that only man can be guilty of violating a law; animals and things cannot. Because of man all creation is under God's curse and desires the completion of the world, at which time, the children of God will be made perfect and the cosmos will no longer bear the curse of God. This does not imply that sin is inactive in the pre-logical modalities, even though their laws are inviolable since they are not normative in character. To understand this point, we need only reflect upon the *principle of universality* of each sphere (See para. 18).

God's plan of creation included in it the expansion through human activity of the normative anticipations ordained in the pre-logical spheres. The earth, the plant and the animal world were meant to be expanded by man for the glory of their Creator. Since the fall, however, man has led this expansion-process in an apostate manner. Not *ad maiorem gloriam Dei*[1] but to the glorification of sinful man. Consequently, there is a disharmony in the *expansion* of nature.

Even though the "Common Grace" of God checks the total demonization of the apostate creation,[2] the earth

---

[1] To the increased glory of God.

[2] We have placed the term "common grace" in quotations, because legitimate objections can be made to this terminology. Klaas Schilder has offered

brings forth thistles and thorns; and sickness and death affect the life of man. Nature itself is free from any guilt; man alone bears the responsibility. He was created as the Master and head of creation, and his fall dragged the cosmos with him (with the exception of angels).

We have said that God's laws have not been affected by sin. This statement must be augmented by the following: In the super-psychical (normative) modal aspects, the principles given by God must be developed into *positive* law. And this positivization is influenced by sin, if carried on by someone who is not obedient to the Word of God. Parents who command their children to do things contrary to the Will of God, errors in the confessions of the church, and the incorrect formulation of the platform of various organized social institutions illustrate the influence of sin upon the development of positive law.

The power of sin has been conquered by Christ. He clearly demonstrated this victory in His resurrection. His death has atoned for our sins. The hearts of His people are, therefore, renewed by the Holy Spirit. Consequently, there happens in their life a twofold change. In the first place: the life of God's children has got now the religious direction to the right, directed to God, to His true service; desiring to fight the good battle against the idols.

Secondly: they have now for God's sake the principle of obedience. They like to keep His commandments, not only the religious law of love, but all the functional laws too. And daily they pray for remission of all their trespasses.

Finally: in their action of norm-positivization they try to stick to the Word of God as a guide for their whole life. For they have a delight in the law of God after the inward man (Rom. 7:22). Moreover, they do not find pleasure in performing only some of God's commandments but they delight in obeying all of them.

such a criticism. For is this "grace" really "common" when it is exclusively related to non-Christians, (the life of Christians is directed and fulfilled by God's special, renewing grace). Moreover, can we rightly speak of *grace* in this connection?

CHAPTER III

THE THEORY OF KNOWLEDGE

21

SEVERAL BASIC PRINCIPLES OF LOGIC

In the preceding chapter we set forth the main features of the theory of the modal aspects of reality. Our present task is to enunciate several of the basic characteristics of the theory of knowledge, as they are developed in this system of Christian philosophy.

Epistemology — sometimes called: critique of knowledge — is the sole object of interest in some systems of immanence-philosophy. Ontology is not discussed. Such systems deify and exaggerate the scientific thought of man. But, because some philosophers exaggerate the role of epistemology, we are not justified in eliminating it from our study. Human life is more than thinking and knowing and the cosmos exists independently of man's knowing it. Nevertheless, thought plays an incalculable role in our life. The knowing-process is an integrating factor in science; we must examine therefore its meaning by the light of the Holy Scripture.

In our discussion of the modalities or modal aspects, we have seen that the analytical or logical modality is one of the many temporal aspects which God has placed in the cosmic order in an architectonic structure.

The structure of the analytical modal aspect is correlative to that of the *other* aspects. It contains a law and a subject side. The law side includes the analytical norm, which briefly summarized, commands us to distinguish the analyzable correctly.[1]

---

[1] We shall not pause to examine the analytical norm further. See section G in Chapter II.

The subject side includes the analytical subject which we can divide into three parts:
1. The knowable
2. The knowing-process
3. The possession of knowledge

1. *The knowable* is everything which can be the subject of knowledge. It includes God, His law, and the cosmos. God and His law are known indirectly as God is knowable insofar as He reveals Himself in His Word and in His works. We know the functional diversity of law by examining in the light of Scripture that which is subject to law. We know solely by direct Divine Revelation the religious fulness of the law — to love God with all our heart. We acquire knowledge of the cosmos by a direct examination of it, namely the earthly part of cosmos.

2. *The knowing-process* or analytical activity is restricted to man. Other creatures, excepted the angels, do not think. They do not possess a subject-function in the analytical sphere. They only possess an object-function in it. The rest of creation is the *object* of human thought. It must be considered as a part of the knowable rather than as a part of the knowing-subject.[1]

Human analytical activity focuses upon the knowable with the intention of examining and determining the boundaries of its diversity. The knowable however exists independently of the relation it sustains to the human knowing-process. We disagree with Kant in his affirmation that the intuitive and rational forms of our reason make the *Ding an sich* (which in itself is unknowable) to be something knowable. The cosmos is objectively knowable independently of its being known by a knowing-subject. In fact the cosmos would still exist even if no one ever made it the object of his knowing-activity. The human knowing activity does not possess any creative power. It observes only the diverse aspects which God has placed within the cosmos. Our

---

[1] The Biblical expression, "An ox knoweth its master, and an ass its stall," does not refer to an analytical subject-function. An animal is psychically qualified; its knowledge is an instinctive emotional-knowledge.

knowledge is always partial as there are so many aspects that we can never fully know them.

Analytical activity is subject to norms. It is subject to the laws of thought and its direction is properly determined by the religious norm of love to God. We do not mean, however, that our analytical activity always takes place in obedience to the norms which properly govern it. On the contrary, our thought conflicts with the analytical norms in a three-fold manner. There is thinking which is in harmony with the modal law, but in conflict with the religious norm. In this case correct thinking is employed in opposition to God. Secondly, we can think in such a way that we violate both the modal and the religious norms. And finally there is thought which obeys the religious norm and violates the modal law.

We can, therefore, speak of errors of thought or illogical thinking. Such modal disobedience can occur when the pre-analytical functional life of a person is disturbed. If someone is psychically shocked by fear or sickness, he will not be able to think logically for the first few moments. It is, however, incorrect to limit analytical error to illogical thinking. A law of thought anticipates and points back to the laws of later and earlier modalities. Consequently, a violation of an analytical analogy or anticipation is a breach of a divinely ordained norm of thought.

A lack of brain power for example, is an infringement of an analytical analogy which refers to the physical modality of energy; a lack of concentration is a violation of a psychical analogy; and an incomplete or incorrect *formation* of concepts is a violation of the historical anticipation of the analytical norm.

The last thing to note in connection with analytical activity is that it is an individual action. Thinking and knowing are always activities of the individual person. To say that analytical activity is *individual*, however, does not imply that it is *individualistic*. If analytical activity were individualistic, no one could utilize and build upon the labors of the past in order to acquire knowledge. Each person would have to make a fresh start. A study of history and sociology shows that this is not the case. An individualistic epistemology is unhistorical and a-social.

The individual character of the analytical activity affirms rather than denies the fact that a person acquires knowledge by building upon the foundations of the past and by utilizing tradition. The results of the past are the product of human labor and consequently they need to be improved and completed.

3. This completes our consideration of the knowable and of analytical activity. We can see that the *possession of knowledge* or error is the result of analytical activity as it is related to the knowable. The possession of knowledge is the fruit of correct thinking about what is knowable. Analytical activity is dynamic in character, but the possession of knowledge is static. The last statement does not imply that our knowledge cannot be increased or decreased.

Knowledge is lost when something is forgotten, and it must be acquired anew by means of analytical activity. Self-correction can also cause a decrease in our knowledge; we can recognize something to be false which formerly we held to be true. Such an instance is not entirely negative. The recognition of error is accompanied by positive knowledge. We constantly learn to employ the laws of thought with a greater degree of accuracy and we learn to avoid following the wrong course in the future.

Knowledge is increased through continual analytical activity. And such activity is related to the wide field of the knowable.

In the following section we shall see that both concepts and judgments are a part of the knowledge that we possess.

22

Several Distinctions in the Theory of Knowledge

In the preceding section we discussed several basic principles of logic. Before we can examine several principles of epistemology we must notice the difference and the connection between logic and epistemology.

Logic is the science which examines the analytical modality. It is a special science.[1] Epistemology is the science concerned with the human activity of knowing, with the results of this activity, and with the laws applicable to the knowing-process, and to knowledge. Every human *act* — see the section on anthropology — functions in all the aspects of the human body, and thus bears a structural totality. Epistemology therefore, can not be restricted to a science of one specific modal aspect. Consequently, it cannot be equated with logic. Epistemology is not a special science; it is part of philosophy.

However, there is a close connection between epistemology and logic. The analytical is an integrating element in all knowledge. Epistemology is not possible without logic but it cannot be satisfied solely with the results of logic. Epistemology must also investigate the knowing-process and knowledge insofar as both exceed the analytical modality and express themselves in other modal aspects.

We can now discuss three distinctions which are of primary importance in epistemology:

1. The distinction between thinking and knowing;
2. The distinction between naive and scientific knowledge;
3. The distinction between learning to know and knowledge.

1. With respect to the first distinction we must note that

---

[1] A special science investigates a specific aspect of reality. It is in this sense that logic is a special science. Logic is usually considered to be a part of philosophy. Many special sciences have previously been thought of as subdivisions of philosophy, and it is only since the end of the middle ages that they developed independently of philosophy. Logic is such a special science. It lacks that *totality-character* which marks philosophy. Philosophy is a science concerned with the totality. It is a science that is concerned with things or structures which, in their inclusions of many modal aspects, bear a *totality-character*. In other words, philosophy is concerned with the whole of reality, whereas a special science is only concerned with one of reality's many aspects.

thinking and *knowing* are not synonymous terms. There is a twofold difference between them.

(a) *Thinking* is exclusively an analytical activity. If we think about something the analytical subject concentrates his attention upon an analytical object in order to observe its diversity. But this does not mean that *thinking* is an act which is limited to the analytical modal aspect. Human acts are so constituted that they function in all aspects. Thinking rests upon its modal substratum. We would also not be able to think without a brain, without our biotic function. Thinking also includes superstrata-functions. It anticipates the historical aspect by seeking to dominate reality logically. And it is also subject to the law of the economy of thought.

Moreover, in practical life thinking occurs within the structure of a specific social relationship. The structure of the school, the church, the family, industry and other organizations all direct or lead our thought. Ecclesiastical thinking, for example, is an analytical activity which is under the leadership of our faith. And, when an industrialist reflects upon the basis and prospects of an enterprise, his thinking is led by economic considerations. Political thinking, which is the task of the ruler of a nation, is an analytical act under judicial leadership. Every case we have mentioned is a form of thinking and is consequently analytically qualified. But, in each instance we have witnessed a difference in *leadership* and in the *end* pursued. The analytical function unfolds or opens by means of a *union* of thought with different social structures.

And what we have said concerning thinking is equally applicable to knowing. Knowing is analytically qualified, but it is not a purely analytical act. More functions are structurally involved in the act of knowing than in thinking. Thinking, for example, commences with the observation of diversity in the analytical object. Its inception as well as its end is analytical in character. Knowing on the other hand begins with *perception*, with the collection of sensory — thus psychical — impressions.

The second phase of the knowing-process consists of

thinking about the material collected through psychical activity. In this phase, the knowable diversities are observed, abstractly analyzed, and logically established. The knower, for example, establishes that a thing is beautiful, motionless, large, and that people enter it, and so on. In the third phase of the knowing-process the diversities which have been established are brought together in a concept, for example, in the concept, *cathedral*. In order to distinguish one concept from another we must employ a *word*. The logical characteristics, which are noted in thinking, are fixed in a concept. The linguistical aspect and the historical aspect — which are presupposed in the *formation* of concepts — play an important role. The next step after the formation of concepts is the formation of *judgments* (e.g., This cathedral is five centuries old). The knowing-process does not end with judgments, for judgments give rise to argument and demonstration. If a person makes a judgment, he shares it with others in social intercourse, and thus transmits knowledge, namely the results of his knowing.

(b) The second main difference between thinking and knowing is that knowing is always related to *truth*. In order for knowing to be knowing, it must obey the laws of the knowing-process. If it deviated from these laws in any phase then the knowing-process does not attain a correct result and knowledge is not increased. The knowing-process is no longer a process of knowing but of error. Thinking also ought to obey the laws of thought, but erroneous thinking is still thinking. Erroneous thinking is still an analytical activity. The notion that the stars are the souls of departed people is possible only because of the analytical function.

2. The second main distinction that we have made is between naive and scientific knowing. Naive knowing is the knowing that occurs in everyday life within the structure of various social relationships. The knowledge acquired by it is not inferior to scientific knowledge. The naive manner of knowing does not present a distorted picture which must be purified by science. As a matter of fact it is impossible for anyone permanently to abandon naive knowledge. One

cannot move solely in the orbit of scientific knowledge. Very often immanence-philosophy makes the mistake of glorifying science and depreciating naive knowledge, which it characterizes as *naive realism,* and then rejects as being uncritical.

It is, however, incorrect to criticize naive knowledge as being an unsound *scientific* theory. The naive knowing-process does not furnish theories. It is a natural and practical manner of knowing, which nobody can deny or abandon, even not the scientific research-worker. Outside of the limited sphere of his science, he cannot lack our naive knowledge. Scientific knowledge is not superior or more accurate than naive knowledge. It is merely different.

How then does naive knowledge differ from scientific knowledge? The relation of subject and object plays the decisive role in naive knowing. By means of this relation the knower, conscious of the reality of a thing in its entirety, takes cognizance of all its cosmic aspects, and without systematic abstraction, he grasps this reality in concepts. These concepts are closely related to the representation which in turn is closely related to our sensory psychical life. The naive knowing-process, as the scientific, is in touch with reality, and is *systatic* and cosmic in nature. It is closely connected with life. Naive knowing is subject to the laws of knowing and therefore has legitimate claim to truth.

Scientific knowledge is acquired differently and is therefore of a different character. Both sorts of knowledge are analytically qualified. The naive knowing-process, however, can have a multiplicity of ends. It can seek to attain an economical end, as in the case of industrial knowledge, or it can have a pistical end, in the case of pistical knowledge. Scientific knowledge, in contrast, always has an *analytical end*; it is concerned with a scientific understanding of reality.

The subject-object relation does not play a fundamental role in the acquisition of scientific knowledge. Scientific knowledge is attained by means of *abstraction* and *synthe-*

sis. The scientist isolates a specific cosmic aspect from the other aspects, and places the isolated aspect in such a position that it sustains an antithetical relationship to his analytical cogitative function. In the act of knowing, the analytical cogitative function is synthesized with the isolated and antithetical modal aspect. As a *field of investigation,* this modal aspect is systematically examined, and its diversity — created by God — is observed and established. And if this examination is conducted in accordance with the laws valid for the acquisition of scientific knowledge, then the resulting concepts, judgments, and demonstrations will be scientific truth. Scientific knowing is, thus, *synthetical* and *cosmological* in character.

In the naive knowing-process, pre-scientific concepts are strongly bound to the psychical substratum of the sensory impressions derived from concrete things. In scientific knowing, on the contrary, cogitative symbolism arises, and concepts emancipate themselves from sensory representations and acquire the symbolical meaning of conceptual terms. Naive knowledge can, therefore, express a specific condition in different ways which are mutually related. Scientific knowledge, on the other hand, seeks to express a certain condition in a *specific term* which is precisely defined and can only be interpreted in one way.

We do not wish to imply that an antagonism or cleft exists between the naive and the scientific knowing-process or between scientific and naive knowledge. Both ways of knowing supplement each other. Scientific knowledge cannot be gained without naive knowledge. And, the latter is *enriched* and *systematized* by the former.

Scientific knowledge critically supplements naive knowledge and seeks to control and to correct it whenever necessary. In this way naive knowledge is enriched, broadened, and systematized.

3. The third main distinction under consideration is that between learning to know and knowledge. The knowing-process is not executed in the single relation of knowing-activity→knowledge, but it occurs in the dual relation,

knowing-activity → knowable → knowledge. In both scientific and naive knowing, the knowing-activity in the knowing-process directs itself toward the *knowable*. A correct examination of the knowable yields *knowledge*. The diversity within the knowable must be noted and fixed or established in subjection to the laws of knowing. Such an examination results in the possession of truth concerning the knowable. The knowable occupies thus an intermediary position between learning to know and knowledge.

The relation between learning to know and knowledge is *indirect*. But the connection between learning to know, the knowing-activity, and the knowable is *direct*. In naive knowing this connection is the analytical subject-object-relation and in scientific knowing this relation is that of the analytical synthesis between the analytical function and one of the remaining modal aspects of the cosmos. The relation between the knowable and knowledge is also *direct*. In naive knowing it is a relation between object and object. For the knowable as well as knowledge is an analytical object. And the internal object-relation is always a *relation of something*; knowledge is always knowledge *about* the knowable. In scientific knowing the field of investigation is not an object, but *"Gegenstand,"* namely, that which is antithetically opposite to the analytical function. And knowledge is the result of knowing the *"Gegenstand."*

In the preceding section we have discussed learning to know as an analytical activity, and we have examined the knowable or analyzable. We can now proceed to consider knowledge as a result of knowing.

23

Knowledge

Knowledge, the possession of truth, is acquired when the knowing activity is focused upon the knowable in obedience to the laws of knowing. Knowledge is fixed or established in *concepts* and *judgments*.

1. *The Concept.*

A concept is the primary possession of knowledge about something knowable. And a concept is norm-determined, since the entire act of knowing takes place under the jurisdiction of norms. However, every concept is not therefore correct. Incorrect concepts or false notions occur when, in the act of knowing, the knower violates a norm of knowing. A concept however is not only determined by a norm, but by the knowable and knowing activity too. Every concept is determined by the knowable and is a concept *about* something that is knowable. The diversities included in a concept should exist in the knowable. And a correct concept is free of elements which do not originate in the knowable and are the product of the mind of the knower.

Every concept is also determined by the knowing activity and is the result of it. Since this activity is individual, a concept is also individual. Do not confuse *individual* with *individualistic*. If concepts were individualistic, conceptual communication would be impossible and one concept would not connect with another. The individual character of a concept does not imply that every concept comprehends the diversity of something individual in the knowable. There are also concepts of that which is universal, for example, of law, and of structures. By saying that a concept is individual we are only implying that each concept is the result of the activity of a certain individual man.

We can classify concepts according to different points of view.

(a) There are simple and compound concepts. The former are formed by one act of knowing, and the latter are the result of more than one act of knowing.

(b) Concepts are distinguished according to their degree of clarity. In a clear concept all the diversities of something knowable are grasped as a unity. If the knowing activity only grasps a part of these diverse aspects, then the clarity of the concept which is thus formed will suffer. This danger is acute in the case of compound concepts.

(c) There are non-scientific and scientific concepts. The former, the naive concept, is strongly bound to the psychical substratum of sensory representations. The latter frees itself from a psychical substratum, and under the leadership of the norm of cogitative symbols, it rises above the level of abstraction attained by a naive concept. Because of its high degree of abstraction, a scientific concept gains in clarity but it loses direct contact with life.

(d) We can also distinguish between primary and secondary concepts. The former establish or fix the diversity of something knowable which itself is not a concept or a judgment. Primary concepts which are formed of the earthly cosmos are related to *kingdoms, structures* and *individual things*. By the word *kingdom* we understand a totality of things, which are qualified by the same modality, for example: the kingdom of physical things, the kingdom of biotic plants, of psychical animals, etc. A *structure* is a certain universal *law-fulness,* which exists in concrete things and that is discovered by abstraction, for example the tree-structure, existing in all concrete trees. *Individual things* are all those things which have concrete existence.

Secondary concepts are concepts formed about another concept or judgment. The primary concept about which a secondary concept is formed can belong to me or to someone else. A primary concept need not be co-temporal with a secondary concept, for example: when I myself form a secondary concept about the concept of individuality by Aristotle.

(e) Finally concepts are correct or incorrect, insofar as they are formed in obedience or disobedience to the norms of knowing.

Thus far we considered the concepts separately. We are now in a position to discuss the mutual relationships between concepts. If two concepts are formed in conformity with the laws of knowing, the one can tolerate the other and they are *compatible*. If only one is formed in conformity with the laws of knowing, they cannot tolerate each other and are *incompatible* and contradictory.

Compatibility is not a criterion of truth. Two concepts can be compatible because both are formed in opposition to the norms of knowing. The sole criterion of truth is agreement with law.

The relationship between simple and complex concepts is that of elements related to a combination of the same sort of elements. The situation is different with respect to the relationship between scientific and non-scientific concepts. It is not desirable that they be intermingled. The appearance of scientific concepts in a non-scientific argument, (e.g., in a sermon,) does not make the latter scientific but only hinders our understanding. The introduction of non-scientific concepts into scientific discourse is equally undesirable, as it weakens the critical scientific character of the argument.

Scientific and non-scientific concepts are not to be mixed. But this does not imply that they contradict each other, as non-scientific concepts are the proper foundation of scientific ones.

The relationships between *primary concepts* are purely *analytical*. Nevertheless, the things about which these concepts are formed are related to each other in countless ways. The original relationships between things are different from the relationships between concepts about things. The latter are purely analytical.

Great care must be taken in the formation of concepts that their contents do not conflict. Antinomies arise if the different modal aspects in the forming of concepts are confused with each other.

Primary concepts are also related to each other in a manner which is dependent upon the extent of their connotation, namely the extension of that which is conceived by the concept. The relationship between the concepts "man" and "humanity," for example, is such that the former concept is subordinate to the latter. Concepts may totally or partially coincide with each other or they may be completely unrelated, e.g., (a) house and habitation; (b) house and room; (c) house and lake.

2. The Judgment

Concepts are a primary constituent of knowledge. Judgments, however, are secondary as they are formed from concepts. Vollenhoven defines a judgment as the possession of analytical knowledge about a state or condition (the predicate of a judgment in *relation* to the subject of that judgment). A judgment consists of three elements, a subject, a predicate, and a relation. The *subject of the judgment* is that concept to which another concept (the predicate) is ascribed as being applicable or inapplicable. The *predicate of the judgment* is the concept predicated of the subject. And, the *relation of the judgment* is the relation between the subject and the predicate. It is positive when the predicate is applicable to the subject and negative when inapplicable.

Judgments correspond to concepts in the following ways. Both are a part of knowledge or error and should be formed in agreement with the norms of knowing. Both contain a relation between the knowing-activity and the knowable. And both are individual and contain truth if they have been formed in conformity with the norms of knowing.

A judgment should be formed in conformity with the analytical norm. This means that the *relation* of a judgment, which is of central importance, may not be contradictory or contain a contradiction. But the fact that a judgment is not contradictory does not prove the judgment to be true. To be true a judgment must be formed in agreement with the norm of knowing in all its aspects and not only to the linguistical anticipation of the analytical norm. A true judgment is never contradictory. The three elements of the judgment are related to the knowable. Consequently, the one making the judgment must form each of these three elements in accordance with the knowable. Whether or not the relation of a judgment is positive or negative depends exclusively upon that which is known. The correctness of the judgment, "this house is new," or "this house is not new," is not determined by any epistemological norm but by the concrete house in question.

Every judgment is connected with the person making it. He alone determines whether or not it is simple or complex, scientific or non-scientific. If the relation between the subject and the predicate of a judgment is one of identity, then the converse of the judgment can be stated with equal validity. The judgment, "the cosmos is the world," may be reversed, and stated in the form, "the world is the cosmos."

Judgments can also be classified from various points of view.

(a) Judgments which are or are not contradictory.
(b) Simple and complex judgments.
(c) Scientific and non-scientific judgments.
(d) Judgments pronounced with more or less subjective certainty by the person who forms the judgment.
(e) Negative or positive judgments.
(f) Universal or individual judgments. (This type of judgment depends upon the range, the extension of the subject in the judgment. "All men are mortal" is a universal judgment. "John is thin" is an individual judgment.)
(g) Primary or secondary judgments depend upon the character of the subject in the judgment. If the subject is related to something knowable that is neither a concept or a judgment, then the judgment is primary. If the subject is related to a concept or a judgment, then the judgment is secondary, for example: the philosophy of Aristotle is an intricate system.

We must still say a word about the relationship between judgments. A contradictory and a non-contradictory judgment are mutually *incompatible* and do not tolerate each other. If two or more judgments are compatible, this does not mean that the argument is necessarily correct; it is only logically closed. Correct judgments are always in harmony with law.

Judgments can be arranged to form a new judgment if they have the same quality, that is, if they are positive or negative, and if they have identical subjects or predicates.

EXAMPLE *I*: "This house is new."
"This street is new."
"This house and this street are new."
EXAMPLE II: "This house is new."
"This house is high."
"This house is new and high."

Scientific and non-scientific judgments ought to be compatible and to agree with each other. If they both seem to be lawfully formed and yet in conflict, then effort should be made to uncover the cause of error. And only a prejudice would warrant the conclusion that the non-scientific judgment is necessarily at fault. Science is not infallible. If two judgments only differ from each other in quality and are otherwise identical, so that the first is positive and the second negative, then they contradict each other, and both judgments cannot be true.

If the subject of a judgment is the predicate of a second judgment, then, a third judgment follows, in which the subject of the second judgment is its subject, and the predicate of the first judgment is its predicate.

E.g., "All men have a soul."
"John is a man."
"John has a soul."

The first two judgments are called premises, the third, the conclusion. The term which appears in both premises is called the middle term. The three judgments considered together are called a syllogism. The judgment which is greatest in extent or quantity is stated first, and is called the major premise. The other premise is the minor premise. The extent (universal or particular) and the quality (positive or negative) of a conclusion depend upon the extent and quality of the premises. There are various possible combinations and a great number of forms or *modi* of syllogisms.

When both premises are universal and positive, the conclusion is also universal and positive.
E.g., "All men have a soul."

"Americans are men."
"Americans have a soul."

If the first premise is universal and positive, and the second is particular and positive, then the conclusion is also particular and positive.

If the first premise is general and negative and the second premise is particular and positive, then the conclusion is particular and negative.

E.g., "Men are not animals."
"John is a man."
"John is not an animal."

Thus within the cadre of the above figure there are 16 modi (ways to form a syllogism) in which the middle term is the subject in the major premise and is the predicate in the minor premise. And, with respect to the place of the middle term there are still three other possible figures. The middle term can be the predicate in the major and the subject in the minor premise. Or it can be the subject or the predicate in both premises. Within each of these figures there are 16 possible modi; thus there is a total of 64 modi of possible valid syllogisms. A valid conclusion follows from each union of two valid premises.

Syllogisms are helpful in establishing proofs, but, in any concrete instance, more is necessary. We must also discover in a concrete case the coherence between the premises and the conclusion. And if such a coherence is lacking the proof is not complete, for in that case we touched a state of matters, which is knowable, but not yet known.

Proof plays a role in practical life as well as in science. However, its importance must not be overestimated. There are many things which do not require logical proof but are immediately and directly known, because also without proof the conclusion is clear; or because along a shorter way the knowledge is possible. Nevertheless, in judging an argument one should always consider the possibility that his opponent has failed to draw the conclusion demanded by his premises, because he has failed to see the connection or because he shrunk from the conclusion implied.

24
The Problem of Knowledge

There is no problem of knowledge in pre-theoretical knowing. Such a problem is alien to naive experience. A person who is not called to engage in scientific activity does not engage in philosophical reflection and does not raise the question as to how it is possible that his knowing-activity can acquire knowledge of reality. This question is a scientific one and it can be answered only by scientific thought. In naive experience we are not concerned with such problems. Pre-scientific knowing is simply in direct touch with reality. Reality is its data. Naive experience is the concrete experience that we have of things and of their relationships with temporal reality in all its fulness. Naive experience does not give an account of the *possibility* of knowledge. However, no contradiction exists between naive experience and science. It is erroneous to maintain that the former is fallacious and deals only with appearance, whereas truth is found solely in science. We must closely guard against such a contention, for it is the product of the deification of science.

The points of difference between scientific and non-scientific experience do not in any way warrant a denial of the ability of the latter to attain to truth. It is equally wrong to condemn science as something superfluous. The person who rejects science, forgetting that naive experience is enriched by it, voluntarily accepts an impoverished life. From science we learn to know with greater accuracy the richness of reality. Science increases our wonder and admiration for the works of God and very often corrects our pre-scientific naive knowledge.

In naive experience we reflect upon concrete reality, which is given to us in an unbreakable coherence as a totality. In science we employ logical abstraction and abstract various aspects of concrete reality. The scientist abstracts the modal aspects or modalities and separates reality into its different aspects. The scientist realizes that feeling is a different function from organic life, and that life is different from motion, and motion different from space. The knowing-process in science properly begins with the analytical separation and division of reality. Science separates and distinguishes one aspect from another. The psychologist, biologist, and the historian can only properly investigate the emotive, the vital, and the historical function of reality after their respective fields have been distinguished. Each science investigates a specific modal aspect by seeking to discover in which creatures and in which way it expresses its very meaning in our experienced world. Each science also discovers the laws to which its respective aspect is subject as well as the relationship which exists between itself and the remaining aspects of the cosmos. The scientist places one aspect of reality as his field of investigation in an antithetical relation to his own analytical function. Scientific thought is, therefore, antithetical thought.

In German the field of investigation is designated by the term, *"Gegenstand,"* meaning what is opposed to my scientific thinking; but English does not have any equivalent term. The term "object" is not suitable to designate the field of investigation, as we have already seen previously. The antithetical relation between a non-analytical and an analytical function is highly important, as scientific knowledge is obtained when a synthesis is made between these polar opposites.

An adequate theory of knowledge must answer the question as to how this *theoretical synthesis* is possible. How can we give a philosophical explanation of the synthesis which takes place in scientific knowledge between the analytical and a non-analytical function? This problem is of a peculiar nature. Such a synthesis can only take place in the innermost structure of the analytical function. It cannot be accomplished by any other function. If this synthesis is to be possible, a deeper coherence must exist between the analytical function and the remaining functions. Contrary to the view of the Marburg school of Neo-Kantians, science does not have creative power. The possibility of this synthesis is not the sovereign creation of science but the result of God's creative work.

The problem of knowledge is to discover how this synthesis takes place. If there were not a deeper coherence between the analytical function and the non-analytical aspects, the analytical aspect could not be in touch with the remaining aspects and would be foreign to them. Scientific knowledge would then be impossible.

Immanence-philosophy considers synthetical thought to be self-sufficient. By absolutizing scientific thought, immanence-philosophy can not give an account of the possibility of theoretical synthesis. It accepts it as a given without even being aware of the problems involved. Immanence-philosophy forgets that reality is only *given* to us in *naive experience*.

A truly critical philosophy must seek to solve this epistemological problem by determining the *conditions* under which this knowledge-yielding synthesis is possible. There are two such conditions, the one is *transcendental* and the other is *transcendent*. The religious root of our temporal existence, the heart, is the transcendent condition. The heart is the religious concentration point of all the cosmic functions of the temporal order. The deepest coherence of these functions lies in the human heart. Consequently, the analytical function is not alien to all the other aspects of temporal reality. We need not appeal to such constructions as "pure thought," "Bewusztsein uberhaupt" ("consciousness in general") or similar ones, in order to solve the problem of knowledge. Such constructions are themselves the results of analytical abstraction. The analytical function can never free itself from its religious root. It is impossible for the analytical function to abstract itself. Every abstraction presupposes the *I-ness*, the religious root of scientific investigation in the innermost depths of the scientist's heart.

The second condition for the knowledge-yielding synthesis is a *transcendental condition* which remains within cosmic time, even though it is necessarily related to the religious center of the knowing-consciousness. This transcendental condition is the *intuitive* activity in the knowing-process.

This intuition is both naive and theoretical. Naive intuition is found in naive experience. It is the *conscious experience of reality as my own.* Naive intuition is the cosmic self-consciousness in which we knowingly experience the modal aspects and their diversity as parts of the same reality. And this reality is not alien to us; we are in touch with it.

This cosmic self-consciousness includes the knowledge that in and above all cosmic functions we are one and the same person.

Intuition lies within the cosmic order between the modal aspects and the religious root of our existence. We have expressed this idea previously when we defined intuition as a *transcendental* condition of knowledge.

Intuition should not be sought in any modal function. Kant and Bergson both violate this principle. The former resolved theoretical self-consciousness and the thinking selfhood in the logical function. And the latter subordinated intuition under the psychical function. We cannot accept this functionalism, for if intuition were actually resolved in a particular function, then the remaining functions would not be our own, but would be strange to us. We must regard *intuition* as a *temporal depth* of the analytical function through which we gain an insight into the cosmic temporal coherence of all functions. Intuition lies on a lower, deeper level than that which is determined by the modal aspects. Because of it each person consciously experiences the diversity of the modal aspects as his own reality; and knows immediately that love and law, thinking and feeling, space and motion, are quite different from each other.

Intuition however is not to be identified with our selfhood, with our heart, the religious root of our existence. Our selfhood is itself cosmically conscious in intuition. The human heart functions by intuition. However, although not identical, there is an inseverable connection between the selfhood and intuition. Intuition does not exist where there is no selfhood. Creatures, such as animals, which lack a religious root, also lack intuition. An animal lacks self-consciousness; possessing instincts alone, it cannot experience reality in its entirety. To an animal much of reality is foreign because an animal is limited to sensory impressions and acts instinctively without being self-conscious. Its psychical life moves in a closed structure; it only knows the psychical *objective* side of reality in a restricted sense.

In contrast to animals man knows all functions as his own by means of his intuition. Nothing in creation is foreign to him. He can knowingly examine reality and experience its fulness, but he is not resolved or exhausted in temporal reality. He has a deeper religious identity, which is intuitively experienced. According to Holy Scripture this super-temporal identity is the consequence of the fact that man is created in the image of God. Man is, therefore, created for eternity; he has an end that transcends everything temporal.

Up until now we have treated naive intuition exclusively. Naive intuition is the transcendental condition for pre-scientific knowledge, which unsystematically grasps the full cosmic reality.

In addition to naive intuition we must also consider *theoretical intuition*. We defined the former as the conscious experience of reality as our own. We can define the latter as our theoretical insight into the temporal cosmic coherence of the modal functions or aspects, the insight that reality in all its temporal aspects is my own. Theoretical intuition is *theoretical self-consciousness*. It affords a solution to the problem of knowledge by telling us how *theoretical synthesis* is possible. By means of this insight we can see how, in scientific knowledge, the analytical function is united with the other functions. By means of theoretical intuition, the analytical function, in its innermost structure, namely the human heart, comes into actual epistemological contact with its field of investigation. This theoretical intuition rests upon the conscious experience of naive intuition. And it is precisely for this reason that pre-scientific knowledge is the very foundation of science. Theoretical knowledge must always start with pre-theoretical knowledge as its foundation.

God has endowed man, who is His image, with so many talents, in order that He, the Creator from mankind, in the unfolding of its culture, would receive honor and glory for the greatness and wisdom of all His works.

25

The Horizon of Human Experience

Our human experience is not unlimited; it has boundaries and a certain horizon. Upon a little reflection everyone will grant this to be true. For we cannot experience things which do not exist. We can imagine things which do not exist; we can experience our fantasy, but not its objects. We cannot even experience everything that exists. As long as we are on earth, heavenly things are beyond the reach of human experience. Our knowledge of them is derived from God's revealed Word. It is a knowledge of faith; we cannot observe heavenly things directly. We can only experience things which belong to the temporal cosmos, and even such things can only be experienced under certain conditions. A baby does not experience political life, nor does a member of a primitive society have any experience of the objects of Western culture. The horizon of our human experience has a *lawful* structural character. It has limits which God has placed in the very structure of things (no one can experience something which does not exist). And, on the other hand, this horizon has a *subjective* character. It can still be closed to various structures of reality, but it need not remain closed. The *subjective* horizon of experience can be opened. The *subjective* aspect of the horizon of experience is necessarily correlative to a *lawful* structural side. For, in the final analysis, this horizon is not merely the horizon of our human experience. It is an horizon of the cosmos itself as it was formed by God. It is a part of the created order.

To speak of the horizon of human experience is to speak of the way in which the knowable is accessible to our knowing-activity. And this is not an arbitrary matter; it is not determined by the knowing-subject but it is a *structural apriori*. It is firmly established in the divine order of creation. To acquire correct knowledge concerning a particular state of affairs and to discover truth, the knowing-subject must not only acknowledge this structural order but he must also place himself in subjection to it.

The apriori element in reality has been perennially discussed in philosophy. In antiquity and medieval scholasticism it was conceived of in a metaphysical sense. It was considered to be the ground of *being* and the basis for the *existence* of individual concrete things. Aristotle sought this apriori in the essential form of things; while Plato sought it in the world of ideas.

Modern Kantian philosophy was anti-metaphysical and spoke only of the *apriori element* in a theoretical, epistemological sense. It considered only the subjective aspect of the horizon of experience and detached the latter from the lawful, structural side of the horizon. Kant declared the structural side to be unknowable. The *Ding an sich* was a hypothetical unknowable magnitude. Under the subjective apriori, Kant subsumed the so-called forms of knowledge: the forms of perception and the categories of thought. With the aid of these forms, the knowing subject is able to construct reality out of the "phenomena of consciousness" (the material of knowledge).

Both the metaphysical and the theoretical epistemological view are unacceptable to us. The former utilizes a form-matter schema which impoverishes and misforms the richness of reality by deifying either form or matter. From a Christian point of view the cosmos does not come to rest in any created aspect but only in God, upholding all things by the Word of His power.

The theoretical epistemological view deifies the knowing

subject. In his knowing-activity this subject is exalted to be the Creator of reality.

Since we cannot accept the ancient or Kantian view, what then is the horizon of human experience? Perhaps an illustration will help to answer this question. In what way can I experience an orchard? In what way can I acquire a correct and pure experience of it?

In the first place it makes a big difference whether or not I view the orchard in question as created by God, or as a product of "Mother Nature." It makes a difference if I see a reflection of God's wisdom in a tree, or if in Kantian fashion, I approach it as an unknowable, "Ding an sich," a *Ding an sich* which arouses in my mind various phenomena which I must arrange and construct until they become concrete and individual reality.

If some one objects that a tree is a tree, no matter if it is viewed by a Christian or a non-Christian, such an objection displays a lack of appreciation of the radical character of the Christian religion. All of a person's experience is influenced by his basic religious commitment. We cannot detach our heart from our experience of reality.

To view an orchard as created is, however, not enough if we are to gain a correct experience of it. For in the second place, my experience is influenced by the knowledge I have of the temporal coherence of the various aspects of reality, wherein this orchard as creature of God expresses itself in cosmic time (I should at least have a scientific view of this coherence). If my experience is to be complete and correct, I must notice the number of trees in the orchard, the size of the orchard, the soil, the weather, the color of the trees, their age and commercial value, the beauty of flowering, the owner of the lot, and so on.

The horizon of my experience is constituted in the third place by the fact that I have a direct consciousness of the peculiar nature of biotic life which qualifies living trees. It is not enough that I have a knowledge of the temporal cosmic coherence of the many aspects of reality within which the orchard expresses itself. For if I were not conscious of the nature of biotic life, I would not notice any difference between trees painted on stage scenery and real trees.

And finally my experience depends upon whether or not I possess an insight into the *plastic* structure of a tree, so that I can distinguish an apple from a pear tree, or a tree from a plant or shrub.

The horizon of our human experience is determined by four different apriori. It has four different dimensions which hang together in an unbreakable coherence. These dimensions are arranged in an order which can be systematically represented as follows:

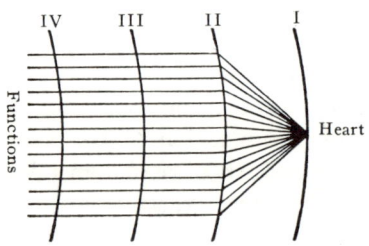

(I) The first dimension, the *transcendent horizon,* is the heart, the religious root of human existence. Our experience, whether it be our knowing-activity, or something else, can never be detached from our heart. Such a detachment would mean the end of experience and the termination of this life.

(II) The second dimension, the *transcendental horizon,* is time. Through it we experience the diversity and coherence of the aspects in which temporal reality presents itself. All experience on earth is bound to time, not only to clock-time or historical time, but to cosmic time. We cannot experience anything which transcends cosmic time.

(III) The third dimension is the *modal horizon.* This dimension includes the structure and the peculiar nature of the modal aspects. If man, for example, did not have an aesthetic subject-function, if he did not have an intuitive insight into the structure of the aesthetical modal aspect, then he would, as an animal, indifferently pass by the most beautiful painting. The richness of the aspects of temporal reality, in its entirety is accessible to our human experience because of the modal apriori's. In contrast to the tremendous diversity of individual things, the modal aspects, because of their apriori character, have a structural constancy.

(IV) The fourth dimension, the *plastic horizon*, is that of the *structures of individuality* of concrete things, events and societal forms. A house and a church building are both things whose last subject-function lies in the physical aspect. Their modal apriori is the same but their plastic structure of individuality is different. Apart from a specific house or church building, everyone has a fixed concept of a house and a church, because both have a constant plastic (moldable) structure which is not arbitrary. The word "house" or "church" does not bring to mind a mountain or a lamp post.

The horizon of our experience has a law and a subject side. Its law-side is given in a structure and is unchangeable because it is rooted in the divine world order. No one can experience anything outside of the four dimensions[1] we have listed. Every person is subject to this horizon and cannot create a new one.

[1] Prof. Dr. H. G. Stoker, from Potchefstroom, S. Africa, who is unanimous with Prof. Dooyeweerd with relation to the foundations of this Christian philosophy, has a different view on the horizon of our human experience. He distinguishes the following structural dimensions:
1. the dimension of modality;
2. the dimension of individuality;
3. the dimension of events (causality);
4. the dimension of values;
5. the religious dimension.

Observable is, that Stoker has no separate place for the transcendental horizon of cosmic time, because he ranges the time under the *dimension of events;* while Dooyeweerd places events next to things and takes both of them together under the dimension of individuality, the plastic horizon.

Stoker's *dimension of values* is a summary of all normative modalities in their polarity of right and wrong, true and false, beautiful and ugly, love and hate, and so on.

See his book: *Principles and Methods of Science.*

The case is quite different with respect to the subject-side. All human insight can be troubled or obscured. From the Christian point of view the fall of man has darkened our subjective horizon. Man's own apostasy causes him to close his heart to the light of divine truth and to deny that all of life is religiously determined. Apostate man seeks certainty in autonomous science or in sovereign human personality. In departing from God, man leaves the true origin of all things and loses his life to that which has no permanence in itself and which is meaningless apart from God. The horizon of human experience and science is thus obfuscated by the fall.

The horizon of our experience is again emancipated and opened by the light of Divine Revelation. For the Christian, Jesus Christ is the Truth, the Redeemer of our whole existence. By faith in Him, Christ again directs our life toward God, unto whom we are created. "In thy light we see the light."

26

Truth

The last subject that requires attention in our discussion of the theory of knowledge is truth. A close connection exists between knowledge and truth. Without the latter, knowledge simply does not exist. When we are uncertain of the truth of something, we do not speak of knowledge, but of conjecture, opinion, or probability. Knowledge is always related to truth. If I say I have knowledge about something, I mean that I, as the knowing-subject, have a true insight into something that is knowable.

The problem of truth is a perennial one. The question raised by Pilate, What is truth? is known to everyone. Different answers have been given to it in all ages. The answer of scepticism is that there is no truth which is valid for everyone. What is true for one person is not true for another. What is true today may be a lie tomorrow. Truth depends upon the thinking and speaking subject. Such scepticism is found in antiquity, for example, in the teachings of the Sophists (e.g., Protagoras and Gorgias). They hold that truth is the certainty of the individual that what is perceived is real. Consequently, every opinion may be called true.

Agnosticism is even more radically subjectivistic. It teaches that all truth is unknowable. The conception of modern *pragmatism* is related to both agnosticism and scepticism and is just as subjectivistic. Pragmatism teaches that truth consists of the effectiveness of an affirmation. That which advances a previously determined end is true, and that which hinders the attainment of such an end is false.

In the history of thought many other subjectivistic conceptions were defended with respect to the problem of truth. Pierre D'Auriol, for example, a Medieval thinker, held that truth is honesty in speech or clarity in distinguishing the contents of one's own consciousness.

In spite of their divergencies all of these subjectivistic theories of truth have a common characteristic. They all deny the relation between knowledge and the *knowable* and only recognize the relation between the knowing-subject and knowledge. The third element, the knowable, is eliminated.

A Christian thinker cannot agree with any of these points of view. One thing, at least, is certain to every Christian: no matter how truth is to be defined, in any case it is not entirely dependent upon the knowing-subject. The criterion of truth is not subjective.

Not every philosopher has tried to solve the problem of truth in a subjectivistic manner. We encounter realism in the history of philosophy. Realists, from Aristotle via Thomas Aquinas, up until present day realistically orientated Christian thinkers, have contended that truth is the agreement between thinking and being, between subjective thought and objective reality.

It is not surprising that many find this definition of truth superior to those offered by subjectivism. Realism is apparently aware of the fact that truth is concerned with something outside of the knowing-subject and is valid as truth for the knowing-subject. Realism is aware of the fact that in all true knowledge there is a relationship between the knowing-subject and the knowable. Realism is, however, not satisfactory, mainly, because it only distinguishes two components of the knowing-process: the knowing subject and the knowable. Realism omits a third factor, namely, law. If truth is merely agreement between thinking and being, law would be identical with the knowable. This does violence to the data of reality in which the knowable is subject to the law of knowing. We can have truth only when the knowing process is executed in *conformity with law*.

The relationship between the knowing-subject and the knowable may not be identified without qualification with the subject-object relationship. The subject-object relation is the cadre within which naive knowing takes place. Naive knowing bears a systatic-cosmic character. And scientific knowing is synthetical and cosmological in character; it engages in a theoretical analysis and synthesis of the modal aspects.

In its theory of knowledge, realism identifies these two essentially different relationships, namely the naive and the scientific knowledge, and forces the epistemological relationship into the subject-object schema.

There are additional objections that can be made to the definition of the so-called correspondence theory which holds truth to be the agreement between thought and being. The word, *"agreement,"* indicates that this theory is only aware of the *logical object-side* of being. It is only aware of that which is logically objective in reality.

According to the correspondence theory this agreement is thought of as being an agreement between the knowing subject (subjective logical) and that which appears as an object in the analytical modality (objective logical). By *only* ascribing being to the *logical object-side* of the things, this view impoverishes reality and overlooks the other aspects of the reality. Furthermore, the statement that truth is an agreement between thinking and being detaches thought from being and elevates the logical function of thought above reality. And this indicates that realism has not radically broken with the apostate tendency of immanence-philosophy. To deify the analytical modality is to seek religious certainty in human thought.

Subjectivism seeks certainty in the logical subject and realism in the logical object. Both seek it within creation and not in God.

The Christian position is that a true knowledge of reality is only possible in the light of true knowledge of God. If a person does not have the knowledge of God in his heart, he cannot know the truth about God's works *in its coherence*. This does not imply that the non-Christian cannot discover moments of truth in a limited sense. In-so-far as he actually observes existing relations within the cosmos, his observation is true. But the interpretation that he gives to these relations, his total view concerning them, perverts the truth.

The truth about the creation is inseverably connected with the truth about the Creator, who expresses Himself completely in His Son and who revealed Himself to us in His Word and works. Thus, the horizon of our experience is free to attain true knowledge of God's works, if, and only if, we believe in Christ as He is revealed to us in the Scripture. Then we are standing in the Truth, that means in the Firmness, which liberates us and also sets free the horizon of our experience, so that we can get to the very knowledge about the great works of God. As Christians we may not divorce our theory of epistemology from our religious faith. Transcendent Truth is the firm foundation of cosmic-immanent truth. Our whole life is religiously determined.

We can conclude from the preceding that truth bears the same perspective character as the horizon of our human experience. The broadest perspective of truth is in the transcendent dimension of the human heart, which is either committed to God or seeks certainty within the created cosmos. To the Christian, the broadest perspective of truth is the Transcendent Fulness of Truth, namely, Jesus Christ. From this transcendent dimension of truth, the light of truth shines into the dimensions of temporal truth, which is determined by the apriori of the transcendental temporal horizon.

The following definition applies to the knowledge of truth in naive experience. *Within this temporal horizon, truth is the agreement of subjective knowledge with the structural laws of human experience.* We can speak of truth when the subjective activity of knowledge takes place according to the analytical laws of thought and according to the remaining modal laws valid for that about which we seek to acquire knowledge. We can speak of truth, but with the understanding, that this temporal act of knowing included within the temporal act-horizon, is open to the light of the Transcendent Truth in Christ.

The definition of theoretical (scientific) truth is as follows: *theoretical truth is the agreement of the subjective apriori synthesis* (the synthesis of the analytical with a non-analytical function) *with the modal structure of the field of investigation.* The field of investigation may not be detached from its coherence with all the preceding and subsequent modal aspects. And it must be connected to the Transcendent Fulness of Truth in Christ.

The criterion of theoretical truth is the *principle of excluded antinomy.* When we encounter antinomies in scientific thought (two contradictory laws), this is a sign that we are proceeding on a false path. We may draw this conclusion because of the fact that every temporal truth (a truth included in the transcendental horizon) must be able to justify itself before the forum of Transcendent Truth. Stated in another way, antinomies act as a warning signal because God is not Yes and No at the same time.

A second criterion for science is this: theoretical truth must be able to give an account of temporal reality as the latter is given in naive experience. Theoretical thought which discards or depreciates the data of naive experience is false. Science does not contradict naive experience and is not detached from it. True science does not claim to be self-sufficient, but recognizes that it has a God-given task to open reality theoretically in order to magnify the honor and glory of God.

Perhaps a quotation from Professor Dooyeweerd is a fitting end to this chapter. "Our philosophy makes bold to accept the 'stumbling block of the cross of Christ' as the corner stone of epistemology. And thus it also accepts the cross of scandal, neglect and dogmatic rejection."[1]

[1] *A New Critique of Theoretical Thought,* Vol. II, page 562.

CHAPTER IV

THE THEORY OF THE STRUCTURES OF TEMPORAL THINGS

27

SUBSTANCE

THIS chapter deals with the theory of the *structures of individuality* of temporal reality. First of all, What is the distinction between the theory of modalities and the theory of structures of individuality? Both theoretically investigate temporal reality, and temporal reality is created by God and is subject to the world order. The difference is that each conducts this investigation in its own peculiar way. The theory of the modal aspects examines the many aspects which, as it were, divide the cosmos into *segments* or *cross sections*. It does not examine things with respect to their own *typical totality*. It examines them according to their modal or functional coherence. The theory of modalities is concerned with everything which pertains to the modal aspects, but it does not consider a concrete thing, as such. It does not view a tree as a concrete living object in order to ascertain its structure. It is not interested in its lawful construction which constitutes the tree as a unified thing and as a peculiar creation of God. The theory of modal aspects focuses its attention, for example, on everything subject to biotic laws, i.e., plants, animals, and man. It notices that in spite of their differences, these things all have a biotic subject-function.

The theory of structures of individuality, in contrast, concentrates upon the fact that God has created *individualities* or *individual structures*. God has made concrete things, and concrete things are structural unities which we experience as totalities with their own typical nature. The individuality of a thing means a thing is more than the sum of its properties and functions. A stone, for example, is more than a certain weight, color, and hardness. It is more than its properties. It is a creature of God and it displays a *unity* of a typical and peculiar nature. A stone is a different sort of a thing from a tree. The *typical* nature of a stone is not arbitrary. If it were, our experience of stones and of other things would not be possible, and the world would collapse into a chaos of loose, disconnected "phenomena." Experience would be impossible unless, in Kantian fashion, it is endowed with a creative faculty.

The fact that the unity of a thing is above arbitrariness permits us to speak of a certain *structure* or construction which displays a *lawful* character in the cosmic order. (This character is ordered by God.)

These structures of individuality determine the very possibility of our experience of reality and belong to what we called in epistemology, *the plastic horizon* of our experience. And as we have seen this horizon displays an apriori character. It is that dimension of our experience which is not related to the modal community of created things, but is related to their typical diversity, to their peculiar unity and characteristic *structure as a totality*.

The distinction between the theory of modalities and the theory of structures of individuality may be described as a distinction between a functional and an individual view of reality. The difference between the two is not antagonistic. The latter supplements the former, and the former is the necessary foundation of the latter. An insight into the structures of individuality cannot be gained without the aid of the theory of modal aspects. And our view of the structures of reality, in turn, enriches our insight into the modal horizon of our experience. Our subsequent exposition will clarify the relationship between these two perspectives.

Before we can proceed further with our analysis, it is necessary to say something about the problem of *substance*. The word *substance* is frequently encountered in systems of immanence-philosophy. Many Christians have borrowed the term and employ it in their scientific endeavors. The term originated in antiquity and has since frequently been proffered as a solution to the problem of the structures of individuality of temporal reality.

None of the divergent uses of the term "substance" are acceptable to us because they all imply that *an ultimate fast point is to be found within the created cosmos.* We affirm, in contrast, that the permanent basis of all that exists is found in God alone. Philosophy which employs the idea of substance does not sufficiently distinguish between the *origin* of the individual, the *structure* of the individual, and the *subjective individual* itself which is subject to cosmic laws within the structural apriori horizon of temporal reality.

The word "substance" (hypostasis in Greek) literally means "to stand or be under." In the New Testament the word has two usages. When used with respect to God (Hebrews 1:3), it denotes a *firm foundation* and, secondly, it denotes that which has permanence and firmness because of this foundation. (2 Cor. 9:4, this confidence.) In the second usage the term derives its stability from God.[1]

In its metaphysical usage in philosophy the term denotes a being that subsists or rests in itself.[2] If a place is ascribed to secondary substances, these originate in the self-sufficient reason or logos.

All metaphysical thinkers are in agreement about what we have said up until this point. The difference between them arises with respect to what they respectively consider to be substances.

[1] See, *Het Calvinisme en de Reformatie van de Wijsbegeerte,* by D. H. Th. Vollenhoven, Aantekkeningen 188.
[2] Cf., H. Dooyeweerd, *A New Critique of Theoretical Thought,* Vol. III.
In Petrus Ramus' (1572) work, *Defensio pro Aristotle adversus Iac, Schecium,* I found the following definition of substance: *"ousia accipitur theologicé et physicé pro eo quod per se subsistit"* (p. 38). (Translation: The essence [substance] is theologically and physically understood as *that which exists through itself.*)
Cf. Spinoza, *Ethica,* Definition III: "By substance I understand that which exists by itself and that which must be comprehended in terms of itself."

The Ionic philosophers of nature sought to discover an eternal primordial stuff which would serve to explain all that is. Thales, Anaximander, and Anaximines respectively sought this world-stuff in water, the infinite, and in air.

Parmenides, the founder of the Eleatic school, thought that all becoming and all change is illusion. True reality is the eternal unchangeable and unmovable "being," which is identical with a "static and bullet-shaped space," and can only be discovered by thinking.

Parmenides was followed by the Atomists who were represented by Leucippus and Democritus. The Atomists taught that substance consists of an infinite number of indivisible, ungenerated, unchangeable, primal bodies, called atoms.

Plato considered this world to be an image or copy of the real world. Beyond the world of sense, he posited a world of ideas, namely: truth, goodness and beauty, with the really existing numbers themselves. He called them super-temporal substances, and considered them as perfect examples the law for all terrestrial things. Aristotle, in contrast, sought "substance" in the things of this world. He included all reality in a schema of form and matter and considered matter and form to be related to each other as potentiality to actuality. Becoming is due to the fact that matter strives after form. The structure of a thing is a correlation or interaction between matter and form. The essence, the substance of things, has a higher reality than the individual things themselves. A horse, the essence of all concrete horses which are, is not only a universal concept, but it is a higher *reality* than a concrete horse. It is a metaphysical *substance*. This substance does not exist apart from and outside of individual things. It exists only in things. *The universal horse,* the metaphysical substance, which rests in itself, is found in many concrete horses because of matter. Form is universal. The principle of multiplicity, of individuation, lies in matter. Aristotle sought the structural principle of each thing in form and the principle of individuation in matter. The individuality of a thing and its structural principle are basically opposed and foreign to each other. For this reason, in our judgment, Aristotle failed to give an adequate explanation of the structures of individuality of temporal reality.

Modern humanism brought medieval thought to an end. Nevertheless, Descartes believed in two sorts of substance, *extended* substance and *thinking* substance. He reduced all the pre-psychical functions to extension and all the following functions to thinking. Immanuel Kant, however, no longer sought substance in an extra-mental reality (which exists outside of our consciousness), but he sought it in the *human* subject. Substance is a form or category of thought by which — with the aid of perceptional forms of time and space — we construct concrete reality from the chaos of our sensory impressions. The concept of substance does not have a metaphysical significance but a purely epistemological one. Metaphysical substance, the *"Ding an sich,"* is not knowable but is an object of faith. Kant deified the functions of consciousness so that autonomous man subsists by himself.

Our objection to *substance* is not merely verbal. A philosophy which operates with it is functionalistic. It only recognizes the functional (modal) diversity of the cosmos. It neglects that which transcends temporal functions and it tries to reduce the plastic horizon to the modal horizon. Functionalism always proclaims one or more temporal functions to be self-sufficient, thereby depriving them of their meaning and character, so that they no longer point to God, the Foundation of all things.

Following Aristotle and Medieval Thomistic philosophy, the concept of substance is employed in order to discover the "essence" of the soul and the body. Also in protestant circles, both these parts of human existence are generally thought of as two hypostasized complexes of relatively arbitrary temporal functions, two substances, instead of learning with the Scripture the full unity of body and soul. Man *has* not a body, but he *is* his own body. This wrong solution of the two substances gives rise to the unsolvable pseudo-problem of the relationships between "body" and "soul." And it darkens the scriptural teaching concerning the heart or soul of man, and loses sight of the fact that, as the religious concentration point of all temporal functions, the soul or heart cannot rest in itself, but only in God, who is the Father of spirits.

The philosophy of substance is consequently apostate philosophy. It does not understand God as He has revealed Himself. And a pure knowledge of God is necessary in order to attain wisdom in daily life as well in science. If we do not know God, in whom the whole creation rests, we cannot rightly know His works.

Philosophy can proceed to the discovery of a correct view of individuality, if it abandons the concept of substance and recognizes that nothing within the cosmos subsists in itself. Everything points to and is sustained by the power of God.

28

Analysis of the Structural Principle of an Individual Thing

The concept of substance rests upon an hypostatization, or a deification of one or more temporal functions which it deprives of all meaning. To be *meaningful* a temporal function must be directive in character and must point away from itself toward Christ in whom the whole creation finds the fulfillment of its meaning; and through Christ toward God, the eternal Origin of all things. Consequently, as Christian thinkers we must reject the concept of substance. However, even in Christian circles some people cling tenaciously to it, and will not break radically with immanence-philosophy. Their arguments in support of the retention of the concept of substance are often weak and confused. Some accuse us of not recognizing the proper essence and created self-sufficiency of creation, and in the course of their argument they identify created self-sufficiency with the concept of substance, which we reject. They argue that the notion of substance is necessary to insure that the creation is independent of the Creator. And they contend that our recognition of God as the sole substance, the sole Fast Ground, leads to pantheism. This contention is without any basis in fact. The concept of substance is not necessary to insure the created independence of creation, and our view does not jeopardize it, because we have not merely propounded a theory of modal aspects, but we have also set forth a theory of *structures of individuality*. The latter supplements the former and emphasizes the fact that the unity of a thing is more than the sum of its functions. The world is not composed of a multiplicity of phenomena. God created things, man, and social relationships, subject to fixed structural laws and woven together to form a vast concatenation. All creation is sustained by God's Omnipresent and Omnipotent power and in this sense it possesses a created independence which is not in any way self-sufficient. The structure of a thing is anchored in the Divine world order and this structure guarantees its identity. In spite of various changes, within certain limits, a thing remains the same and is not a complex of arbitrary functions.

The structures of individuality of temporal reality, as the modal aspects, are not the invention of science. Everyone intuitively perceives the different modal functions in his naive experience. Similarly, without theoretical analysis, we experience reality, in its concrete plastic structure, as things.

We speak of a "table," a "tree," a "picture," a "family," and a "church." As linguistical symbols these words point to various individual things each of which displays a constant structure which determines its unity. We do not use the term "table" to denote a certain energy-mass in a certain form and weight, but we use it to refer to a concrete thing with an internal unity which is subject to specific structural laws. Naive experience *systatically* experiences the structure of a thing and focuses its attention on temporal reality in its fulness. The task of philosophy, in contrast, is to investigate these structures theoretically through systematic analysis. Theoretical investigation starts with the data of naive experience and seeks to explain it. Philosophy is not opposed to naive experience, nor does it try to push it aside and replace it by a purely scientific view. Naive experience cannot be replaced. Philosophy ought to abandon all pride and join forces with naive experience and accept the God-given task of scientifically disclosing the structures of individuality.

To investigate the lawful structure of a concrete individual thing philosophically, it is first necessary to see how far it can be scientifically penetrated if it is only considered functionally. After this investigation we can draw our conclusions with respect to the structure which determines the unity of a concrete individual thing.

To begin our functional analysis, let us consider a specific tree growing in a certain place. By means of theoretical thought we can abstract this tree from its natural habitat and retain a "loose" thing which is capable of being analyzed further. For in naive experience we never deal with "loose" things but with totalities in which a multiplicity of individualities are woven together into a rich unity. We know that this tree at least functions as a subject in the first four modal aspects, the numerical, spatial, kinematic and physical. No thing has its qualifying end-function in the first three modal aspects. A spatial figure, for example, a circle, which is characterized by the spatial modal aspect, is not a real individual thing. It only exists on other things. It is drawn on a piece of paper or is the form of a wheel or something else. Also a moving thing — without physical energy — is not existing, except in abstract thinking. Thus a tree, as a real existing thing, has at least four subject-functions. It functions in the numerical and spatial sphere, as its leaves can be counted and it occupies a certain place. And it also functions in the kinematic and physical sphere. It can be moved and chemically analyzed and can be contemplated by the physicist as a moving mass of energy built up of atoms and electrons. But, from these four perspectives alone, one cannot meaningfully speak of a *tree*. A stone or a book can also be described from the view-point of the first four modalities. The structure of individuality of this specific thing therefore remains a mystery to anyone who refuses to go further than a physical explanation. The physical explanation is not incorrect but it is not sufficient to comprehend theoretically this living thing in its true nature.

It is only meaningful to speak of a "tree," if we notice that it is subject to the laws of organic life and therefore functions as a biotic or organic subject. A tree displays its vital-aspect in the processes of growth, metabolism, and reproduction, and since this biotic subject-function is its last subject-function, we can say that the biotic modality qualifies a tree. In other words a tree is biotically qualified because the last modality in which it functions as a subject is the biotic sphere, and it is from this sphere that a tree claims its peculiar nature and original individuality. The biotic function therefore occupies a cardinal position in the structure which constitutes a tree as a thing. Although a tree is *biotically qualified*, its real structure is not shut off or arrested in its organic vital aspect. The reality of *a thing* is not shut off in *any single modality*. And the structure which constitutes a tree as a thing is also individually expressed in the remaining modalities. In all the post-biotic aspects, a tree functions as an object rather than as a subject. Thus, we can say that the *structure* which constitutes a tree as a thing has an *objective individual* expression in every post-biotic modality. In the psychical modal aspect it appears as an *individual sensorily perceived image* which represents the perceived object to us. This perceived image is individual. It does not consist of a jumble of disconnected impressions which are formed into a unified thing or unity by the perceiving subject of the observer. It is rather the *thing* which appears to us in an individual form, in the perceived image. It is the thing which gives to the perceiver an individual objective-psychical expression of its structure as a thing.

In the analytical modality a tree functions as an *individ-*

ual conceptual object, an object accessible to our individual *cogitative function.* And this conceptual object has an individual form. For the difference between the concept "tree" and another concept is not due to our analytical cogitative function, but it lies in the *thing* which is the object of our thought.

In the historical modality a tree appears as an *individual cultural object,* as an object which furnishes the material used to construct usable objects. And in the linguistical sphere, a tree functions as an *individual symbolical object.* Naming is not an arbitrary activity, but it is based upon the fact that the structure which constitutes a thing expresses itself in the linguistical modality in an individual and objective way. A tree functions in the social modality as an *individual social object.* Trees planted in gardens and along lanes are attractive to human society and increase the richness of social intercourse. A tree functions as an object, in an individual way, in the social modality. And it possesses this function independently of human subjectivity.

The tree also functions in the economical modality as an *individual article of value.* It functions in the aesthetic modality as an *individual aesthetic object.* For while our tastes may differ, the beauty of God's creation does not depend upon our subjective likes and dislikes. The aesthetic function is not reducible to a psychical function, just because there is an inseverable connection between the two. God has made everything with an aesthetic object-function.

A tree is also an *individual juridical-object* in the juridical modality. It has a lawful owner and its ownership can be the subject of litigation. And, in the ethical modality, a tree is the *individual object of love* or hate. And finally, in the modality of faith, a tree is an *individual object of faith.* We believe that a tree is created by God, and the createdness of it does not depend upon our faith but is objectively true, independently of our faith. In our faith we subjectively confess objective-pistical facts to be true. A tree points beyond itself to God whose Name is glorified by His creation. God is above the creation and because of Him creation has meaning. And this meaning is disclosed to those who view the cosmos in the light of God's Revelation.

29

Concluding Remarks Concerning the Structure Which Constitutes a Thing

In the preceding section we analyzed an individual thing functionally and we used as an example a tree, which is qualified by its biotic subject-function. We saw that a tree functions in an *individual* manner in all the modalities of the cosmos. In the first five modalities, it functions as a subject; and in the ten remaining spheres it functions as an object. We can conclude that a tree has a modal *individuality* in every modality.

Now, the modal individuality of the object-functions of a tree or of its post-biotic functions is grounded in the original modal individuality of its last subject-function, which happens to be biotic. The last subject-function of a thing, therefore, is of a *qualifying* nature, and it plays a primary role in the structure which constitutes a tree as a concrete thing. A functional analysis however, cannot terminate our inquiry into the structure of a thing. A thing is *more than the sum of its modal functions*. If we forget this fact, we are in danger of falling into a fatal functionalism which can consider only functions and which would unravel the world into a bundle of loose phenomena. Without even noticing the deeper unity from which functions arise, this sort of functionalism, in consequence, loses all contact with reality. A functional analysis does not supply us with an adequate explanation of the unity of a thing, and, insofar as it is possible to do so, it is the task of philosophy to explain this unity. So let us notice first of all that the qualifying function of a tree is at the same time the individual *leading function* of its *internal unfolding process*. By internal unfolding or opening process we refer to the inner coherence and cooperation that exists between and directs the subject-functions of a tree in the first five modal aspects. It directs them in a certain individual way in order to fulfill a certain individual end. Whether or not a tree takes nitrogen, lime, or phosphorous as nourishment is indifferent from a *modal* physical-chemical standpoint; for, seen from this modal standpoint, all these chemical matters are possible; no one of them has preference. However, in reality, one plant needs more nitrogen, and another more phosphorous or lime. And, the physical subject-function of an individual thing follows the direction of its biotic subject-function so that if the biotic subject-function needs nitrogen for growth and nourishment, it directs the physical-function, *in an individual manner,* to this specific end. The biotic function leads the unfolding process, as it causes the moments, which anticipate the biotic aspect in earlier functions, to work in a certain manner and direction. This internal unfolding process takes place within every individual thing in the cosmos. Through it the modal functions of a thing acquire a mutual inner *structural coherence,* because of which *every* individual thing displays a necessary *inner unity.* We have seen that a tree expresses itself objectively in the post-biotic modalities. Its structural, non-arbitrary unity maintains itself also in these object-functions and prevents man (or animals, and these only in the psychical modality) from treating those object-functions of the tree in an arbitrary manner. In other words, man is limited by a tree's internal structure.

The qualifying biotic subject-function which is the leading function of a tree is also its *destination-function.* In the internal structure of a tree all pre-biotic functions seek to further the tree's life in an individual way. The furtherance of the life of the tree is, therefore, the end or goal of the pre-biotic functions. And this end is not to be confused with the fact that a tree serves an external purpose, such as providing shade. An external purpose does not portray the uniqueness of what we call a tree. The end-function in question is a veritable structural factor in the internal construction of trees. The end-function of a thing distinguishes it from all other things with a different end-function.

We have frequently stated the thesis that a thing is more than the sum of its modal functions, and that the unity of a thing is not to be found in the plurality of functions. If it is correct to speak of an individual unity in the diversity of modal functions, then the unity of a thing cannot itself be of a *modal* character. It must lie deeper in another dimension of the horizon of temporal reality. From our theory of knowledge, we know that behind the modal apriori there lies a transcendental apriori of cosmic time. Cosmic time guarantees the intermodal coherence between the functions of temporal reality. The structural principle of a thing is grounded in cosmic time as a typical principle of totality. *The unity of a thing is not modal in character, but it is to be found in the continuity of cosmic time.*

The identity or unity of an individual thing is rooted in the depths of cosmic time. A tree, pruned of a third of its branches, is still the same tree. And a tree retains its identity after being transplanted. A year old sapling does not lose its identity by waxing into a mighty oak. And this identity is not functionally determined. Modal relationships can undergo all possible changes without affecting identity. Identity is rooted in the continuous temporal depths of reality. The deepest dimension in which perishable things are rooted is the transcendental temporal horizon. Perishable things do not have the religious depth possessed by man. God has placed the human heart in contact with eternity.

Theoretical thought cannot further penetrate the structure of temporal things. This limitation of science discloses the fact that it is not self-sufficient. Science must appeal to naive experience in order to grasp the unity of a thing which is in and behind modal diversity. Naive experience is the foundation of science and science cannot and may not disregard it with impunity. Even philosophy can never replace naive experience.

Since the identity of a thing is rooted in the transcendental depth of cosmic time, the unity of a tree is not exclusively biotic in character. This unity expresses itself in a very special and characteristic way in the biotic modality, because this aspect is its qualifying-, leading-, and end-function. Nevertheless, the inner unity of a thing is not enclosed in a specific modal aspect, but it binds together all the temporal functions of a thing into an individual structural whole. All philosophy which utilizes the notion of substance commits the error of seeking the "essence" of living nature in the *biotic function,* conceived of as being self-sufficient. The attempt to reduce all other functions of a plant to the biotic function results in vitalism. And if substance is sought in the psychical aspect, a *psychologistic* view of reality results which does not recognize the supermodal unity of a thing. Instead it encloses a part of creation in one aspect, so that it no longer starts from the truth, that all things are of God and through Him and unto Him.

30

Structure-Types

We have employed a tree as an example of a specific structure constituting a thing. A tree is a biotic qualified thing of nature. We could just as well have chosen a stone, or an animal, which respectively are physically and psychically qualified.

There are *structural-types* or different *kingdoms* of things in cosmic reality. Each kingdom is composed of individual things of a peculiar type. Things belonging to the same kingdom possess a common type of structure which differs radically from the type of structure of things belonging to a different kingdom. It is difficult to distinguish between animals and plants in the micro-animal world; nevertheless, an animal is essentially different from a plant. In spite of variation, all animals possess a structure of the same type. They are all qualified by the psychical function.

We employ the term *"radical-types"* (types which differ in their *roots*) to designate foundational structural types of an elementary nature. A radical-type cannot be reduced further. A radical-type is a type of structure of individuality under which are joined all individual things which have their destination-function in the same modal aspect. And the totality of things whose destination-function lies in another modal aspect, belongs to another radical-type and thus forms a different *kingdom*. A radical-type indicates the modal aspect which contains the destination-function of all the things which belong to this type. Next to the radical-type which includes within itself physical things, there is a radical-type *plant*; and next to this a radical-type *animal*. All things which belong to the same radical-type constitute a *kingdom*. We can speak of a *kingdom* of natural physical things; a kingdom of plants and a kingdom of animals. These three radical-types do not include all existing radical-types but for the present we shall restrict ourselves to them. A *kingdom* corresponds to a radical-type. It is the greatest sphere of unity which exists within cosmic reality. Of course, we can unite the kingdom of plants and animals and speak of a "kingdom of living beings," but in the strict sense, this is not a kingdom, but a general logical concept which does not correspond to reality. The so-called "kingdom of living beings" is an arbitrary functional bipartite of created-things. All created things qualified by a pre-biotic subject-function are placed then on the one side, and the remaining creatures are placed on the other. This division is purely arbitrary. We could just as well draw a dividing line at the psychical function. We would then have a kingdom of emotive beings on the one hand, and a kingdom of emotionless beings on the other. If such a course is taken the word "kingdom" is without meaning. If its meaning is to be retained, we must employ it solely to mean the totality of individuals which display the same radical type.

These three kingdoms together with those not yet mentioned are woven together in cosmic reality. This fact is very important and meaningful, but it does not do away with the radical and typical structure of the things which are interwoven. A stone covered with moss belongs to the kingdom of physically qualified things of nature, and the moss belongs to the plant-kingdom. From the fact that both are woven together, we can see that the biotic *object*-function of the stone is correlative to the biotic *subject*-function of the growing moss.

Within the same basic structure of a radical type, we can distinguish *group-types*. Under a *group-type* we understand a narrower principle of structure within a specific kingdom. Things belonging to the same group-type possess structural peculiarities that are foreign to other groups within the same kingdom. This distinction is not arbitrary but is required by the plastic horizon of reality. It is not the product of our desire for logical classification. It gives an account of actual structural relations which God has placed in the cosmos. Within the radical-type, animal, there are group-types, such as, mammal, bird, fish, and so on. The typical peculiarities of such group-types do not depend on *external* factors, but are guaranteed by their internal structure. A mammal never becomes a bird, nor a bird a fish through change in external conditions. The group-types display an inner constancy which depends upon the order of creation. On the other hand, within every kingdom, there are certain spheres of variation in which a type of structure undergoes change through external factors. In this sense we speak of *variability-types*. There are, for example, plants and animals, which in another milieu, develop external *phaeno-typical* characteristics.

Within the various kingdoms the group-types differentiate themselves into sub-types until we finally arrive at *individual subjectivity* or the individual thing that is subject to the lawful structure of the radical-type. Within the radical-type animal, we can distinguish the group-type, bird; within this group-type, we can distinguish the sub-type, bird of prey, within which we can distinguish a further sub-type, eagle, until we finally arrive at a specific eagle perched on a mountain.

Up until now we discussed the kingdom of natural physical things and the plant and animal kingdoms. These structures of reality are of the *first-order* as their radical typical destination-functions are subject-functions. There are also kingdoms of things whose radical-type is determined by an object-function. These are *second-order* structures of reality, as they presuppose primary structures of individuality. For example, we cannot understand the meaning of a bird's nest, if we seek its destination-function in the biotic modality; it would then be only an arbitrary conglomeration of dead twigs and branches. To understand the meaning or purpose of a bird's nest, we must seek its qualifying destination-function in the same modal aspect in which the bird has its destination-function, namely, in the psychical aspect. In this aspect, the nest lies on the objective side. The bird's nest is qualified by a psychical object-function. Together with all other objects formed by *animal* activity, a bird's nest belongs to the kingdom of *objective things of nature.*

Similarly the destination-function of things formed by *human* activity, paper, tables, sculpture and countless things more does not lie in the physical modal aspect, which is the last sphere in which these objects have a subject-function. At the very least, the destination-function of these objects lies in the historical aspect. They are the result of *free human forming.* The destination-function of these objects must be *objective* in character if their meaning is to be understood. The destination-function of semi-manufactured paper, which is intended to serve as newspaper, lies in the historical sphere. Such paper belongs to the kingdom of *objective-historical* things under which is subsumed all semi-manufactured things. A table and a chair, in contrast, have an *objective social* destination-function; they are objects which serve human intercourse. They belong to the kingdom of useful objects. In the case of art objects, it is again different, their radical type is objective-aesthetically determined.

And although we shall postpone our discussion of them, we should notice that there are also radical-types of societal relationships (e.g., state, church, family and so on). These radical-types differ one from each other, because the destination-function of these relationships is in each instance radically different.[1]

31

Structural Analysis of an Object of Art

We have already tried to give a structural analysis of a natural thing, (of a tree) whose end-function is biotic. And to illustrate the fact that natural things exist as objects in cosmic reality, we chose a bird's nest which is qualified as a psychical object. Our discussion would not be complete, however, if we did not examine things which are qualified by a *normative object-function*. We must examine the structure of a thing which has an object-function in a normative modality and is thus normatively qualified. As an example of such a structure we have chosen a *work of art*, which we shall now submit to philosophical analysis.

There is a kingdom of works of art which is radically and typically qualified by the aesthetic destination-function. This kingdom is further sub-divided into such group-types, as architecture, music, literature, and sculpture. Each of these *group-types* of art are divided in turn into *variability-types*. In sculpture, there are the variability-types of marble-plastic, copper-plastic, and so forth. Let us analyze a concrete work of sculpture which portrays a human form and which belongs to the *variability type*: *marble plastic*.

The last subject-function of this marble statue is undoubtedly physical. As a work of art, however, the thing is not qualified physically but is qualified as an aesthetic object. Moreover, this individual thing has an object-function in all post-physical modalities.

We must notice the *relation of representing*, which plays

---
[1] Human societal forms are also *second-order* structures because they presuppose the primary unity of the human race.

an essential role in this work of art. The artist's *aesthetic vision* of the living human body found an objective expression in this statue. It would be obvious to contend, that this marble statue is only a copy of the living model. Such a notion would be wrong, because it eliminates the *aesthetic forming-activity* of the artist, which is an essential factor in the production of any work of art. This factor may not be neglected, for sculpture is not to be equated with photography. The human body possesses an aesthetic function and can therefore serve as a model for the artist. But a statue cannot be a mere copy of a living model, because the human body is not aesthetically *qualified*. The human body does not find its *end*, its destination in the aesthetic aspect and is, therefore as such, not a work of art.

The aesthetic fantasy of the artist occupies an intermediary position between the living model and the marble statue. The artist produces his *aesthetic conception* or fantasy-image through his aesthetic fantasy. The representing relation has two poles, the aesthetic conception and the marble statue. The sensory side of the statue is related to the sensory form in the fantasy of the artist. If a person wishes to appreciate a work of art as art, he must have an eye for the fantasy-picture of the artist. It is this fantasy that is objectively realized in the statue. In other words, the art-observer must possess a *reproductive* fantasy. One of the gifts of human nature is the ability to live into a work of art aesthetically. This gift must be developed and cultivated in order to judge a work of art seriously. When this talent is rudimentary, superficial judgment results. The observer, then, considers a work of art to be a copy of a living model and judges it according to the degree in which it resembles the model.

The fantasy-image of the artist possesses an aesthetic objectivity. It is the product of his subjective aesthetic fantasy. This productive aesthetic fantasy is based upon a *feeling* of fantasy. And in this *fantasy-feeling*, with which we view the model in sensory perception, we are productively *objectifying*. The fantasy-feeling accompanies our perception of the model and we objectively produce in this feeling. We project namely the fantasy-picture which is the *objective* sensory side of the product of our imagination, so that it acquires an objective *aesthetic* form in the conception of the artist. The *objectivity* of the aesthetical fantasy-picture of the artist is still only an *intentional would-be objectivity*. The aesthetic fantasy-picture is not yet embodied in a concrete thing; it has only a *would-be* relation to the object-side of temporal reality. It has the intention to become expressed in a concrete thing. The aesthetic fantasy-picture or *phantasm* is the would-be object which the artist portrays in marble as a plastic work of art. And this phantasm is *objectified* in the statue rather than the aesthetic subjectivity of the artist. For it is impossible for a specific subject to become an object in the same modality in which it is a subject. The objective work of art, the statue, is a representation of the intentional aesthetic object which is in the fantasy of the artist.

The leading structural-function of the statue is thus objective-aesthetical in character. Now the leading destination-function of natural things displays an *original individuality*. The individuality of an animal, which is psychically qualified, possesses a psychical originality. The individuality of an animal does not issue from the pre-psychical aspects. This is not the case with a thing which is qualified by a normative *object-function*. In this instance the leading destination-function does not have an original individuality. The individuality of a work of art does not bear an *original* character in its aesthetic aspect, for it points back to the original individuality of an earlier function, which we shall call the *foundational-function*. To approach the structure of a thing characterized by a normative object-function, we must therefore start with unbreakable coherence between the *leading* and *foundational* functions.

In the case of a marble statue, What is the foundational function in which the individuality of this work of art is grounded? Its individuality cannot be grounded in the physical function, in which marble is qualified as a product of nature. There is nothing inherent in marble that implies that it will be made into a statue. Marble can serve many other purposes. The statue is the product of an aesthetically qualified phantasm which, in its intentional objectivity, rests upon the psychical feeling of fantasy. It would appear that the foundational function lies in the objective-psychical function of the marble-statue. But this is not the case. Such a position would deny the depicting activity of the artist by which he gives concrete form to the phantasm which he intends to render objective. The individuality of a work of art is founded in the free *formational work* of the artist. This is the origin of the individuality of the statue. The foundational-function of a work of art is *historically qualified*. The objective-aesthetical destination-function is indissolubly connected with the objective-historical foundational function. Together they form the structure of individuality of the marble statue. The style-moment of all art rests on an historical foundation. Style is an aesthetical analogy of the historical function.

The radical-type of the entire kingdom of art-works is historically grounded. No art is possible without the productive free formational-work of the artist, who must technically master and dominate his material.

Now a dualism may not exist between the structure of individuality of the material and the objective expression of the aesthetic conception. The unruliness of the material must be completely dominated by the artist. But the technical formational function may not overshadow the aesthetic structural function, in which marble is qualified as a product of art. Where this is the case, the work of art makes us admire the technical ability of its author, but we do not admire its aesthetical harmony, which ought to be its proper end.

32
Structural Analysis of Usable Objects

We have seen that the structure of an object of art is qualified as an aesthetic object. In this section, we shall seek to discover the structure of individuality of the kingdom of usable objects. This kingdom is made up of a great variety of group-types, such as tables, chairs, clocks, dishes, clothes, houses, streets, automobiles, etc. All such objects owe their existence to *human forming*. They are not things of nature but things of culture. They also have in common the fact that they are made out of a certain material, e.g., wood, iron, and rubber. We must guard against thinking that the structure of individuality of these objects is determined by the structure of individuality of the material out of which they are made. If such were the case, a hopeless confusion would result and philosophy would conflict with naive experience. In naive experience we know directly that the meaning or purpose of a house is entirely different from the meaning of a building stone. We also know that the destination of a church is different from that of a private dwelling. This difference would be denied if philosophy identified the structure of individuality of the material with that of the objects constructed out of it.

In dealing with the relationship between the material and the usable objects we are dealing with two separate structures. The structure of the material is interwoven with the structure of the usable object. Dooyeweerd calls this an *enkaptic* relationship, so that a state of intertwinement exists between the two structures. A similar *enkaptic* interlacement exists in the relation of the work of art to the material out of which it is made. The material of such an object is variable; a table need not be made out of wood, nor a house of stone. In this *enkaptic* union of two structures, the structure of individuality of the usable object is grounded in the structure of individuality of the material.

In their structure of individuality, natural materials such as iron, wood, and marble are not all qualified by the same modal aspect. Iron ore and marble, for example, are physically qualified by their last subject-function. Wood, however, is qualified by the biotic aspect, since it is derived from a living organism. Even though dead wood is separated from the total structure of the living tree, it remains an organic product that is constructed of cells.

Ordinarily, natural material is not made directly into usable or other objects. It is generally formed into semi-manufactured articles, such as planks, iron plates, and hewn stones. And these semi-manufactured articles have a different structure of individuality than the natural material out of which they are constructed. Their structure is typified by technical forming. The objective foundational function of a semi-manufactured article is, therefore, found in the historical modality. Again we are dealing with two separate things or structures which are woven together, so that the structure of the material is *enkaptically* bound to the structure of the semi-manufactured articles. The *internal* foundation within the structure of individuality of the semi-manufactured article lies in its objective-historical function, but the entire structure of the semi-manufactured material is *externally* founded in the structure of the material that is *enkaptically* interwoven with the technical semi-product.

A peculiarity of this semi-manufactured article is that it does not have an actual destination-function. Everything can be made out of it. Out of a piece of cedar we can make a crucifix, a pencil, or a work of art. The destination of a semi-product lies in its further formation, and is thus historical and technical in nature. The destination-function is potential; it changes into the actual destination-function of the object made out of the semi-product.

There are at least two structures of individuality *enkaptically* joined in usable objects, namely, the structure of the natural material and that of the semi-manufactured article.

What is the internal structure of such a usable-object? The qualifying function of the natural material out of which the object is made is the last subject-function of the thing. The following internal functions of a usable object are, therefore, of an objective character. A chair has an objective-biotic function, as it is an object used in human life. And it also has a psychical object-function, because a tired person who sits on it has the psychical experience of rest and relaxation. An animal can also have this psychical feeling of rest, but in contrast to man, an animal cannot sustain any relation to the analytical object-function of a chair. An animal cannot form a concept of a chair as a *piece of furniture.* An animal does not have an analytical experience. Man, in contrast, experiences a chair in its individual structure as a totality and distinguishes it from other objects.

The historical object-function of a chair is the *foundational function* of its internal structure. The structure of all usable-objects is based upon human forming. And, as we have seen, human forming is characterized by *historical domination.* All objects, including usable objects, which are grounded in the historical aspect, are designated by the general term, *"cultural-objects."* The end-function of a chair does not lie in its psychical aspect. The need of rest does not have to be satisfied by a chair. We can also sit on the ground. The destination-function of a chair is in every case to be found in a post-historical aspect and this can only be the *social.* The group-type, furniture, is subject to the social norms of intercourse; furniture cannot be omitted from human society. It helps to create a sphere within a house and depends upon style which is a positive norm of social intercourse.

Not only the group-type furniture, but also the broader radical-type, *usable objects* has an objective-social destination-function (e.g., a house serves a social function as a dwelling place; clothes are originated from the sense of shame of the sinner about his nakedness in relation to other people). The fact that the internal destination-function of usable objects lies in the social aspect does not mean that the individuality-structure of these objects is not expressed in the post-social spheres. It is obvious that these objects have an economic and an aesthetic object-function, since they are subject to the norms of value and price and can in some instances be elegant.

Historically considered hand-work gave rise to the development of so-called *"bound"* art. Bound art is art connected with objects which have another destination than the aesthetical. Pure art in contrast is qualified by the aesthetic object-function. This pure art has loosed itself in later times from the bound art. If a usable object is aesthetically unenjoyable, this does not infringe upon the structure of individuality of this thing as a usable object. It can still fulfill its end. In addition, these objects can have an ethical and a pistical object-function. We can be attached to them for certain reasons (e.g., a ring or heirloom). And we can accept them out of the hand of the Lord as a sign of God's favor and goodness.

CHAPTER V

THE THEORY OF THE STRUCTURE OF HUMAN SOCIETY

33

THE CENTRAL QUESTION

OUR previous discussion of the structures of individuality of temporal things disclosed the fact that the construction of individual things is dominated by structural principles which are rooted in the divine world order. In this chapter we shall see that what has previously been said of structures of individuality of temporal things is also applicable to the structure of the temporal relationships of human society.

How are these relationships to be understood? Our naive experience makes us aware of the rich number of ways in which we are associated with our fellow man. A single person may be a member of a family, a citizen, a factory worker, a union member, a church member and a member of various clubs. This same person is also a friend, a neighbor, a customer, and a salesman. The task of philosophy is to reflect upon the extremely complicated data of social life. We experience such relationships as the family and the state as structural unities which possess their own typical nature and character. A philosophic view of human society must clarify the peculiar character of these structural unities. Philosophy may not eliminate existing differences in order to preserve a preconceived generalizing theory. It may never mutilate or discard the data of naive experience, darkening in this way the many-colored wisdom of God, that shows in all His works.

In the third volume of *A New Critique of Theoretical Thought*, Dooyeweerd, in discussing the structure of human society, distinguishes between *authoritative societal rela-*

tionships and *free societal relations*. The former possess an internal communal character and an inner solitary unity that is to a certain degree independent of the coming and leaving of its members and is marked by authority, (e.g., the immediate family, church, state.) Free societal relations, in contrast, are of an *external* nature and are much freer. In free societal relations persons are coordinated next to each other without the relation of authority, as for example, in the case of a buyer and a seller, or in my relationship to an acquaintance whom I casually meet on the street. Authoritative relationships and free relations are inseparably interwoven in various ways. Not only is a member of one family (an authoritative relationship) related to a member of another family, but the relation between two authoritative relationships, such as the church and the state, is external in character.

It is impossible to divide all of human society into authoritative relationships and free relations. The marriage relationship and the family-relationship (broadly conceived of) do not fall into either of these classes. Both the marriage and the family (considered broadly) bear a communal character and display thus an internal unity. And in marriage authority even plays a role. Nevertheless, they are not *internal* authoritative societal relationships. In marriage the communal band is so closely connected with the individuality of two married people that as soon as one of the parties leaves, this temporal community disappears entirely. The unity of marriage is not to a certain degree independent of the change of its individual members.

The family-relationship (broadly considered in contrast to the immediate family which bears the structure of an internal authoritative relationship) lacks any element of authority. Therefore, we shall, henceforth employ the term *community* to designate the relationship of the family (broadly considered) and of marriage.

Communities, and authoritative relationships and free societal relations are of a secondary order based upon a reality of a primary order, upon the unity of the human race. This primary unity of mankind is not only biotically based upon the blood-relationship of all people, but is besides religiously anchored in the communion of covenant, which God gave to His mankind in Adam and restored to us by grace in Jesus Christ.

Now any theory dealing with the authoritative relationships of human society is confronted by this central question. *What is it that guarantees the authoritative relationships of human society their internal unity, or their own peculiar structural nature, and what is it that insures the identity of such a relationship in spite of change in its individual members?* Philosophy must seek to discover the structural principles, which are different in each sort of relationship, and it must seek to explain the richness of the relationships of society. A societal relationship is not a conglomeration of different people. And within certain limits the change of its individual members does not destroy its identity and unity. Children who marry and leave home do not abolish the authoritative relationship of the immediate family, even though they decrease its number. And the United States of 1966 is the same as that of 1820 even though its citizens are different. Several people who agree to live together do not constitute a family. There must be principles, therefore, which are based upon the Divine world-order and which express themselves within an authoritative societal relationship and determine its structure.

Philosophy has perennially sought to answer what we have called the central problem of societal relationships. In the main it has offered two solutions which we shall call *universalism* and *individualism*.

The theory of universalism recognizes the unity and the reality of authoritative societal relationships, but elevates one relationship above the others and considers it to be an all-embracing totality which includes the lower relationships as dependent parts. The lower relationships are related to the higher as means to an end. The relationship precedes the individual. The individual person is not self-sufficient. His *being-human* unfolds itself solely in the relationships in which he appears. The highest relationship possesses autonomy, is self-sufficient, and is the goal of all life and historical development.

Plato and Aristotle taught the existence of such a universalistic societal relationship. Human society, according to them, has a universalistic foundation, which for Plato was found in the *idea* of the state. Aristotle sought the universalistic foundation of society in the *substantial essential form of man*. This substantial essential form of man is for him the human "rational soul" which made man a social being. And since the synthesis-philosophy of the Middle Ages sought to unite Aristotelian philosophy with the basic tenets of Christianity, this notion of Aristotle was preserved in a modified form. If we examine the schema, nature and grace, we find that nature and grace are two spheres related to each other as the higher is to the lower. The goal of the state is to supply man with temporal goods. The state is the highest relationship in the sphere of nature. But the holy influence of the church overshadows the state, as the church is the highest community in the sphere of grace. The church, as an institute of grace, is a perfect community, and since temporal goods are the foundation of the seeking of eternal blessedness, the state serves the highest goal, namely, the church.

Hegel expounded a universalistic theory in modern philosophy. He considered the state to be as an *Ueberperson,* the highest revelation "of objective Spirit." His idealistic universalism was rooted in the trans-personalistic trend of the humanistic ideal of personality. This trend does not hypostasize the post-analytic functions in the individual but in a super-personal being or *Gesammtperson*. Universalism is the philosophical background of national-socialism and fascistic theories which make the folk and the state the deified goal or end of all human intercourse. The same tendencies lurk in socialism and communism. Especially in communism is in force the tenet: the individual is nothing, the state is all.

In contradistinction to all universalistic conceptions, in-

THE THEORY OF THE STRUCTURE OF HUMAN SOCIETY 193

dividualism denies the existence of any real unity and universalistic root of societal relationships. It maintains that the *individual is self-sufficient* and precedes any societal relationship. A societal relationship is a *collection* of self-sufficient, independent, individuals, who together conclude a compact in order to attain a certain goal. The tie uniting individuals in society is *external*. Individualism conceives of society as a function (e.g., as a psychical or a juridical phenomenon). In the former, societal relationships are thought of as complexes of psychical interaction between individuals, and in the latter as juridical contracts which are freely made by equal parties. Because of their functionalism, individualistic theories overlook the plastic horizon of reality, and consequently deny the structure of individuality of authoritative societal relationships. In antiquity we encounter such theories in Epicurus and in late Stoicism. Epicurus taught that a community of men did not exist in a state of nature but arose by a voluntary gathering of individuals. The later Stoics viewed the unity of a societal relationship as an external-juridical tie. The Stoical theory of natural law did not base the state upon the essential nature of man but upon convention. The goal of the state consisted in restraining the dissoluteness of man.

Similar views are expressed in the humanistic theory of natural law (e.g., Hugo de Groot and Thomas Hobbes) which holds that societal relationships arise through a social contract and thus equates law with the general will of individuals. A societal relationship is a *societas*. And the difference between societal relationships is solely external. It lies in their objective or aim and not in any *essential* structure. Modern existence-philosophy (Heidegger, Jaspers and Sartre) is totally individualistic. An authentic man lives in perfect freedom and does not let his existence be determined by ties of societal relationships. Otherwise he is apostate from the authentic existence.

Neither individualism nor universalism recognizes the inner structure of societal relationships. However, universalism is less incorrect than individualism as it accepts the reality of societal relationships. But even universalism misconstrues the internal structural differences of societal relationships, as it thinks that it can comprehend human society in a schema which would relate the whole to its parts and deify the highest relationship as the total-relationship.

Individualism denies the reality of societal relationships and considers them to be the name of an arbitrary union between sovereign individuals. Individualism deifies one of the human subject-functions. The dilemma universalism — individualism lies within the cadre of immanence-philosophy and is foreign to Christian philosophy. We cannot make here a choice. Both views we have to reject.

A Christian view of societal relationships is based upon the religious root of the human race. And this truth is a revealed truth. The unity of the human race was originally anchored in Adam, the head of the first covenant, and in view of the fall of man it was renewed by the free grace of God in the Redeemer and Mediator Jesus Christ. In Him and through Him humanity is held together as the *body of Christ*. Contrary to the Roman Catholic view, the body of Christ is not to be identified with the temporal institution of the church which, as the highest relationship, absorbs all lower relationships as means to further its end. The body of Christ is the "Una Sancta," the *transcendent religious* root of all temporal relationships. Temporal society is brought to fruition in the body of Christ, from which it derives its meaning. The body of Christ, in other words, reveals itself in the structure of all those societal relationships, which in principle are renewed by Christ and directed toward Him. The institution of the church is not the only temporal revelation of the body of Christ, but a Christian family, state, and industry are also such a revelation. The revealed truth of the religious fulness of society in the body of Christ frees us from the prejudices of immanence-philosophy. It frees also society itself from the tyranny of a temporal relationship (e.g., the church, the state which ascribes divine power to itself) and from the sovereign individual who clothes himself with Divine glory. Only the truth can make us free. Only this truth is sufficient to disclose to us the internal structure of temporal relationships. And this disclosure serves to advance a pure form of *communio sanctorum* (communion of the saints) in all forms of social life in this era, which will pass one day in the full revealing of the sons of God.

34

THE STRUCTURAL PRINCIPLE OF AUTHORITATIVE SOCIETAL RELATIONSHIPS

NEITHER universalism nor individualism can truly explain the *internal structure* of societal relationships as both misconstrue or eradicate their peculiar nature and character. Reformed Christians have strongly opposed those who would violate the peculiar character of the different relationships. They opposed the domination of the church over the state, organized their own Christian schools, and opposed the interference of the state in family matters. Reformed Christians have opposed the domination of science by the state or church and have opposed Marxism and socialism. We are indebted to Abraham Kuyper[1] for the development of the principle of sphere-sovereignty which opened our eyes to the fact that each societal relationship is endowed with its own vital laws. These laws are not arbitrary; they can be discovered by examining the various societal relationships in the light of God's Word. It is a fact of naive experience that different societal relationships display different structural types. This fact is a datum of pre-theoretical experience and it cannot be disregarded with impunity by scientific analysis. A person who is not a philosopher and who simply follows the precepts of the Bible is immediately aware of the fact that the proper

[1] Abraham Kuyper was a Dutch thinker and Statesman. He warned against the danger of accepting any theory which is not grounded upon the Word of God. He had a great influence upon the Christian life of the Dutch people in all sections of existence. He died in 1920. He was also the founder of the Free University of Amsterdam, The Netherlands.

nature of the family is not determined by the state or the church. He knows directly that a statement defining the family as a societal relationship designed to raise good citizens or church members does not do justice to its structural principle. In other words the structural-types of the several societal relationships must be sought within the relationship itself. Individualism and universalism disregard the difference between the structures of individuality of societal relationships. Philosophy must guard against this error. Each societal type (e.g., family, industry, church) has its own structural principle which cannot be functionally grasped as it is *super-modal*.

It is illegitimate, for example, for a person to consider the state as a *purely juridical* phenomenon enclosed within the juridical modal aspect. Then the structure-principle of the state is not well understood. Some one else could with equal validity consider it to be an historical or economic phenomenon. Nor is the truth of the matter to be found in a middle course; it is not a question of being one-sided. The structural principle of the state lies beyond the modal aspects. It is super-modal and stretches over all the modal-aspects within cosmic time. The structural principle of a societal relationship lies on another niveau than the modal horizon: it is anchored in the plastic horizon. Every structural principle bears a *lawful* character to which the subjective individuality of societal relationships is correlative as subject. This individuality is rooted in the transcendent horizon of cosmic time, which is the deepest level possible, since all societal relationships are temporal. The body of Christ is religious, endures all centuries and remains eternally, though the forms in which it expresses itself are temporal. In the root of his existence man cannot be absorbed into temporal relationships. Individualism rightly defended this principle against universalism. The structural principle of societal relationships can be theoretically approached by gaining insight into its *destination* and *foundational* functions. The former is determined by the radical-type of the relationship and directs all its functions in an individual manner, so that they acquire an internal structural coherence. The *foundational function* is the function in which the individuality of a relationship has its foundation.

From the Christian point of view it is incorrect to consider societal relationships as enlarged human persons; think of the term: legal personality. The personality of man, full human existence, has a transcendent religious root in which it transcends temporal reality. Human societal relationships are subject to the cosmic temporal order and cease with the termination of earthly life in this era. And at the end of the ages, when consummation has come, there is no more life of family, industry, state or church, like it is now at present. Human personality does not form a *component* of societal relationships, as man is not resolved in them. Man transcends temporal society in the root of his selfhood. Moreover, a Christian is a member of the body of Christ through faith and, as such, possesses personal religious freedom. This ought not to be taken away from him by any temporal societal relationship.

In contrast to things whose structure we have already analyzed, societal relationships have characteristics in common. They all have a *subjective structure*, a *subject-function* in all modal aspects. This should be directly evident, since societal relationships are groups of *men*, structures of man's own temporal existence. Man, created in the image of God, transcends all temporal relationships in his transcendent religious root. But in his temporal functions he lives together with others in society, from which he cannot and may not withdraw himself. Man is *subject* in all modal aspects and as such he cannot be *objectivized* or made an object. Consequently, since all societal relationships are constituted by man, they function as subject in all modalities. This does not mean to say that a subject-object-relation does not exist within a societal relationship. A societal relationship, as subject, can sustain a relation to a thing as an object. A family that occupies a house is, for example, a *subject*, and as such it sustains a relation to the house as an object. This relation is *qualified* in the social modality since the house is qualified by its social object-function.

A *societal relationship* does not have any *internal* object-functions in view of the fact that all of its internal functions are of a *subjective* nature. In its individual totality as subject, a societal relationship can only appear in all sorts of *external* subject-object-relations, such as the relation of a family to the house in which it dwells. But as an individual totality a societal relationship can possess all sorts of *external* object-functions. If I observe a family, in a psychical subject-object-relation, in its all-sided totality, then my observation of it constitutes this family as a psychical *object*.

An authoritative societal relationship is subject in all modalities including the normative spheres. Consequently, a societal relationship has a *normative task, the task of continually realizing itself through its own members*. The family, through mutual love, ought to maintain the bonds of love between its members. Authority and harmony ought to be preserved, social intercourse sought, and communion in thought and speech upheld. If this normative task is neglected, the family disintegrates, is divided and broken up. By violating the ordinances of God, life is directed away from Him and the end of it is a tearing up of community, discord and dissolution. This form of sin has two dimensions which need not accompany each other.

Primarily the heart may be religiously turned away from God toward an idol; or secondarily the typical norms of the societal relationships may be modally violated. But our life only prospers when God's laws are obeyed. Thus societal relationships are *dynamic structures* which have to serve the Kingdom of God or otherwise serve the kingdom of darkness.

Another common characteristic of societal relationships is that they not only have a leading-destination function which discloses their radical-type, but they also have a foundational function in which the individuality of the relationship is grounded. The destination-function of a relationship, however, does not have an *original type* of individuality. An international conference of Christians, for example, does not constitute a church, because it lacks the foundational function upon which the individuality of a church is based. Or, if various people who love each other decide to live together in one house, they do not constitute a family because they lack its foundational-function.

An investigation of the internal structure of a specific societal relationship must first disclose its destination- and foundational function. This disclosure must be followed by a demonstration of the individual manner, whereby the internal structure of a relationship expresses itself in the remaining modalities. This internal structure expresses itself in an unbreakable correlation of its destination- and foundational functions.

The main distinction between societal-relationships is that the foundational function of some lies in one of the natural aspects of reality, while that of the others is grounded in the historical modality.

35

Structural-Analysis of the Immediate Family-Relationship

Before we begin our analysis of the immediate family-relationship it is appropriate that we define our use of the word "temporal." We do not mean to imply that, because societal relationships are temporal, they are historical phenomena relative to each age. We are not suggesting that societal relationships lack a constant structure. If they did, a medieval state would be unrelated to a modern one. Such a theory is not Christian. It denies the normative structural principles which are rooted in the divine order of creation. Our reference to societal relationships as temporal means that such relationships, at least when subject to the Kingship of Christ, reveal the religious and everlasting body of Christ, in which earthly society finds its Transcendent Root and Fulness. By temporal we mean to imply that these relationships will not exist in the future world of glory. Neither the family, the church, nor the state may be elevated out of the order of temporal things and identified with the body of Christ. They are not super-temporal or eternal. The error of universalism must be avoided, or we shall lose our heart in temporal things and separate ourselves from Jesus Christ.

The structural analysis of the family-relationship must first discover the normative structural principle of the family in its unbreakable correlation of destination- and foundational function. And this must be followed by an investigation which discloses the individual manner in which this structural principle expresses itself in all the internal functions of the family.

The family is frequently referred to as the "cell of society." If this expression is intended to convey the thought that the family is the cornerstone of temporal society, then our only objection is that it is ambiguous. The richness of human society cannot be grasped in a concept derived from the biotic modality. However, if this expression is conceived of as an explanation of the structure of the family and is meant to convey the idea that the family is the *germ* from which the whole of society springs forth, then we must take issue with the correctness of the expression. If it means that all other relationships develop out of the family, which is the primeval-relationship, then such a view of the family absolutizes it. And we cannot accept it because it denies the peculiar nature of the other relationships and deprives their structures of the normative principles which are anchored in the Divine world order. For normative structural principles are not the product of historical development. That would be subjectivation of the norm.

It is, however, perfectly transparent for us to maintain that the foundational function of the family lies in the biotic modality. The family is built upon consanguinity as the inner relationship between parents and children, grounded upon a blood relationship.

Though the individuality of the family is founded in the biotic sphere, the normative structure of the family cannot be explained in terms of consanguinity. Naturalism tries to deduce the normative modalities from their natural substratum. It opposes our contention that the norms of our temporal existence proceed from above, and not from below. A naturalistic view seeks to construct the family relationship out of mere biotic relations.

In addition to its foundational function we must consider the leading destination-function of the family relationship which lies in the *ethical* modality. The family is *qualified as an incomparable* community of love. God requires parents to love each other and their children. He also requires children to love their parents and each other. The inner temporal end of this relationship is the mutual love between the members of a family. The Bible represents this love as a reflection of the relation of God the Father to His children in Christ. *The family is, therefore, a constant individual community of love based upon the natural ties of blood between parents and children.*

The moral norm of love may not be denaturalized to an emotional affection or impulse. Love has an analogy in the psychical emotive life but it is ethically and not psychically qualified.

The *internal* destination of the family must be distinguished from its *external* end. The former lies exclusively in love, whereas the latter signifies, for example, that the family serves to raise citizens, preserve the church, and advance economic life, etc.

The structural principle of a family guarantees an unbreakable coherence between its destination and foundational function. Sin is active in human society and destroys all sorts of temporal community life. Nevertheless, it does not affect the structural principles of societal relationships. Even if the community of love were not realized in any concrete family, the norm of love would remain and the destination of the family would not be changed. God's common grace, however, enables men to realize this communion of love so that it is even present in pagan society, though such communion under common grace is on account of the apostasy of the human heart directed to the left, religiously bound to an idol.

The coherence between the destination and foundational function of the family-relationship characterizes also the structure of *authority* which typifies the immediate family. Authority is present in every real relationship (e.g., ecclesiastical authority, authority of the state, and of the owner of a factory). But in each relationship, this structure of authority is of a different nature, because its destination or foundational function, or both, are different. The bearers of authority in the family-relationship, which authority is grounded upon consanguinity, must exercise their authority with love, and those required to obey must also be motivated by love. The structure of authority expresses itself in all the functions of the family-relationship and dominates all the internal relations of the family. It is primarily expressed ethically in the relations of love between its members. Family love is of an essentially different structure of individuality than the love between friends. The love between parents and children is not the love of equals. Parents must command and children must obey. Moreover, the love that children bear for each other is affected by the love that they together bear for their parents. If one child no longer loves his parents, his relationship to his brothers and sisters will be impaired. The fifth commandment, which requires that children honor their father and their mother, corroborates the fact that the love that children bear their parents is marked by authority.

We have seen the way in which the normative structural principle of the family expresses itself in the ethical modality. It remains for us to discover the way in which the family-relationship expresses itself in the remaining modal aspects.

The structural-principle of the family is as well typically expressed in the *juridical* aspect of the family relationship. The family has its own peculiar internal juridical relations.

Within the family, parents have the right to exercise discipline, and children have the duty to subject themselves to it. Parents have the duty of supporting their children, and children have a right to this support. These *internal* juridical relations are *not derived from any authority outside of the family*. The origin of the *internal* right of the family does not lie in the state. The state is not the source of all law. It is erroneous to maintain that all the forms of law found in other relationships are derived from the state. Legal authority does not exist by the grace of the state. Such a totalitarian theory of the state destroys the structural principles of all other relationships. By disavowing the sovereignty of each sphere it violates the divine order of creation. And in practice its universalistic starting point leads to a tyrannical standardization which reduces many relationships to an all-inclusive state. No temporal power has the right to interfere with the internal authority and the duties of the members of a family. Any tendency to interfere must be immediately recognized and violently opposed by Christian parents.

Of course it is true that a family also has *external* juridical relations insofar as it is interwoven with other relationships such as the church or state. Naturally, these other relationships are competent to lay down positive rules for the external *juridical* functions of the family. The state may require that children procure the permission of their parents if they desire to marry below a certain age. And the church can require that parents who desire that their children be baptized promise to bring them up in the nurture and admonition of the Lord. But the *internal* juridical relations of a family possess a sovereignty within their own sphere. The internal law of the family is different from the law of the state, the church, or of industry. It is intrinsically connected and directed by the love which exists between parents and their children. Mere support is not enough; parents ought to be motivated by love, and they ought to be obeyed solely because they are loved.

In the *aesthetical* modality the family relationship also

has a typical function determined by its structural principle. There is harmony in a family if mutual love exists between parents and children. Harmony exists where parental authority is exercised in love and children respond by honoring their parents in an affectionate manner. The disruption of this relationship results in disharmony and causes family life to lose its charm.

The management of a family household has an internal typical *economic* function; the manner in which it is financed is essentially different from the financing of a business. A business is given up if it shows no prospect of yielding a profit. Profit is not the motivation of household management, nor do losses or debts dissolve the family. Housekeeping is motivated by a desire to supply the members of a family with their material needs. Love and harmony must guide parents so that they will exercise their authority by giving preference to necessities. And by focusing our attention upon the internal *social* relations between the members of a family household, we can see that the family also functions in the modality of social life. Social intercourse between its members is different from that occurring between equals and strangers. It is intimate and should be directed by love. And, since the distance which marks social intercourse in general is lacking in the family, its social intercourse should take place in a sphere of mutual trust. Trust and love, however, do not cancel the respect and honor that children owe their parents.

The family functions in a typically individual manner in the linguistical sphere too. Its language and manner of expression has a character which is inappropriate in other forms of society. And the language of the family may not clash with its character as a relationship of love, nor may it violate the normative authority of the family. Children may never be permitted to speak disrespectfully to their parents.

The internal culture formed within the family gives evidence of its *historical* function. A family has its own style and customs. What is permitted within the family circle may be intolerable outside of it. Of course everything is not permissible. Its customs and habits must be formed by love in such a way that none of its members feel oppressed and seek refuge outside of the family sphere. The structural principle of the family is also expressed in a typically individual manner in the *logical* or analytical modality. Within the family there is a typical community of thought which is pre-theoretical in character and is grounded in the internal emotive relation between its members. The manner of thinking of the individual family member is mutually interwoven in this community of thought. It is not necessary that all members of a family think alike; there can be a difference in development and opinion on various matters, but on fundamental issues there ought to be a basic agreement, so a free exchange of ideas can occur. If love rules, the thinking of a family is enriched and a far greater agreement on basic matters is attained than when love is lacking. Filial respect will serve to guarantee that the common bond of thought between family members is not broken by polar tensions. Antinomy does not have a place within the common internal life of the members of a family; the *concept of authority* should be central.

The family relationship also has a typical *psychical* function in the emotive relations between its members who are united to each other by a feeling of oneness. When everything is in order, the members of a family feel that they belong together because of their blood relationship and mutual love. If this feeling of oneness is active and is not destroyed by sin, it will express itself in reciprocal dependence which requires an interchange of personal feelings. And if this interchange is lacking, the feeling of oneness will suffer, and the unity of the family will be impaired. Authority is psychically expressed in the parental feeling of authority and in the filial feeling of respect. Authority distinguishes the family's feeling of oneness from the feeling which friends have of belonging together. Authority endows the family with its typical character.

The structure of the family also expresses itself in the biotic function, which is the foundational function of the family. Its basis lies in consanguinity and heredity. The family has its original individuality in vital organic communion. The latter is the basis for the communion of the family on all other levels and can only develop properly if led by love.

The structural principle of the family also expresses itself in an individual way in the *pre-biotic* functions. Also the *physical* aspect of a child's body proceeds from and is supported by its parents. The *kinematic* function of the family becomes apparent in the many alterations which daily occur in each family-member himself and between them mutually. By dwelling in the same house, a family displays a *spatial* unity. And the feeling of homesickness is a psychical analogy of the spatial modality.

Finally, the unity of the family as a diversity of individuals is an expression of the family structure in the *numerical* aspect. Human arbitrariness cannot remove the fact that a man and his wife constitute a unity from which a child is born, creating a richer unity composed of a multiplicity of constituents. The twofold unity of the marriage relationship is thus enriched in this manifold unity.

We have not yet discussed the way in which the family structure expresses itself in the *modality of faith*. The faith of a Christian family is expressed by the prophet, priest, and kingship of the father of the household. This father-office does not exclude that every Christian — also each member of a Christian family — is endowed by God with the threefold religious function of prophet, priest and king. If the family's tie of love is not directed by faith and does not point toward the eternal Father of our Lord Jesus Christ, then the family is in the bondage and service of the kingdom of this world and does not have any future. But if in the tie of faith, the family-bond points beyond itself toward Jesus Christ, who also renews the family, then it is a temporal expression of the religious fulness of the communion which believers have with God. But in contrast to the church, the family is not *qualified* as a household of faith and can never take the place of the institution of the church.

36
The Structure of Marriage

In the preceding section we have considered the relationship of the immediate family with its biotic foundational- and ethical destination-function. There are, however, several other structures which hang together with the immediate family relationship and are *enkaptically* interwoven with it, but which are at the same time different from its structure. The family — in-general — is a separate structural unity which unites the living kin on the side of the mother and of the father. As in the case of the immediate family, the family — in-general — is biotically grounded and has an ethical destination. Moreover, both, namely the immediate family and the family in-general, exist solely in *simultaneity*, in the contemporaneity of their members, and both can lose or gain members by death or birth without destroying their identity.

The difference between them is that in the family-in-general authority is lacking; it is a *community* rather than a relationship.

The structures of the family-relationship and of the family community are closely joined together. Under certain conditions members of the family-relationship can become members of the family-in-general. If parents die, their children no longer constitute a *family-relationship* even though they continue to live together. And children who marry or leave home for other reasons are then bound by the bond of the family community to their parents and brothers and sisters who remain at home. They are no longer in the immediate family-relationship.

We must also consider the structural unity between ancestors and posterity. Just as the immediate family is *enkaptically* interwoven with the family-in-general, the latter is interwoven with ancestors and descendants. The family, composed of past and future generations, is also biotically grounded but it differs from the immediate-family and the family-in-general in that its unity is not realized by contemporaneity but by the succession of its members.

Finally we must notice that in the marriage-*community*, the unity of man and wife is to be distinguished from the structure of the immediate-family. Dooyeweerd does not consider marriage to be a relationship but a community. Since authority is still present in marriage, it lacks the character of a relationship for an entirely different reason than the family-in-general. Marriage is not a relationship because relationships exist to a certain degree independently of the change of its members. Therefore relationships are always a manifold unity; whereas marriage is a twofold unity. If one of its members departs, a marriage no longer exists.

The *marriage-community* is *enkaptically* interwoven with the internal family relationship, so that a close coherence exists between them without their being identical. The family-relationship is inseparably joined with and onesidedly founded upon a specific marriage community, without which a family is not possible. A childless marriage is not yet a family. The family-relationship presupposes the mutual bond of love between parents and children. When two people marry the end in view is the formation of a family. This end is only accomplished by the birth of the first child. The family-relationship is an enrichment of the marriage-community and occurs when a twofold unity develops into a manifold unity.

The normative structure of marriage is a typical unity of love occurring between two people in *their full temporal existence* and thus expressed in all the modal aspects. With respect to its internal structural principle, the marriage community is more than a biotic (sexual) communion; it is also emotive, analytical, historical, linguistical, social, economic, aesthetic, juridical, ethical, and pistical. Marriage is ethically qualified as its destination is love. In the fifth chapter of Ephesians, for example, husbands are exhorted to love their wives "even as Christ loved the church and gave Himself for it." Husbands are also exhorted to love their wives "as their own bodies." And the apostle concludes, "let everyone of you in particular so love his wife even as himself; and let the wife see that she reverence her husband." The fact that the Apostle commands the husband to love his wife does not exclude the wife's obligation to love her husband. Paul is here seeking to remind wives of their obligation to recognize and respect the authority which husbands bear within the marriage-bond. In concrete situations women are tempted to forget this admonition.

Since the destination-function of marriage is ethical, its essential character is not legal. The state does not conclude a marriage, but a marriage is established by the promises of the bride and groom to love and remain faithful to each other. The state is concerned with marriage solely because marriage — in addition to its *internal* functions — also functions *externally* as a civil legal institution. Marriage is *enkaptically* interwoven with the state, and with the church if both parties or at least one party involved are church members. For this reason the church ought to perform the marriage ceremony. However, *this function is also external,* and only a civil ceremony is also a **marriage** (contrary to the Roman Catholic view).

It is not valid to argue that marriage is not a community of love because love as a subjective activity is transitory and can quickly vanish. Such an argument forgets that love is a permanent *norm* that ought to be subjectively realized, but which is not destroyed as a norm by an anti-normative attitude on the part of the parties of a marriage. This argument identifies love with an erotic feeling and, because of a basic psychologism, it loses sight of a normative view of life. Romanticism took this course in its depreciation of marriage as an institution and in its idolization of "free love."

Thomistic philosophy seeks the end of marriage in the reproduction and procreation of posterity. This view obscures the internal structure of marriage by confusing it with that of the immediate-family.

A childless marriage is a real marriage. The proper character of a specific relationship or community cannot be derived from its being interwoven with another relationship. The family-relationship does not determine what marriage is.

The structure of marriage implies a *structure of authority*. The authority in marriage is a Divine ordinance and is not to be derived from a civil external legal function. Even if the laws of the state no longer recognized authority in marriage, they could not abolish its normative structure, as the latter is anchored in God's Sovereign Will. God has ordained that the husband is to be the head of the wife and that the wife should permit herself to be led by her husband. This authority must be exercised in love; it is not tyranny and it ought to be accepted in love by the wife. The feelings of a woman are naturally disposed to accept and rest upon the direction of her husband. And a man is naturally inclined to lead.

In the juridical modality the structure of authority of marriage is expressed in the fact that it is the husband, as the head of a family, who must make decisions for which his wife is equally responsible even though she may not have agreed with them.

The authority of marriage is also expressed in the aesthetic modality. When a man and his wife are compatible with each other, we speak of a harmonious marriage. And this harmony is disturbed when a wife — even when compelled to do so — assumes the authority which rightfully belongs to her husband.

Authority in marriage is also expressed in the social and linguistical aspects by the manner in which a married couple associate with and speak to each other. The marriage relationship must be directed by love, but this does not exclude the fact that a wife must respect her husband as the head of the family, while the husband in his turn has to give honour unto his wife as unto the weaker vessel.

In the historical modality, marriage has a typical cultural-forming task, since it must assist in the development of culture in various ways. The children of a marriage are raised and formed to meet the cultural task of the future.

And, in addition, a married couple have the task of forming each other culturally.

Marriage is also a peculiar community of thought and feeling. There should be a continuous interchange of ideas and feeling between the married pair. Love is the guarantee that agreement will be reached in both thought and feeling. It guarantees that both parties will not be foreign to each other and that their individual differences do not cause dissension or lack of harmony and shall not grow into separation.

The marriage-structure is biotically founded; two are one flesh, and this sexual aspect is as such not sinful. My former teacher, Geesink, was fond of saying, *"naturalia non sunt turpia,"* natural things are not shameful. The unfolded marriage relation differs from the mating of animals in that the biotic aspect of marriage should be led by the normative anticipatory spheres. The sexual side of marriage is then *controlled* by a biotic anticipation of the historical aspect. Sin is present in all aspects of reality, but it is not to be combatted by eliminating one of the aspects (this is an anabaptistic and a gnostic tendency, which has also its adherents in circles of fundamentalism). Sin is to be combatted by employing all aspects in obedience to God's ordinances in order to advance the Kingdom of God. This is what is meant by keeping the Covenant in marriage.

Marriage is also a typical community of faith. It is either apostate or serves God. Apostasy and the service of God are mutually exclusive. And it is for this reason that a marriage between a Christian and a non-Christian is reprehensible in the sight of God. There cannot exist real unity between faith and unbelief.

The communion of the Christian faith directs marriage beyond its temporal significance toward its religious fulfillment in Christ, that — because of the tie with the heavenly Bridegroom — will exist throughout all eternity. As members of the body of Christ, husband and wife eternally belong to each other, not as man and wife, but as children of God.

37

The Structure of the Relationship of the State

Today it does not require a long demonstration to show that the theory of the state is of great importance. The normative structural principle of the state rests upon the divine world order and not upon the will of the people. In recent years we have seen the results of theories which — under the slogan of sovereignty of the people — derive their authority from the authority of the people. Also the appeal to a universalistic myth of omnipotence of the state tyrannizes society and destroys freedom. A totalitarian state is an idol which robs all other societal relationships of their sovereignty and presses them into slavery. It is, therefore, extremely important that we investigate the normative principle of the structure of the state. Such an investigation will enable us to judge its concrete life and will enable us to discover the way in which a state can live peaceably with the other societal relationships without seeking to dominate them. We have time to recall only a few of the many theories which have been advanced concerning the state.

The universalistic ideal of Plato and Aristotle is well known. They conceived of the state as a whole which includes all other societal relationships as dependent parts, in need of the whole in order to be complete. Society is thus thought of as a relation between a whole to its parts. The individual is preceded by the state. The state is the highest good and everything must serve it. The state has a metaphysical basis. It rests upon the rational essential nature of man who is a social being (Aristotle). This ancient universalistic conception of a state lacks any circumscription of structure. The state is a great *Moloch*. Everything else is sacrificed to it. This view overlooks the fact that the state is not a thing of nature. The state is grounded in the historical aspect. This ancient view was generally retained and modified in the Middle Ages. It was accommodated to Christian thought by means of the schema of nature and grace. The state was considered to be the highest relationship within the sphere of nature, and the church was considered the highest relationship in the sphere of grace. The church was above the state and the latter must serve the former. A church-state rather than a state-church was considered ideal. The state ruled by the grace of papal authority.

This idea of the state was developed by Thomas Aquinas only to be undermined by the nominalism (William of Occam) of the late Middle Ages. Nominalism considered nature and grace to be contradictory rather than supplementary. A Christian may externally keep the ordinances in the sphere of nature; internally, however, he is free and above them. Law is abolished by grace. Nominalism opposed the church's domination of the state, but not with the intention of binding the latter to the Word of God. It merely secularized the state and considered it as something arbitrary.

Martin Luther never broke entirely with the position that grace is opposed to nature. And in modern times, this motive is expressed by such dialectical theologians as Karl Barth and Emil Brunner. Brunner distinguishes three factors in a state, the community-moment, which is an ordinance of creation; the coercive system of law, which is due to sin; and finally a half demonical element of power. The essence of the state is to be found in the third element. The state is a worldly order. It is not holy; its very essence is sinful. A *Christian* state is a contradiction in terms. These notions arise from an irrationalistic philosophical position and they clearly show that Brunner does not distinguish between the *normative* structural principle of the relationship of the state and its subjective realization in a sinful world, in a concrete state. For Brunner the very structure of the state is sinful and evil. This notion is not accidental but it is deeply rooted in his whole system of dialectical theology, because the latter maintains that creation as such is under the judgment of God.

Another reformer, John Calvin, radically broke with the

nominalistic as well as the Thomistic schema of nature and grace. He considered all creation to be subject to the laws of God and held that sin is active in all spheres of life. Its curse is spread over the whole cosmos. But since Christ *redeemed the world,* His Kingdom rules in the hearts of believers and has to reveal itself in all the societal relationships. Calvin did not develop these ideas into a theory of a state or a philosophy, but his views paved the way for such a movement.

Soon after the Reformation, the views of Calvin were replaced by Humanism, which derived the totality of life from the non-Christian basic religious motive of freedom and nature.

Humanism was driven by the double ideal of the all-powerfulness of science and the ideal of human personality. In this motive humanism tried to harmonize and to synthesize the Greek motive of form and matter, the Christian motive of creation, fall, and redemption, and the medieval schema of nature and grace. Humanism is diametrically opposed to the basic principles of the Reformation. Yet the fact that it could acquire tremendous power in European thinking is not due solely to remnants of medieval and non-Christian philosophy in the thought of Luther or Zwingli. But, to a large extent it is due to the fact that Melanchton consciously made an alliance with non-Christian philosophical motives.

Humanism advanced its own theory of the state in the theory of *natural* law. This theory reached its focal point in the idea of a legal civil state. The civil state was originally preceded by a state of nature in which abstract individuals lived in full freedom and equality, until the want of common necessities caused them to feel the need of a civil state containing authority. Consequently, all the free individuals in the state of nature entered into a *social contract,* in which they agreed to give up all or a part of their freedom and equality to be governed by authority. The individual is sovereign; the authority of the government is derived from the will of the people.

The humanistic theory of natural law developed a conception of a legal state, in which certain legal limitations were imposed upon the government.

We shall briefly distinguish three periods in the development of this humanistic idea of the state. In the first phase the task of the state was limited by the theory that the social contract had been entered into in order to insure the organized maintenance of natural human rights. The sole task of the state is to protect the absolute rights of free individuals, namely, freedom, life, and property. And any interference of the state in private or public life was viewed as an encroachment upon the sovereignty of the individual. This view is not at all related to the Christian principles of the sovereignty of each sphere. Many people have, for example, erroneously sought to discover a connection between the theory of natural law (with respect to the state) and Christian principles. There is no such tie. The Christian derives the sphere sovereignty of the modalities and of societal relationships from the Sovereign Will of the Creator, whereas the humanistic theory of natural law is based upon the sovereignty of human personality. Thus, according to humanism, the state is to refrain from interference; it must only guarantee the individual dissoluteness within the formal limits of civil law. History has shown that in practice this theory leads to tyranny and the oppression of minorities.

The *non-interference* theory of the state did not remain unchanged. Historical development made new demands upon the state and required it to enter into the various spheres of public life. The state had to interfere with the labor conditions of industry, education, traffic and commerce. Consequently, the idea of the civil state was changed to mean that the state is competent to further cultural ends, public health, well-being and prosperity of the public. The state however must act in strict obedience with law, and this safeguard was to protect its citizens from arbitrariness of the state. The power of the state was thought of as being limited by a legal system. In practice, however, this view did not stop arbitrary action. Legislatures were free to enact whatever law they desired. And this led to a third period in which the idea of a legal civil state was totally undermined. In this third stage the state was identified with law; it no longer had any juridical limits. For all that the state performs is simply right.

This phase robs the idea of a legal state of all content and formally sanctions totalitarianism. Our experience during the five years that Holland was occupied by the Nazis' regime was more than sufficient to acquaint us with the misery which arises when man is subject to the tyranny of rulers who have forgotten God. It bears witness to the tremendous dangers for human society which are concealed in anti-Christian philosophy. In this connection Dooyeweerd speaks of a "crisis in the humanistic idea of the state." Under the influence of positivism and historicism, modern theories of the state no longer have room for a normative structural principle of the state. The state is considered to be only an empirical product of arbitrary human power.

We are now in a position to discuss the normative structure of the relationship of the state. The Christian idea of the state must not be based upon the dualistic schema of nature and grace. If it is, history has shown that either it will not recognize the presence of sin in the state, or it will consider the structure of the state to be sinful in itself and, in consequence, will be unable to offer resistance to revolutionary theory and practice. The Christian view of the state must proceed from the contrast between *sin* and *redemption*. The destructive power of sin is present in human life in its entirety, and this includes communal life. No single form of communal life is sinful *as such*. The structure of societal relationships rests in the Will of God, our Creator and Redeemer. The temporal relationship of the state exists because of sin (Rom. 13) but it never exists apart from our Lord, Jesus Christ, who is the Ruler of the kings of the earth. The life of the state is basically directed toward God or away from Him. If it is an apostate revelation of anti-Christian power, it works against the Kingdom of Christ. It works for the Kingdom of God, if the Transcendent Body of Christ is revealed, in a more or less pure fashion, in the communal life of a Christian state.

Therefore now we always must be careful to recognize the difference between the *direction* taken by a state and by societal relationships and the *structure* of the relationships. The structure of societal relationships bears a normative character and expresses the Will of God. Consequently, societal relationships can never be set aside by human arbitrariness. The actual life of a particular state may be antinormative. Certain norms are not applied in a concrete situation, but this does not imply that norms do not exist. Sin does not exist without law.

It is noteworthy that in all the possible theories and forms of the state we always encounter the structural factors of *law* and *power*. In spite of the various constructions in which the relationship between law and power is theoretically construed, no theorist or politician can deny their presence, as they respectively indicate the destination and foundational function of the structure of a state. The relationship of the state is grounded in history, and rests upon historical formational power. The family, a relationship grounded in nature, existed at the beginning of history but the state did not. Different kingdoms have arisen and passed away in history. Recall the proud kingdom of Augustus. The historical foundation of the state makes it possible for it to assume various forms. The foundational function of a natural relationship, in contrast, is free from human formation, and therefore is a natural relationship, like family and matrimony much more invariable.

In every relationship in which historical formation is the foundational function, its form is always an organizational-form, a form in which the historical factors of power are brought together through intentional organization into a constant cooperative unity. A democratic state has a different organizational form than a dictatorship. Natural societal relationships do not have an organizational-form. The form of a family, for example, is independent of cultural level and milieu. Organization is not to be confused with organism. To speak of the state as an organism is to speak figuratively in order to compare it with biotically qualified things. Romanticism idealized the organic at the expense of what is formed through organization. Such naturalism is to be avoided. That which is the result of organization is not of less value than that which is the product of organic growth. The corruption of creation through sin does not originate in the historical modality, but permeates all modalities and lies primarily in the heart of man. Historical organization in societal relationships signifies an enrichment and development of its natural substratum which includes the organic.

To characterize the foundational function of the state it is not sufficient to say that it rests upon historical formational power. The same can also be said of the church and industry. Historical power is a modal concept which can be predicated of a multiplicity of structures of individuality. The historical power that a specific relationship possesses as a foundational function depends upon the structural principle, that determines this *type* of historical power. *The typical foundational function of the state is the monopolistic organization of the power of the sword over a specific territorial cultural sphere (orbit).*

From this definition of its basis, it is evident that the state exists because of sin, so that together with its coercive power the state is a characteristic institution of common grace. The Roman Catholic view, which grounds the state in the sphere of nature, does not do justice to the fact of sin.

This foundational function in the structure of the state bears a normative character. Each state has the task of organizing the power of the sword, so that it can properly function both at home and abroad. A state which neglects to organize this power commits national suicide.

Do not misunderstand. We do not mean to imply that the historical aspect of the state consists *exclusively* of organized coercive force. The power of the sword is the form of power which *characterizes* the state and this form of power is the foundational structural function of the state. The power of the sword is not found in any other societal relationship. However, a state has additional forms of historical power, namely, anticipatory forms in which the historical structural function of the state anticipates later functions. Such anticipatory forms of historical power are, for example, economical monetary power, and moral and pistical force. Without these anticipatory forms of power, the formation of an army would not be possible. Do not confuse the anticipatory forms of power of the state with the forms of power of other organizations. The monetary force of a state bears another character from the monetary power of a business venture. Both forms of power are typified by the structural principle of the societal relationships to which they belong. The state is interwoven with other forms of power which are qualified differently. But a state with a weak army is never powerful because of being strong in anything else, such as, industry, business, science, and art. The error of a totalitarian idea of the state is just that it seeks to reduce all other structures of power to internal components of the power of the state.

The historical foundational-function of the state displays a *subject-object relationship*. The object of the power of the sword is the military equipment by which the organs of the state exercise power. These objective means only have value if they are employed when necessary by the *subjective* organization of the army or police force.

The territory of the state is also an object within the historical structural function as it is the sphere in which the state is authorized to exercise its formational power. As we bring our analysis of the foundational function to an end, notice that National Socialism wished to ground the state in the German Folk, upon a community of blood. It invented the myth of an Aryan race and considered the "Folk" to be a primeval community from which all other communal life originated. The highest peak of attainment was thought to be achieved in a deified state which enslaves all other forms of society in a universalistic manner.

Dooyeweerd distinguishes Fascism from National Socialism by the fact that according to the former the state creates the nation, and calls the folk into existence, whereas in the latter the process is reversed. Both absolutize a temporal relationship which ought to disclose — after its own fashion — the Kingdom of God.

Now the *destination*-function of the state. This function must not be confused with the objectives which are striven for in a particular state. The *destination*-function is not determined by changing objectives. On the contrary, the objectives that a state has to try to reach, ought to be judged and determined by its normative destination-function. Objectives change according to the historical circumstances under which a state has to fulfil its task. In times of prosperity objectives are different than in times of crisis. Nevertheless, the objectives and the manner in which they are to be attained, always remain joined to the normative structure of the state. If the Netherlands decided as a state to force all subjects to become protestants, then all protestants should abhor such an action, as it would exceed the authority that God has given to the state.

The *internal structure* of the destination-function is primary; and the external objective of a state is secondary. The destination-function of a state is juridical. A state is qualified as a juridical relationship. Law (justice) and power (destination and foundation) are the two roles in the structure of the state. Power without law degenerates into arbitrariness and tyranny. A power-state which disavows law as its *leading*-function degenerates into a well-organized band of gangsters. On the other hand, the state cannot continue to exist if law is separated from its historical basis of power.

The correlation between law and power expresses itself in the structure of authority of a ruler over his subjects. It is a misconception to identify the state with government. A state also has people; the government and the people are essential elements of a state. We must further make a few additional remarks concerning the law which is the destination-function of a state. Other societal relationships, such as the family and church, have an internal function of law, which is characterized by their non-juridical destination-functions. The law-function of the state, in contrast, itself is the qualifying one. To act according to law is the destination-function of the state. The destination-function of the state is identical with its law-function. The church, as an institution, has a law-function too. We can speak of church law. The bearers of ecclesiastical authority must act according to law, but law is not the destination of a church. It is meant to serve only the operation of the power of faith in the Word and Spirit of Christ.

Dooyeweerd defines the juridical function of the state as follows: *The internal law of the state is the law which a government enforces in a particular territory; it is the law of a sovereign state. And it is based upon the organization of the armed forces governing a territory.* The State law embraces the relationship of the state in its entirety. This law does not only belong to the government, nor only to the people, but to both. And it must be put into effect by the government and justly enforced upon the whole territory.

By reason of its *typical destination* the state is a legal-community. Its law is public law. Therefore, it is not qualified by a non-juridical *destination*-function, as is the law of the church, school, family and industry.

The nuclear moment of the juridical aspect is judgment, *the well-balanced harmonization of a multiplicity of interests*. The public law of the state ought to be a well-balanced harmonization of all the interests *within a particular territory*. No single interest within the borders of a state can be ignored.

The legal community of the state has its own universality, a universal relationship of law, which in *a certain sense* encompasses all other societal relationships. We are not making any concessions to universalism, as the state only spans other relationships *in public law*. Other relationships are not merely subordinate parts of the state. The state does not have a voice in the internal law of the family, school, church, science, or industry. Other relationships are entitled to the protection of the state. The state is called to protect their individual interests against any encroachment, thus enabling them to develop in peace (cf. 1 Tim. 2:2 "that we may lead a tranquil and quiet life in all godliness and gravity"). This is the political principle of totality or *integration*.

The question arises as to whether or not what we have said in the preceding paragraph eliminates the sphere sovereignty of the law of the state. Does the principle of integration endow the state with the power to interfere in other relationships?

No, the state ought not to interfere, as the law of other relationships is qualified differently. Their internal law is beyond the jurisdiction of the state. However, all relationships have an *external* as well as an *internal* juridical function. A church, for instance, is affected by a noisy factory, so that the latter is prevented by law from interfering with public worship. A state must seek to harmonize such *external* legal interests, but it must also respect the internal sovereignty of other relationships and promote justice as a whole by utilizing public law in order to balance the external legal relations of societal relationships. A state is limited by the sovereign law of other relationships which is determined by their internal principles of structure.

We have discussed the destination- and foundational function of the state, but have not yet seen the way in which its structure is expressed in the remaining modal aspects.

In the *aesthetical* modality the structure of the state expresses itself in a harmony that exists if a people and a government are united in a closely knit community. A state ought to be a political harmony, or a community in which various interests are held in balance by the strong arm of government. If the government neglects its task and permits one interest to dominate, not only is law violated, but harmony is disturbed and the policy of the government is aesthetically disrupted.

In dealing with the *economic* function of the state, it is of primary importance that we distinguish between it and that of private industry. The latter is economically *qualified*, whereas state-economy retains the same qualification as does the state. A state exceeds its power if it seeks to absorb industry and economic relationships. It exceeds the limits God has imposed on it. The state lacks any basis in public law if it seeks to nationalize industry. The economy of the state is distinct from that of private industry, because the state lacks the motive of profit without which industry cannot exist. The expenditures of a state must be gauged by the necessity of its internal economical measurements. A state must purchase military equipment which yields no profit. Its economy is led by its juridical destination-function and is a coerced economy.

The *social* function of the state is expressed in the social form between a government and its subjects. Citizens ought to respect their rulers, not through fear or because they are eminent people, but because God has endowed them with the power to rule. ("Liberty, equality, and fraternity" is a meaningless, asocial, revolutionary slogan.) Moreover, a government must uphold the honor of a nation. National disgrace violates the social norms of the state.

The *language*-function of the state does not only include its national language or languages, but also its objective symbols, such as flags, standards, titles, and medals. The government is not called to form or suppress a language, but it can take measures to insure uniformity in spelling and language, insofar as this affects public justice and the furtherance of the general welfare.

In the *logical* modality, a state expresses itself in national thought, in a political coherence of thought which unites the people and their government. Public opinion does not express the agreement of all individuals, but it is a community of thought, which points to formation. Party slogans express public opinion if, and only if, they are a part of the convictions of the people. Public opinion is a factor which should not be confused. In a healthy state it supports the government. A government, which continually opposes it, gradually loses its power. Nevertheless, public opinion should not rule; its function is foundational and not directive.

The structure of the state is also expressed in political feeling, in the citizens' feeling of belonging together and being subject to the government. In contrast with natural feeling (e.g., desire), political feeling is *cultivated,* as the psychical anticipations of the historical and juridical functions of the state are opened.

With respect to its *biotic* aspect, the state is a political vital community which, as subject, sustains a relation with the objective political *Lebensraum* within which a certain type of people are gradually formed.

Concerning the *physical* function the state is a dynamic community which points toward continual actualization. And the activities through which this occurs are *founded* in the physical modality.

In the *kinematic* sphere of motion the state expresses itself in the fact, that it is continuously changing in all respects. Officials and subjects are coming and going. Laws and relations are altered. In short, the life of the state is passing through its history. Only the structure of the state is as divine ordination elevated above all alteration.

In the *spatial* modality, the state expresses itself in its territory. The latter possesses a subjective spatial function. The state is subject to the laws of space even though its territory functions as an object in all later modalities. As a juridicial territory, for example, it is the object of the subjective legal function of the state, and as a territory of power it is also an object within the historical function of a state.

The state also has a *numerical* function, as the number of its citizens and rulers can be counted and registered in a census.

We have not yet discussed the two post-juridical functions, the ethical and the pistical. The state possesses a typical juridically qualified subject-function in the ethical and pistical spheres.

The structural principle of the state expresses itself in the *ethical* modality in the love which binds a people to their country and land. This love is not identical with the love one has for his place of birth. The latter is biotically and not historically grounded. One can love the place of his birth without bearing any affection for the state containing his birthplace. Primitive people do not possess patriotism but very often have love for their place of birth.

And finally we must consider the way in which the structure of the state typically expresses itself in the function of *faith*.

Many deny the possibility of a Christian state, either because they think that faith is the exclusive property of the church, as an institution, or they are convinced that a Christian state would only be possible if all its citizens were Christians and this ideal can never be realized. Others accept the idea of a Christian state, and see its possibility in a specific relation in which the state supports a church or an ecclesiastical confession. The Roman Catholic view, for example, believes that in spiritual matters the state must accept the pronouncements of the church and exercise its authority to promote the church's welfare.

This same sentiment is expressed by those who would have the state accept a certain confession to which its office-bearers must subscribe.

None of these solutions are satisfactory. The first denies that the structure of the state is expressed in the sphere of faith, thus shutting off its individuality in the ethical sphere. The second also believes that the state lacks an *internal* pistical function but it seeks to compensate for this by *externally* binding the state to the church. This view commits the error of denying a real Christian character to the state as such.

Now we do not deny that the state can sustain external ties with churches within its territory, but, such bands must not infringe upon the sovereignty of the church or of the state.

Every created thing, including the state, functions in all

modalities. The structure of the state has indeed a typical pistical function too. Not only the Christian state, but the non-Christian as well, functions in the modality of faith. Unbelief does not signify a lack of a function of faith. Unbelief is only the wrong employment of faith. It seeks its final certainty in a lie rather than in the truth. Every state functions in the modality of faith and is either Christian or non-Christian.

The destination-function of the state is juridical and not pistical. Even in a land in which there was an ideal Christian state, the state would not be identical with the church. The church is a pistical and the state a juridical relationship.

In investigating the pistical function of the state as a community qualified by law, Dooyeweerd commences with the *law-side* of the pistical structural function of the state and shows that the revelational principle, which bears a specific pistical character, since revelation must be believed, is here specified as a *political* principle of revelation. This means that God, who reveals Himself in His works as well as His Word, also reveals Himself in the life of the state. This revelation can be understood and confessed only in the light of God's Word. Divine revelation in the state means that God is the *Origin of all authority;* law and power come from Him. He is the Law-giver, the Judge, and the Avenger of evil. This revelation is *general* revelation, revelation in His works, in contrast to His Word. However, it is incorrect to think that the state is completely independent of God's Word. For general revelation can only be discovered and believed in the light of the Holy Scripture.

Dooyeweerd calls Divine Revelation in the state the political *norm of faith,* because each state is subject to it, and ought to confess the sovereignty of God. The state ought to make this confession, but in a different way than the church. This brings us to the subject-side of the pistical structural function of the state. The confession of a state should be a *political* confession. No matter what the personal faith of its members is, a Christian state ought publicly to confess — for example in the opening words of laws or in proclamations or on solemn occasions — the sovereignty of God and recognize Christ as the Ruler of the kings of the earth.

A neutral state is a fiction. A non-Christian state also makes a confession. But it closes its eyes to the light of the Word of God and no longer correctly understands the general revelation of God in the life of the state. Consequently, the political norm of faith, the political principle of revelation forces the people and their rulers to bow before the idols of law and power. The life of the state is pushed in an apostate direction, and a political confession is made in the sovereignty of the people, or in the omnipotence of the state, or in what other gods there may be.

We have returned to our starting point. All temporal authoritative societal relationships ought to be earthly manifestations of the religious body of Christ. A Christian state is a temporal manifestation of the Kingdom of God and it must struggle against the kingdom of darkness. An apostate state has no future. By ascribing sovereignty to itself or another creature it serves the kingdom of darkness. On earth we never can find a societal relationship that purely manifests the body of Christ. Consequently the struggle against the forces of evil, which seek to obscure the Kingship of Christ, is both internal and external. This conflict will continue until His Kingdom has come in perfection.

Finally we must note two things. First, a Christian state is only possible if the idea of it is rooted in public opinion. To form a basis of power for a government which can actualize Christian political principles, the idea of a Christian state must be deeply embedded in the life of the people.

Secondly, it is correct to say that the state arises from common grace, since it exists because of sin, and since even an apostate state displays the structure of a state in every respect. But common grace, through which God maintains the temporal world order and checks the power of sin, is rooted in special grace, rooted in Him who gives life to the world. Life may never be divided into two spheres. Both common and special grace permeate all of the life, which is renewed and maintained by Christ.

38

The Structure of the Institution of the Church

Before we can discover the structural principle of the church as an institution we must examine the relationship between — what often is called — the visible and invisible church and then determine the manner in which both are related to the church as an institution.

We can say that there is only one church of Christ, the "Una Sancta," and secondly that there is a multiplicity of church institutions, a multiplicity which exists because of geographical, linguistical, and national differences and because of different confessions and different views of basic doctrines.

These two facts, the faith in one church, and the reality of many institutions, are not contradictory if both are not placed on the same level. Systematic theology has, therefore, traditionally distinguished between the invisible and the visible church. This distinction, properly understood, expresses something which we must never lose sight of and which we must not think of as denoting two churches. God's Word only recognizes one Bride of Christ. The True Shepherd has only one flock. Therefore, when we speak of the "visible" and "invisible" church, we understand that the "Una Sancta" can be viewed under two aspects. It can be sought in two dimensions, in the transcendental temporal dimension of earthly life, and in the transcendent religious dimension which is the deepest root of this earthly life.

The invisible church is the church in its religious fulness, composed of the elect of all ages. We cannot see it. It is ever only an object of our faith. The invisible church is the true body of Christ purged of all hypocrisy. The invisible church transcends our human earthly horizon. The

"Una Sancta" is invisible in its transcendent fulness, but it reveals itself as the visible church in the many forms of our human society. The visible church may not be identified with the church as an institution. (We purposely spoke of earthly forms of human society.) Kuyper taught us this when he distinguished between the church as an *institution* and as an *organism*. This distinction is not identical with the visible and invisible church but is exclusively applicable to the former.

If the visible church is equated with the church as an institution then the Roman Catholic dualism between "nature" and "grace" cannot be avoided. According to it, temporal life belongs to the sphere of nature. Christ is not the direct King of secular life. The sphere of faith is separate; it is a sphere of grace. Society is not a part of the body of Christ, but in its inner structure society is worldly and devoid of grace. It has its origin and end in temporal existence and, as such, does not lead to eternal life. The only tie that the sphere of nature can have with the sphere of grace is indirect. Society can be bound only to Christ by grace. That means it can only approach God through the institution of the church. The latter alone can afford a haven for the sphere of nature. "Nature" is not "idle in the Lord," insofar as it is connected with the church. The latter cannot rest until it dominates human life in its entirety. If the consequences of the dualism between nature and grace are to be avoided, we must unequivocally maintain that the invisible church includes more than the institutional life of the church. The "visible" church is all of temporal society insofar as it derives its life from Jesus Christ and employs its energy to advance His Kingdom. A Christian marriage, a Christian family, state, school, or any other Christian relationship which acknowledges Christ as the King of heaven and of earth, belongs to the visible church. Thus, the church as an institution, as a household of faith, is on the same level with all other relationships. The visible church, or the Kingdom of God, manifests itself in a multiplicity of forms, forms in which the Body of Christ is revealed. The church as an institution is not *the* revelation of the Body of Christ, but it is one revelation of it. The Body of Christ is revealed in other forms. (Compare Ephesians 5:32, where the apostle, speaking about matrimony, says: this mystery is great; but I speak in regard of Christ and of the church.)

The institutional church is not called to dominate any of the other forms of the Kingdom of God, as they too are endowed with internal sovereignty. The task of the institutional church is rather to serve God in a way in which He has prescribed, in harmony with other forms of society.

The church as an institution, as one of the many forms of the visible church occupies, nevertheless, a central place in the Christian life. It has the task of proclaiming the Word of God to all creatures, individually and collectively, and the task of administering the sacraments to believers and their children. In this way the institutional church influences the whole Christian life in all forms. Its task is, therefore, much more inclusive than a Christian organization for charity or youth work. Such organizations have a different nature and a more restricted task. They would not even exist without the proclamation of the Word of God, which stimulates Christians to act in various fields.

With the exception of the institutional church, all societal relationships, such as the family, state, industry, and schools do not *necessarily* have to be revelations of the Body of Christ in order to exist. If they are not Christian in character, they are disclosures of the kingdom of darkness and belong to the "*civitas terrena*." But, in spite of their apostasy, they still retain their own structural principle. A non-Christian family or state is still a family or state. A civil marriage between unbelievers is still a marriage and even an anti-Christian state is still a state.

It is different, however, with respect to the institutional church. The institutional church no longer exists as such if it ceases to be a revelation of the Body of Christ. A non-Christian church, a false church, is no longer a church. It may be a "religious society" or an association for the furtherance of religious needs and worship but it is in no wise related to the church which Christ instituted on this earth. It is not just a question of terminology. The character of an institutional church is essentially different from the character of a non-Christian religious society. The latter is not an institution but a free societal relationship which arises from the voluntary association of equals.

In order to exist the institutional church must be a revelation of the Body of Christ. The Confession of Faith of the Reformed Churches of the Netherlands and of several churches of Dutch origin in the U.S.A. ably states in Art. 29: "We believe that we ought diligently and circumspectly to discern from the Word of God which is the true Church, since all sects which are in the world assume to themselves the name of the Church." This same article discusses the characteristics of the *true* church and of Christians. And from this discussion it appears that the Body of Christ must reveal itself in the church. A *false church* is not a church.

The church can become decadent in many ways. No institutional church is free from some forms of decadence, because the characteristics or signs of a true church are inseparable from the distinguishing features of Christians who belong to it. There must, therefore, be a continual internal reformation which seeks to purify the church and advance the Kingdom of God within its institutional life. If a religious organization completely departs from the Word of God, is not a revelation of the body of Christ, and does not factually acknowledge Christ as its head, then it is no longer a church.

What we have said of the church is true, because the church is an institution of *special grace*. To understand this more fully, we must examine the relationship between special and common grace. Neither Vollenhoven or Dooyeweerd deny this distinction. In his work entitled, *Het Calvinisme en de reformatie der Wijsbegeerte*, page 47, Vollenhoven writes that "the distinction between special and common grace is fully justified . . .," and in Vol. 3 of *A New*

Critique of Theoretical Thought, Dooyeweerd refers to the distinction and coherence between common and special grace. He writes, "common grace consists of the maintenance of the temporal world order with all its structures in opposition to the destructive activity of sin. In this sense common grace includes both good and evil and is limited to temporal life."

The only observations that we have to make with respect to the doctrine of common and special grace concern the terms and their relationship to each other.

The terms "general" and "special" are scholastic and Aristotelian in origin. It is not wrong per se for a Christian philosophy to employ terms of a non-Christian origin. But there is a danger in this case that this terminology will give rise to the notion that special grace operates in the specific sphere of the inner spiritual life of grace, whereas *"gratia generalis"* includes the general sphere of natural human life, as such.[1]

Vollenhoven expresses the same opinion when he writes, "There is a danger that the distinction between general and specific grace will be identified with a dualism in the life of an individual person. Therefore, it is better to speak of objects of grace rather than of spheres of grace."[2]

Dooyeweerd proposes that we replace the term "common grace" by *temporal conserving grace* — the grace of God in Christ by which the temporal world order is preserved by limiting the consequences of the destructive power of sin. Thus, temporal life with its family, state, marriage relationships is preserved, even when renewing, regenerating grace is absent. Even when men deny God, His goodness enables them to perform civil good, to love each other, and have social virtues. God's conserving grace enables apostate culture to develop and unfold. Instead of "special grace," the term *renewing* or *regenerating grace* can better be employed to designate the grace of God in Christ by which

---

[1]Dooyeweerd: A New Critique of Theoretical Thought.
[2]D. H. Th. Vollenhoven: *op. cit.*, p. 47.

God radically changes the life of a sinner and places him in Christ, thus renewing his whole life in principle.

With respect to the relationship between *conserving* and *renewing* grace, this Christian philosophy teaches that there is no grace or goodness of God in this sinful world apart from the Lord Jesus Christ, the Mediator of the Covenant. He is the sole source of all blessing and the Savior of the world. His grace operates in a twofold manner as conserving and renewing grace, both of which operate throughout the entire sphere of human life. There is no division in the sphere of operation of conserving and renewing grace. Life is not divided into two spheres. The Christian does not live in peace and harmony with all men in one common sphere, and, at the same time, also live in another sphere in which he is separated from the rest of mankind. The only line of demarcation which transects the world is that of the sin which God restrains and of the sin which He forgives. In order that His Kingdom may come, Christ restrains sin by His conserving grace. His Kingdom must develop as long as world history endures. His renewing grace is effective, and wherever sin is forgiven, He organizes a new societal relationship, the institutional church, a temporal instrument for the operation of the power of His Word.

The institutional church is qualified by the function of faith; its *destination function* is *pistical*. The church is a community of faith. Its members have a common faith, even though they may differ in nationality, age, knowledge, sex, class and profession.

The function of faith differs from all other functions in that it bears a *border-character*. Negatively this means that the function of faith does not have any modal anticipations. Positively it means that in the function of faith, all of creation points toward the Origin of all things, toward God who made and redeemed the world through Jesus Christ. Apostate faith also points toward the religious, toward a pseudo-god. It honors a deified creature as the origin and end of life.

The destination of the institutional church lies in the border-function of faith. Consequently, all the modal aspects of this relationship point by faith to the eternal Origin of all things. All the structural aspects of the church point beyond the created cosmos.

The *foundational* function of the church is *historical*. The institutional church is free from the necessity of nature and rests upon its own official organizational form.

We have given a modal description of the *destination* and foundation of the church. We must still investigate their type of individuality as both of these functions determine the structure of the institutional church as an individual relationship.

The foundational function can be further described as the *historical power of the Word of the Lord,* the power of Christ, who rules His people through His Word and Spirit. The Lord has organized the power of the Word of God by giving the office, namely apostles and sacraments to the church. The power of the Word is a *power of faith.* For, as the qualifying function, the destination-function impresses its own character upon all other structural functions. The Word of God has the power of a two-edged sword. Its power is different from juridical power because it knows no limits. Christ demands that all of His people subject themselves to the Word of God in faith. Those who refuse to believe will be judged by the power of His Word, which aims at the *spiritual domination* of the world, and seeks to subject all men in faith to Christ. The spiritual domination of the world shall be fully realized and revealed on the new earth, when the Savior returns; then everyone will know and serve Him continuously.

The institutional church is a *temporal organizational* form of the pistical power of the Word. It is temporal because the power of the Word of the Spirit is organized in the institutional church in this era unto the end of the world. The church is an institution for the operation of this power, in the entire temporal existence of believers, among their posterity, among those who have departed from the covenant (evangelization), and among those who never belonged to the New Testament church (missions).

All believers have an office in the institutional church, namely, the *office of believers*. Therefore, they must assist in the formation and reformation of the church. Reformation is not limited to a few periods in history. It ought to be a continual internal process which does not cease until Christ returns. The church can only fulfill its task properly and be a blessing to all of society, if all believers cooperate with the special office bearers of the church.

The type of individuality of the pistical function of the institutional church may thus be defined as an *institutionally organized community of Christian believers who are bound together in the service of the Word and of the sacraments.* Faith in human wisdom and subjective inclination can give rise to associations which are religious in character (even though directed away from God) but it cannot constitute a *church*. An apostate church is a *contradicto in terminis*.

The church as an institution organizes Christian believers and their children, the people of the covenant, in the service of the Word and the sacraments. This community of faith, which is founded on the historical power of the Word of God, is only possible on the basis of a common *confession*. A church which abandons its confession destroys itself. The idea of a national church is the idea of a false church, since the covenant of grace is made with believers of all peoples and nations. This does not mean that a church cannot exert a blessing upon the life of a people. The church and nation are not separate from each other. The confession of a church is the *central positive norm of faith* of a congregation and it contains the central revealed truths of Holy Scripture. The Bible is not given to us in the form of principles but it is given in a positive form by God Himself. No human confession is an absolute norm but it is a norm which in conformity with the Word of God is formulated by the Church. It is not infallible or irrevocable; nevertheless, it is a norm. The members of a church are bound to believe its confession. However, confessions are quite different from the scientific theological pronouncements of systematic theology. The former is normative, the latter is subjective, and non-normative. Systematic theology is itself bound to the norms of science and to the norm of the confession. Theology is a science and as such is a gift of God. It has its place and is not to be depreciated but it is never to be given an equal footing with the confession of the church. It is not normative and has no certainty in itself. The church must never exchange the certainty of the Word of God for scientific formulations even though they may be the pronouncements of Christian science.

To complete our consideration of the structure of the church as an institution, we must still discuss several points. The first is the pluriformity of the church. We cannot go into detail and must be content with a few observations.

The term *pluriformity of the church* is used equivocally. It sometimes means that different institutional churches exist in the same place. At other times it means that institutional Christian churches in other lands display a different *type* than our own. A third meaning unites the meanings just given into a third notion of pluriformity. Obviously confusion can only be avoided if we define the sense in which we employ the term. The view that pluriformity exists between churches in the same place who are divided because of major doctrinal issues or petty differences, is quite different from the fact that a Reformed Church in Java with the same confession and form of government, is slightly different from a Reformed Church in Holland. If we call the latter case pluriformity, then the former can better be referred to as *divisions* of the institutional church.

The difference between the Reformed Church in Holland and the Greek Orthodox Church in Russia under the Czar is not to be explained in terms of pluriformity, but in terms of a fundamental difference in confession.

The division of the institutional church is not reducible to the pluriformity of the church. If this reduction is made, the Truth of God's Word which is contained in the confessions is made relative. Nevertheless, the division of the church may not be set aside by stating that only the Reformed churches are churches of Christ, while other groups, which purport to be churches, are merely sects whose membership may include Christians. Behind such reasoning is hidden the fatal identification of the universal invisible church with the institutional church, which is only one of the many temporal forms of the visible church.

In our opinion the distinction between the division and the pluriformity of the church is best stated as follows. Division is a result of sin and must constantly be combatted. It can be recognized when the differences between institutional churches occur with respect to the *internal structure* of an organized body of Christians. Pluriformity, in contrast, is present when differences exist with respect to the *external* church-type, because of the interrelationship which exists between the institutional church and another type of people, language, and culture.

A second matter which requires our attention is the distinction between the authority of the church and the state, and between an *office* of the church and an *office* of the state. The office bearer in the church is the servant of Christ. It is also true that the government serves under the sovereign authority of the Almighty God, but its authority is primarily ruling rather than serving. It is founded in the power of the sword and is juridically qualified. The authority of the office bearer of the Church is not ruling but that of service. It is *pistically* qualified. The juridical structural function of the institutional church is pistically determined. Church law is concerned with the spirit rather than with the letter of church order. The pistical function always points toward the Transcendent Root of creation, namely, Jesus Christ, the Sovereign Ruler of the church. Therefore, even in the juridical function of the institutional church, the character of authority of its office bearers is determined by service to Christ. The fact that the government of a state must serve God is not due to the juridical destination-function of the state, but is due to the ethical and pistical functions of its structure. These ethical and pistical functions go beyond the destination-function of the state in the cosmic order.

It follows from what we have said, that forms of civil government may not be merely taken over by the church. Democracy or aristocracy deprive the church organization of the authority of Christ. The authority of the church does not lie in the congregation (democracy), nor in its most excellent members (aristocracy), but it is vested in those office bearers who are called by Christ in accordance with the precepts laid down in His Word.

In our subsequent discussion of other societal relationships we shall see into detail how the structure of the church expresses itself in the various modalities. For the present, the reader can easily see that the institutional church is not only a community of believers (pistical function). It is also an ethical and legal community. And we can also speak of harmony in the church, church economy, social intercourse, church-language and symbols such as the cross. We can think of the power of the church (historical function), its concepts (analytical function), feeling (psychical function) and we can think of the church as a living organism (biotic function) and as dynamic (physical function). A relationship is not static, but is full of movement and change (kinematic function). Lastly we can consider the territory of a church (spatial function) and its unity and multiplicity (numerical function). All these structural functions are determined by faith and may not be thought of as ends in themselves. They must work together in harmony to further the same destination, namely the furtherance of the sovereign grace of Christ by His Spirit and Word, until the temporal norms of the visible Church shall pass away to make room for the full revelation of the body of Christ in glory upon the new earth, where the bride will see her King in His beauty.

39
Free Societal Relationships

Up until now we have considered only authoritative societal relationships which are institutional in character and do not owe their existence to human initiative. The institutions of marriage, the family, state, and church are established and sustained by God Himself. A society which tries to eliminate them destroys itself. To a certain degree institutional relationships include human existence *independent of individual volition*. According to divine prescription, marriage binds the parties together for their entire life, and one is born into a family, a church, and a state without making any choice. Anyone who tries to explain these relationships as a voluntary association of self-sufficient individuals is basically wrong, and as an individualist seeks his religious certainty in the sovereign individual.

Human life is very rich. It contains a great diversity of other sorts of relationships which are not institutional, but arise from the free voluntary intercourse of equal people. (e.g., business, clubs, lodges, etc.). We call these relationships which arise through free association, *free societal relationships*.

The church, state and society are not to be placed on the same level. The church and state are both *authoritative* societal relationships. On the other hand *society*, in its generality, is a part of human life, but it is not such relationship. We can define society — at least as it appears in its open individual structure, excluding primitive people — as *the broad field of personal freedom*, outside of institutional relationships, in which men associate with each other as equals and freely organize together. On this broad field of human freedom we encounter in the first place the free societal *relations* and next to them the free societal *relationships*.

Free societal relations are associations, not only between free men, e.g., the relation between a buyer and seller, or between the physician and his patients, the wife and her neighbor, but also the relations between relationships mutually, which are sovereign in their own sphere, e.g., the relation between two or more families, between churches, between nations, or between the state and a church, a club and a family, and so on. These societal relations do not possess an organizational form. From the *organization* of free people the various *free societal relationships* spring into existence, e.g., a factory, a school, a club, etc. These relationships are *historically* grounded, since they originate through positive organizational formation, on the basis of a specific power. A business, for example, is formed on the basis of the power of capital.

The destination-function of free societal relationships can be very different, but it is always connected with the specific *goal* or purpose for which the relationship is formed. Institutional authoritative relationships in contrast, are not effected by arbitrarily chosen goals. A family is not formed in order to further philosophy; a church is not instituted to promote public welfare. All free societal relationships, however, have a goal which determines the type of relationship that is formed. If some people, for example, form an organization to provide for their own recreation, then the choice of this goal determines the destination-function of the organization, consequently, in this instance, a recreational organization would be *socially* qualified. But, if these people change the goal of their organization from recreation to music, then the destination-function is no longer social, but *aesthetic*.

However, in spite of this close relation, we must notice that the goal and the destination-function are not always equivalent. For while the destination-function is limited to the internal life of the relationship, its goal may be much broader and may stimulate activity outside of its internal sphere. A society for the prevention of cruelty to animals, for example, is not satisfied if its own members are kind to animals, but it seeks to further their well-being among as many people as possible.

We have already seen that free societal relationships can

only arise if in human life the sphere of personal freedom has developed outside of institutional relationships (authoritative). This presupposes an opened level of culture, or — as Dooyeweerd calls it — a *process of individualization* in *human associations*. The cultural level of primitive people is closed, so that the entire life of the individual is completely absorbed in an undifferentiated tribal relationship. Life is limited to the rudimentary association between different families of the same tribe and between the members of the tribal relationship as such. As soon as the unfolding or opening process begins in a primitive culture, there is set in motion the process of *differentiation* in human life, and the process of *individuation* in human associations. The process of differentiation means, that in the history of a primitive people there can start a development from the one undifferentiated tribal relationship into the institutional relationships of state and church, as well into several free societal relationships of business, school, factory, hospital, etc. Concerning the process of individuation, which occurs at the same time, it must be stated, that it is further advanced in the culture of a large city than it is in a rural district. In a rural area there are still various remnants of undifferentiated life (e.g., the patriarchal household of a farmer).

The process of individualization has nothing to do with the theory of individualism. Individualism is the view of human society which takes as its starting point the sovereign self-sufficient individual. The Biblical view of society, on the contrary, maintains that the religious unity of the old humanity in Adam and the new humanity in Christ exists above all temporal relationships and free associations as their religious root. This transcendent radical community of humanity makes social intercourse possible and is the necessary prerequisite of its individualization. The unfolding-process in free society, in which free societal relations individuate themselves, is not based upon sovereign individuals. On the contrary, this process increases the needs of the individual and detracts from his independence.

Because of it the individual becomes more dependent upon others.

Up until now we have spoken exclusively of *free societal relationships* which appear in large numbers in opened *individuated* society (e.g., businesses, schools, clubs, and lodges.)

We shall end this chapter by briefly noticing individuated *free societal relations.*

We have seen that the free societal relations are only present in a rudimentary form in the primitive tribal relationship. However, in the life of cultured peoples, they are strongly individuated in the sphere of personal freedom that is guaranteed to man in an opened culture. Besides all the institutional (authoritative) relationships, a man of culture is related to other people in numerous ways, for example, as a customer, neighbor, acquaintance, colleague, and patient, etc. These *free* or *societal relations* have their own typical *internal structure,* which expresses itself characteristically in all aspects of temporal reality, and which are qualified by a destination-function and rests upon an *historical* foundation. The relation between the buyer and the seller, for example, is economically qualified. But this internal structure of free societal relations does not unite people into a *unified relationship,* nor does it rest upon an *organization* as its foundation, as is the case with *free societal relationships.* On the contrary, a free societal relation permits people to be coordinate to each other and incidentally to be active with each other.

There is a great diversity of *individual structures* which appear within free *societal relations,* for example, the free market, advertisement, sport, style, and the press. All of these structures only appear in *opened* society and have an historical basis. We must, therefore, seek to determine what is the destination-function by which such a structure is qualified. Style as a *societal* phenomenon is qualified by the *social* function, and the free market is qualified by the *economical* function. It is here also necessary to see how these structures, which are led by their destination-function and are historically grounded, express themselves characteristically in all aspects of reality.

Finally, we must observe that in all these free individual societal structures there is a twofold tendency. An *integrational tendency,* which aims at international expansion and is cosmopolitan, and a *differentiating tendency.* For example, the style of national and local customs tends, on the one hand, to integrate and become more cosmopolitan; and at the same time they tend to give rise to further differences in sport clothes, evening dress, robes of office, uniforms, etc.

This section should make us aware of the rich variation and many sidedness of the society which, under God's providential guidance, has developed in modern life.

CHAPTER VI

THE THEORY OF STRUCTURAL INTERRELATIONS

40

THE UNIVERSE

WE have analyzed the structure of things and forms of society in detail, but have not yet finished our discussion of the main features of Christian Philosophy. Philosophy is the science which seeks to acquire also a total view over the whole cosmos. It cannot end with a structural analysis of individual things and relationships which are momentarily abstracted from the total coherence of the whole cosmos. A structural analysis naturally gives rise to the question of the coherence of the creation. How are we to view the universe in which God has given all things their proper place?

Non-Christian philosophy, since antiquity, has given a twofold answer to this question. Some consider the universe to be an all-inclusive structure which unites all diversity into a higher whole. This is the answer of *universalism*, which is represented in antiquity by Plato and Plotinus, and in modern times by Spinoza, Hegel and Othmar Spann. The universalistic view of the world considers all individual structures as parts of the one all-spanning structure of totality. A part only has meaning as a part of the whole. The whole dominates all structural parts and is the real being. A part has its purpose in the unity of the whole. The unity is the higher being, the diversity the lower one.

In this respect many philosophers like to speak about the universe as a macrocosmos, in contrast to man, who is a microcosmos (*makros* means great, and *mikros* is small). Plato and Plotinus ascribed a world soul to the macrocosmos.

The world-soul is the principle of motion of the universe which it permeates and envelops.

The macro-micro-theme, however, is not more a *pure* universalistic view, because it indicates that the universal and the individual are independent from each other, placed next to each other in the cosmos, provided that all that happens in the macrocosmos, happens in the microcosmos too. We call this conception: *partial universalism*. Both conceptions, pure and partial-universalism, obviously do not have room for the sphere sovereignty of *individual structures*. Universalism recognizes only one sovereign structure and denies internal self-sufficiency to any subordinate parts which are fully dependent on the total structure.

Universalism views the universe as an animated totality. Individualism, in contrast, denies the totality of the universe. All individualists agree in this denial but they disagree in their positive notion as to what the universe is. The individualistic humanists are divided in accordance with their acceptance of the ideal of science or the ideal of personality. Individualists who are dominated by the ideal of science, whether they be rationalists or empiricists, conceive of the universe *functionalistically*. The concept of the cosmos is for them only a modal concept; the conceptual unity expressed by the term "cosmos" exists only in the fact that all creation can be subsumed under one specific function, which can be physical (rationalistic naturalism) or psychical (empirical psychologism). Both rationalists and empiricists view the cosmos as an all-inclusive *system of relations*. Individualists dominated by the ideal of personality (Kant, and others) affirm that the universe is not a given of experience but is a *limiting concept* of reason. The universe is not reality outside of human personality; it is only a subjective limiting concept that does not even enrich our knowledge, but only has regulative significance for thought. An experienceable reality does not lie at the foundation of this subjective concept.

Christian philosophy cannot accept the solution of universalism, individualism, or a partial-universalism. This does not mean that we do not recognize *moments* of truth within individualism and universalism. On the contrary, it is our contention that every system of immanence-philosophy can only exist because it contains *elements* of truth. Nonetheless, these elements of truth may not tempt us to accept such a system, which in its basic tenets is foreign to the revealed Truth of God. Nor may we seek to effect a *synthesis* between our Christian faith and a conception of immanence-philosophy, for such a synthesis is inseparably connected with the starting point of the latter. However, every element of truth contained in immanence-philosophy can, in principle, be recognized and incorporated into Christian philosophy. Christian philosophy is not a voluntary poverty, but it is a part of the rich blessing which God gives to those who keep His covenant in the field of science.

Universalism contains an element of truth with respect to the structure of the universe. The universe, as the sum of all God's creatures, is a *unity*, which is grounded in the plan of creation and not in human reason. Moreover, God's creation, of which man forms the crown is in spite of the Fall in its root still a unity, a unity which is not to be found in a temporal thing or sphere or relationship, but in the *religious center* of the cosmos, namely Jesus Christ, our Lord. "For in Him were all things created . . . and unto Him. And He is before all things; and in Him all things consist" (Col. 1:15-17). In time this unity of God's creation unfolds itself in innumerable diversities, each of which possesses its own structure of individuality and retains its sphere-sovereignty. Absolute sovereignty can never be ascribed to the universe, as a totality. If such an ascription were made, sphere-sovereignty would be innerly contradictory. Nor can it be ascribed to a part of the universal and to a part of the individual. Absolute sovereignty can only be ascribed to the Almighty Creator, who gave, since the Resurrection, all authority in heaven and on earth unto His Son, our Lord. He is and remains the purpose of all creatures.

Nevertheless, the transcendent unity of the cosmos expresses itself in an immanent cosmic sense in a *temporal universal interwoven-coherence,* within which all individual structures function.

The universal interwoven-coherence of individual structures does also justice to the elements of truth in individualism. God created the terrestrial and celestial bodies as systems of individual structures which are physically qualified, but not merely physical. As all other *individual structures* they function in all modalities. And by acknowledging that all individual structures within the cosmos are interwoven with *human existence,* Christian philosophy also does justice to the truth found within the conceptions of the adherents of the ideal of personality. God has connected the entire creation with the human race. The first Adam was given the earth as his kingdom, and by his fall the earth was cursed. The second Adam, Jesus Christ, redeemed the whole cosmos by His death and resurrection. Thus earthly labors will not appear to have been in vain on the day in which God will make a new heaven and a new earth.

41

The Interwovenness of Structures

We have already concluded that God created the universe in a universal interwoven-coherence which joins together all individual structures of things and relationships according to a cosmic law-order. In his naive experience a person is convinced of the *interwoven-coherence* of all things. We often say that a thing never exists in itself. We can speak of a tree in abstraction but *a* tree in *itself* is nowhere to be found. Every tree stands and grows already on a piece of soil. If a tree is cultivated, then someone planted it to bear fruit or furnish shade. A coherence exists between the tree and other things, and between it and human life (e.g., the eating of its fruit, and the enjoyment of its shade).

Similarly, coherences are everywhere to be found in the

cosmos. Dooyeweerd calls them *interwoven-coherences* or *enkapsis*. Not every relation in the cosmos, however, bears the character of an *interwoven-coherence*. Therefore we have to answer the question: what is interwoven-coherence, or enkapsis? What are the characteristics of this kind of coherence?

Enkapsis can be defined negatively and positively. Negatively, we can say that individual structures are interwoven into a coherence of enkapsis, when this coherence cannot be described as a relationship between a *whole and its parts*. Positively, it must be added that the things or societal relationships which are woven together into a coherence retain their own *internal structure* and thus their structural sphere-sovereignty. This needs further explanation.

Interwovenness, enkapsis, is not a relation of a whole to its parts. Every thing that is a whole has its parts. A piece of stone can be broken into parts. A plant has a stem and leaves, and an animal, organs. But the parts of the whole have the same *destination-function* as the whole and are determined by the same structural principle. A stone is a physical thing; one of its pieces is also physically qualified. A plant is an organic thing; its leaves are also organic in structure. Similarly, the state is a juridically qualified authoritative societal relationship, and its parts, counties and local districts, have the same juridical destination-function. From the fact that parts possess the same destination-function as the whole, we can conclude that the parts of a whole possess *a relative autonomy* but not sphere-sovereignty. A leaf of a plant enjoys its independence insofar as it has its own function in the whole. The stem and flower have different functions. A leaf, a flower, and a stem lose their own functions when cut off from the rest of the plant. They are not sovereign in themselves. A part is only relatively independent as it exists in relation to a whole. If a part is separated from the whole, then it becomes *another thing*, which very often has a different destination-function. A leaf that falls from a plant and becomes humus is no longer an organic thing but a physical thing.

The relation between the whole and its parts cannot be called *interwovenness,* because *interwovenness is the coherence of individual structures, in which the latter retain their internal sovereignty in their own sphere, but are opened in their external functions.*

An illustration of *interwovenness* is the coherence between a bird and its nest. The destination-function of the bird is *subjective* and *psychical.* A bird is subject to the psychical laws of feeling. The nest, in contrast, is *objective and psychically qualified,* namely in correlation with the bird. But apart from the bird the nest as a collection of dead twigs is subjectively qualified as an *organic* thing. The nest does not itself have feelings but it is the object of the feelings of the bird.

Both individualities, the bird and the nest, retain therefore their own structure in this interwoven-coherence. If we had been dealing with the relation of a part to a whole, the nest would have had to possess the same destination-function as the bird and would have had to be subjectively and psychically qualified.

Another example is found in the fact that although the business of a state is in itself a business, but displays an interwoven-coherence with the life of the state, it retains its own structure and remains an *economically* qualified societal relationship in which the state is the proprietor and does not change in a juridical relationship.

42

Types of Interwovenness

This Christian philosophy distinguishes different types of *enkaptic* connections. The first is the *one-sided foundational interwovenness.* This type of enkapsis is present in the interwoven coherence of two structures when one structure is based upon another structure and cannot exist without it. The *interwovenness* of the marble-material in a work of sculpture is such a type. In its *enkaptic* union in a work of art, marble retains the structure of a *subjective*-physical product of nature. In time it will show signs of deterioration due to the effects of the weather. The work of art, in contrast, is objectively and aesthetically qualified. The statue cannot exist apart from the marble, but the marble can exist independently of the statue. In addition it must be noted that although the *enkaptic* union of the marble does not violate the individual structure of the marble, yet this union does affect it. For by technical forming, the structure of the marble is *opened* and *enriched* by the actualization of its anticipatory spheres. For instance: this piece of marble, interwoven in the sculpture, evokes a *feeling* of admiration by the observer of this work of art. The natural marble-material on the contrary is unable to evoke such admiration.

This same type of one-sided foundation is also found in the structure of chemical compounds. In a compound chemical material, for example, table salt (NaCl) sodium and chlorine are joined together. Both elements are *enkaptically* united in this chemical union. They can be separated from the salt compound, but table salt never exists apart from the composite elements.

This type of *enkapsis* can also be ascertained in the composite structures of the plant and animal kingdoms. A plant, as a living organism, is one-sidedly founded in the structures of the materials which constitute it. These materials are physically and chemically qualified. The chemically qualified materials, such as fats, carbohydrates, and proteins are *enkaptically* united in the biotically qualified body of the plant. In the enkaptic interwovenness of the plant these materials retain their internal sphere-sovereignty. But, within the structure of the living organism they acquire an *enkaptic function* as they must follow the internal structural law of that organism. For, in the unfolding of their objective-biotic anticipatory spheres, they are led by and directed toward the organic vital function of the plant.

The body of animals is even more complicated. Here too, the physical-chemical individual structures of the materials, composing the animal body, are *enkaptically*

THE THEORY OF STRUCTURAL INTERRELATIONS 251

interwoven. They constitute namely a one-sided foundation for the individual structure of the *living organism* as a second and more complicated foundation for the existence of this animal. For that living organism of the animal is interwoven, again in the way of one-sided foundation, with *the psychical structures* of individuality of the animal. The plant lacks a psychical structure, but the psychical function is precisely what characterized the structure of an animal. An animal reacts to external impressions in a sensory-motor manner. The external impressions are psychically actualized by an animal in a psychical center or reaction-centrum thereby giving rise to independent bodily motions.

Everywhere that *one-sided enkapsis* is encountered, the individual structures, which are united in the way of enkaptic interwovenness, become bound together as a complicated total-structure or *enkaptic structural whole*. This *enkaptic* structural whole is qualified by the highest of the composite structures, insofar as these structures possess a different radical-type, and displays a typical unity of form. And, in the case of plants, animals, and men we call this unity a *body*.

Secondly, we find *correlative interwovenness* in the cosmos or a *coherence between two interacting structures*. For example, consider the relation of a tree to its surroundings. The tree has a subjective and biotic destination-function and the surroundings are objective and biotically qualified. The objective-biotic anticipatory sphere of the surroundings is opened in its *state of being interwoven* with the tree. The richness of God's creation unfolds in *enkapsis*. Interaction is evident from the fact that the tree cannot exist without surroundings, and surroundings without the tree cannot be the surroundings *of the tree*.

In this *interwovenness* of a living organism with its environment, this organism displays its so-called *phaeno-typical variability*. The same plant exhibits a different form in different surroundings. This difference is external in character as its internal structure remains intact. Consider the shape of two pine trees, if the one is planted on a wind swept plain and the other in a peaceful valley. Phaenotypical variability is a proof of the relation of mutual dependence between an organism and its environment.

In the third place we encounter *symbiotic interwovenness*. *Symbiosis* means the association of a plant with other plants, of an animal with other animals, or of plants and animals; e.g., the relation of a bee to the bee-colony or the relation of a plant to the collective-structure of a forest in which it lives.

In the fourth place there is the *interwoven relation between subject and objects*. The example of the bird's nest illustrated this, as does the relation of the snail to its shell and of cows to a dairy farm; cows are economically qualified objects. A congregation is related to a church building in such a manner that the latter is qualified as a pistical object.

In the fifth place we must mention *territorial enkapsis*. We shall discuss this type of interwovenness in the following section by the discussion of enkapsis in human society.

43

Interwovenness in Human Society

The phenomenon of *enkapsis* is not restricted to the structures of things but it exists also in the structures of human society. We have frequently referred to it in our discussion of societal relationships. Recall that the *external functions* of the different relationships interact (e.g., the relation of church and state, family and church, school boards and the school).

The important question arises as to whether or not the *enkaptic* relation of interwovenness between the family and marriage, on the one hand, and free societal relations, on the other, is *foundational* in character. In other words, can free societal relations only develop on the basis of marriage and the family-relationship? If the question is answered in the affirmative, then it would appear that family and married life are possible without free societal relations. Human existence could thus be exclusively absorbed by the family and marriage, without finding any compensation in the societal relations. Moreover, this answer would lead to the consequence, that all *structures* of society, namely the remaining relationships and free relations, would have *developed* from family and marriage. This consequence, however, that the structures of human society originate from each other, leads to a *relativistic evolutionism*, which is incompatible with the Christian confession, that all the *structures* of temporal reality rest upon the Will of God, the almighty Creator.

We must, therefore, answer the above question in the negative, however, with the understanding that there is a genetic coherence in the *form of genesis* between marriage and the family, but not a genesis of *structures* which — as normative principles — are grounded in the will of God. The form of genesis (origin) is related to the *subject-side* of societal relations and relationships; the structures in contrast, represent their *law-side*. According to the divine order of creation, natural and communal relationships only exist in correlation to free societal relations.

Thus we are here dealing with the type of *correlative enkapsis*. Historically viewed societal relations preceded the marriage relation. God gave Eve to Adam not to be his sister, but to be his wife in the fulness of her existence. And still always is in force for every marriage, that the man accepts his wife in the sphere of societal liberty: therefore shall a man leave his father and his mother and shall cleave unto his wife. Human existence is not resolved or absorbed in any single relationship of society; the relations of the authoritative societal relationships are supplemented by the free societal relations, and they are interwoven with each other in many ways.

There is no *enkaptic foundational relation* between the natural communal relations and authoritative societal relationships on the one hand, and the free societal relations on the other. But this type of interwovenness is present between the free societal relationships and the free societal relations. For the former, a business or a club, for example, is only possible on the basis of the latter. A free societal relationship is only brought into existence by people who are on equal footing. Free societal relations acquire a beneficial connection in these free societal relationships, because too much personal freedom is not conducive to a healthy development of human society, which means: living together. Correlative *enkapsis* rather than genetic coherence also exists between the state and society. Opened society is impossible without a state, and a state is impossible without opened society. In this connection, Dooyeweerd defines society as the *enkaptic interwoven coherence of all particular free societal structures*.[1] In principle society cannot be closed. Society is comparable with the environment, the "*Umwelt*" of natural organisms. It is the environment of the authoritative societal relationships in their mutual structural interwovenness. A special type of *enkapsis* is the previously mentioned *territorial interwovenness*. This term denotes the interwovenness between the state and all societal structures within its territory, but has nothing to do with a universalistic subordination of the latter to the former. The state is not the highest goal. This territorial *enkapsis* is *external* in nature and does not in any way affect the *internal* structure of relationships and free societal relations. The government is authorized to harmonize particular interests with the general interest, so that the former will not injure the latter. If the government does not exceed the limits of its authority, the sphere-sovereignty of all other societal relationships is guaranteed.

44

Form as a Junction of Interwovenness

We must still consider the *contact-points* or *junctions of enkapsis*. We have seen earlier that the phaeno-typical variability of the living organism points us to the interwoven-coherence between organisms and their environment. This holds for the individual structures of all things, namely,

[1] *A New Critique of Theoretical Thought.*

that their changing form is a point of contact of interwovenness. Not only is this true of natural things, but it is also true of cultural things. The variable form of a piece of furniture, for example, points to its interwovenness with human subjectivity in society. In its *origin* there is an *enkaptic* relation between a piece of furniture and the firm of industry which produced it; while in its *existence* there is an enkaptic relation between this object of culture and the family which uses it.

In human society there are also *enkaptic* points of contact, which are to be found in the *positive forms* in which societal relationships are realized. Societal relationships are based on human formation, and positive formation rests on an historical foundation and is only possible in the coherence of the internal and external side of the structure of a specific relationship.

Each societal relationship has in the first place a positive *form of existence*, which is the contact-point of *enkapsis*. The Christian church, for example, has a different form in different lands, which is determined by internal and external factors such as the relation between the church and the state, the church and the family, etc.

Secondly, the positive forms of existence are based upon positive *forms of genesis* by those societal relationships and relations which are historically grounded. These forms of genesis are also contact-points of enkapsis.

The trade agreement, for instance, which Abraham entered into when he purchased the first piece of ground of the promised country, namely a cemetery, bore an entirely different form of genesis than a trade agreement in our time. This *form of genesis* is externally bound to the positive norms of all societal relationships within whose sphere of influence a specific societal relationship or relation is called into being. In our illustration concerning Abraham, the formal genesis of that trade agreement was interwoven with the structure of the Canaanite society of those times. In our day a trade agreement, in contrast, is interwoven with the civil legal system of the state within whose domain such a contract is made.

Human life displays a tremendously rich *enkapsis* of structures by God ordained and by Him maintained. But even in the most complicated enkaptic interwovenness the sphere-sovereignty of each individual structure is guaranteed by God who has created all things for His own glory.

CHAPTER VII

FINAL REMARKS

45

THE SEARCH FOR A PHILOSOPHIC ANTHROPOLOGY

WE have completed our examination of the *individual* structure of things and of human society. The question remains as to whether or not man, as an individual personality, has a temporal *individual* structure. Is the individual unity of man enclosed within the transcendental temporal dimension or is it guaranteed by the transcendent concentration point or religious root of his whole temporal existence?

The task of philosophical anthropology is to answer this question and to furnish us a theory of man which is in keeping with the structure of his temporal existence, as God's image. Such a Christian philosophical anthropology has not yet been fully developed by them, who laid the foundations of this philosophy. We must, therefore, be satisfied with a general indication of the course to be pursued and of the principles from which this anthropology has to arise.

In any case we can say that from what God's Word reveals to us concerning the origin and end of human life, it is clear that man does not have a temporal destination-function, since he transcends all temporal structures in the root of his existence.

Man is created for eternity, he has an eternal destination. His existence is not terminated by death, but continues in heaven or in hell. When Christ returns, the souls of the deceased will be reunited with their bodies. The faithful shall inherit the earth in eternal life, but unbelievers will be cast away from God.

The leading-function in human life is the temporal pistical function. However, this function does not include the *end* of humanity. Man is not created *in order to* believe. He is created and redeemed in order to serve God and to glorify Him through faith in community with the whole world.

Man is fundamentally distinguished from all other creatures through this eternal end. The structures of other creatures have a temporal destination-function; they are perishable.

On the basis of Scripture it further can be stated that, because of the place God gave man in the world, he is the *religious created center* of the whole cosmos. The whole creation is centered in him in the service of God. This truth can only be understood if individualism is excluded from anthropology and a place is made for the covenantal relation which God has instituted between Himself and the human race, and which is represented by the Covenant heads (the first and second Adam).

Man is certainly not *qualified* as a rational-moral being. For this qualification rests upon an hypostatization of single isolated temporal functions. This wrong qualification is only to be understood on the basis of the immanence-standpoint.

In the next place we must notice that a philosophical anthropology cannot inaugurate a scientific investigation to determine the nature or the structure of the human *soul as the transcendent center* of all our temporal functions. God can only teach us in His Word what the soul is. Science is incompetent to furnish knowledge of the soul. It can only examine a theoretical *Gegenstand-relation* with the temporal modal aspects of reality and relate the individual structures in its field of investigation; for these structures of individuality have a typical function in each of these modal aspects. What transcends the cosmic temporal boundary falls outside of the reach of science. It can only be known so far as God revealed it in His holy Word.

The limits have been placed there by God. If science does

not recognize these limits, but seeks to present a theory of the human soul, then the result is either an unjust speculation, which is in no way related to truth and therefore lacks any convincing power; or it results in a view, in which the complex of normative bodily functions are hypostatized to "spirit" or "soul," which as a "spiritual-substance" is then opposed to the complex of lower functions, considered as the substance of "matter." Moreover, such a separation of the many-sided bodily structure of man into two self-sufficient substantial parts results in the unsolvable pseudo-problem of the interaction of matter and spirit.

We can conclude:

(a) that the field of investigation of philosophic anthropology is limited to the *temporal bodily structure* of man;

(b) that this *bodily* structure may not be viewed as an abstract complex of human physical-chemical functions which may or may not be augmented by an organic vital function. This bodily structure is the *whole structure of all human temporal functions,* all the functions from the arithmetical to the pistical. Our body is extended as far as our individual existence is temporal. There is no *dichotomy* in our temporal body. All functions are united into a wonderful whole. Dichotomy can only in a way be spoken of in the Biblical sense of body and soul, the former being understood to mean the structural whole of the many-faceted body and the latter as the transcendent concentration point of our temporal functions; with the understanding that the unbreakable *unity* of body and soul remains maintained;

(c) the structure of this body can be understood only on the basis of the heart which lies on a deeper level. Consequently, the scientific formulations of Christian anthropology concerning the body rest upon a *transcendental idea* of the human soul as a religious presupposition derived from Holy Scripture.

46
The Structure of the Human Body

The human body, as well as the body of plants and animals, is not simple, but is a *complicated structure of totality*, in which additional *individual* structures are enkaptically interwoven, in a one-sided fashion.

The enkaptic structural whole of the human body includes the temporal individual human existence in its entirety. The following *individual* structures are enkaptically united within this structural whole of the human body:

1. The individual structure of matter, which is *physically* qualified and necessary for the construction of the human body.

2. The *individual structure* of the living organism which is qualified by the *biotic* function. In this biotic structure of individuality the autonomic nervous system, which involuntarily regulates functions of life as digestion and circulation, plays a dominating role.

3. The individual structure of the human sensory emotive (affective) life is psychically qualified. The so-called animal nervous system has here the central place, as the organ by which man rules the processes of his sensory feeling and all his voluntary motions.

4. The so-called *act-structure* of the human body unites and directs all post-psychical bodily functions in a typically individual manner. Within this act-structure, human act-life takes place in three basic ways: *knowing, imagining,* and *willing*. This act-structure is typically human. Animal life does not have it since animals have only object-functions in the post-psychical spheres.

What do we mean by human acts? *Acts are the inner activity of man, by which — under the influence of post-psychical, normative perspectives — man is intentionally active with reality and makes it his own by relating reality to himself, to his I-ness or soul.*

To say that one is intentionally occupied with something means, that in an internal way a person directs his knowing, imagining or desiring activity towards it, but does not yet actualize or perform an external deed. He is only *intentionally* engaged in it. *Intentional* activity is the opposite of *actual* activity. The latter does something to reality, causing a real thing to undergo change. If I think about a house, that is performing an *act of thinking*. I do not change the construction of that house nor its owner, yet I am intentionally occupied with the real house.

Although different, an act is closely related to an *actual action*. Our acts are realized in the external world by human actions. Every act is internally directed toward the external world. Now this intention realizes itself by action in the external world.

For example. If I desire a house, I perform an *act of willing*. But when I make that desired house my property by purchase, I realize the act of desiring in the purchasing action. Between desiring and buying there is still the *decision* of buying. Such a decision is a complicated act. For in each decision the three basic-types of act-life, knowing, imagining and willing, are mutually connected. Only after the decision the act passes into the action and the intention is realized in the external world.

From this it follows, that every human action is preceded by acts. Consequently, our actions are *responsible deeds*, which must be normatively judged. They are qualitatively different from psychical reflex movements, which occur independent of acts and decisions. However, all acts are not followed by actions. Numberless acts are never realized. One may have knowledge of something and never employ it. So that this knowledge remains an act without being realized. The same is true of pious wishes which may never be executed.

47
The Act-Structure of the Human Body

The act-structure of the human body is the last or highest *individual* structure of the enkaptic structural whole of the human body. But this act-structure is not limited to the post-psychical or normative bodily aspects. It is not enclosed or shut off in a part of the human functions, for then it would be abstract rather than real in character. The act-structure functions in *all the aspects* of the human body. An act of faith, for example, is not restricted to the pistical function but is active within the other normative functions and also has a physical, biotic and psychical side. In every act the entire human body is engaged in internal action. Accurate investigations have established, that during an act of thought electrical current is generated in the cells of the brain. And any injury to the cells of the cerebral cortex disrupts normal human *acts*.

It should be clear, therefore, that it is incorrect — as occurs in the accepted conception — to conceive of *acts* as pure "spiritual" activities of the soul-substance (read: the hypostatized complex of normative functions), which is supposed to be independent of the human body (degraded to a material-substance). This view is based upon the non-Christian anthropological schema of spirit and matter. It is non-Christian because it is based upon pagan religious presuppositions. The acts are naturally connected with the human soul or spirit. They proceed from the deepest religious center of our existence, from the transcendent heart, and they express themselves in all the aspects of the human body, in the entire enkaptic bodily structure. Human acts are distinguished from the movements, reflexes and processes of life, which take place in the lower bodily structures, by the fact that acts are related to the religious center of our existence. An act cannot occur apart from the soul. And it is equally impossible for the soul — while bound to the earthly body — to express itself outside of the structure of acts. The human soul or spirit expresses and realizes itself in acts which are corporeal in character. As a result, *acts* lack a *fixed qualifying function*. The act-structure is not qualified by the pistical function, but is directly led by the human spirit, which in complete freedom can express itself in *acts*. Consequently, human acts can assume *all the possible qualifications* of the normative aspects. A scientific act of knowing is analytically qualified; an act of love ethically, an act of prayer pistically and an artistic act of imagination is aesthetically an act of speech symbolically qualified. The qualification of a particular act is principally determined by the typical qualification of the individual structure of human society, in which the act arises. If a storekeeper takes an inventory of his stock, then the acts of knowing executed on this occasion are economically qualified. If in social life, one acquires knowledge of human nature, then this knowledge rests upon socially qualified acts of knowing. The corporeal act-structure grants full freedom for these and other normative characterizations, since the act-structure, as such, is unqualified.

Human acts are characterized by the three directions of knowing, imagining, and willing. Knowing, imagining, and willing must not be conceived of as independent self-sufficient faculties. For they are woven together and in reality never appear in isolation. An act of will, for example, cannot occur without an act of knowing and of imagining. If a person wishes to buy a house, he has some knowledge concerning its purchase and has already imagined himself as the owner.

It is true, however, that certain aspects of life are particularly related to a certain type of act. The analytical aspect is particularly related to the act-direction of knowing; the aesthetic aspect to the direction of imagining, and the juridical aspect to the act-direction of willing. But these three act-directions also lack a fixed qualification in the act-structure. They lack an *original* typical act-character, because they are all grounded in the *psychical* corporeal structure of the three intentional experiences, namely: sensory knowing, sensory imagining and sensory desire. These three sensory experiences are also present in the psychical corporeal structure of animals. Animals do not have a transcendent root in a religious concentration and are not subject to the normative aspects. Consequently these intentional psychical experiences of animals cannot be acts. But in human act-life the three directions of sensory experience are related to the soul and are led by normative perspectives.

The individual soul or spirit of man expresses itself *characteristically* in the *enkaptic* structural whole of man's body.

Here we are concerned with the human *character* and with some questions concerning it.

First question: What does it mean, when we speak of the character of a person? Dooyeweerd answers: *"Character is the typical temporal expression of the individuality of the human spirit in the act-structure or border-structure of the human body."*

Hence it follows, that man's character itself is not spiritual, but *corporeal*. For it is a corporeal expression of the spiritual individuality of man's soul, his Ego or I-ness, in his *normative functions*, which are the highest enkaptic structure of the body-totality.

Second question: Is one's character changeable or not? The answer has to be: partly it is and partly it is not. That our character is a matter of the *normative* functions of our body, indicates, that the human character can develop in an *abnormal* way. For instance: if a person's character is thrifty by nature, this trait of character itself cannot be changed. But the man with this disposition has to guard against a development of this trait of thrift into the direction of avarice. For on this point he can degrade his given character by offending against the divine norms.

There exists in mankind a very great multiplicity of character-traits, such as: cordiality, liberality, faithfulness, thoughtfulness, spontaneity, reticence, seriousness, accuracy, etc. Therefore we encounter among people so many types of character in diversity of traits.

The spiritual individuality of the human soul also expresses itself in the *psychical* structure of the human body. In this respect we don't speak of character, but of the human *temperament*. Temperament is the way in which the individual human personality bodily reacts by means of the psychical function of feeling. One can react in his emotional function *primarily*, while other persons in this respect react *secondarily*. Our temperament is a totally unchangeable datum, because psychical laws are not norms, but *fixed rules*, fully independent of our will. Though character and temperament are essentially different, they are bound together in the way of foundational enkapsis. Temperament is the base of character.

In the third place. Our spiritual individuality also expresses itself in the *biotic* structure of our body. Here our *biotic dispositions* appear, namely: the difference of sex, the experience of sickness or fitness, the mood of languor, of vital strength, and so on. Also these biotic dispositions are in a foundational enkaptic way connected with character and temperament.

Finally, there is still a typical expression of our individual personality in the lowest physical structure of our body. Here arises man's *tempo*, the corporeal disposition of our energetic moving, the rhythm of life. This tempo is with temperament and biotic dispositions in a foundational way connected with a person's character.

In contrast to animals, man displays a *spiritual form*. This appears morphologically from the *form-totality* of his body. For his movements are plastic, his body is not specified in one way, it can as it were, be used on *every* side, run in *all* directions. The morphology of man has certain specifically human features. Man walks upright, his eyes and his facial expressions reflect the operations of his soul. Man was created as the ruler of the earth. He must freely rule all things in normative subjection to the ordinances of God. This lordship stamps the form of his body, which is typified through the act-structure.

Human acts have two depths or levels: that of *consciousness* and of *unconsciousness*. Both levels encompass all the aspects of the temporal body. We may not introduce a dualism in these aspects, in which dualism the highest aspects are reserved for consciousness and the lowest for unconsciousness. In consciousness we relate all temporal aspects of reality to our deepest ego, while in unconsciousness — think of sleep — all aspects can sink under the threshold of our consciousness. Our unconsciousness has a tremendous influence in our life. It guarantees, for example, continuity to our acts, since man's memory enables him to recall that which had become unconscious and incorporate it in his present acts.

If a person acts *normally*, the unconscious is subordinate to the conscious. Desires and appetites which are forbidden from a normative viewpoint are normally relegated to the unconscious. In abnormal cases these desires create disharmony and disturb conscious acts. This can result in the unconscious dominating the conscious, or in the breaking of the central tie between human acts and the soul in *consciousness*. Disharmony can also arise between the several functions in man's act-life. Nervous disorders can result from neglecting emotional life by an excessive use of the analytical function.

Human unity of the body is expressed in human acts. The remaining individual structures, which are bound together in an enkaptic structural whole, retain their internal sovereignty with respect to the central act-structure, which accentuates man's exceptional place in the cosmos.

The pre-normative bodily structures permit themselves to be ruled by the will of man only insofar as they have *enkaptic* functions within the act-structure of man. In all his actions, a Christian ought to seek to honor God in his body and soul.

48

Conclusion

We have finished our introduction to Christian philosophy. The question can be put: what is the use of this system of Christian philosophy? Its use lies primarily on a scientific level and there it has as well a negative as a positive side.

Negatively, we trust that this philosophy will serve as a warning to Christians, so that they will not attempt to effect a synthesis between the Christian and the immanence standpoint in the field of science and philosophy. For the whole history of philosophy shows that such synthesis always results in a ruling of un-Scriptural ideas and principles.

Positively, we hope that we have furnished a scientific and Biblical answer to the last questions, which call for an answer in every science and in philosophy.

The usefulness and significance of Christian philosophy, however, is not limited to scientific activity. The results of every science affect our practical life. This is especially true of philosophy since it affects the view of life held to by the masses of people who are not directly concerned with science. Therefore we may pronounce our expectation, that this philosophy may be fertile world-wide in the practical life of many Christians, who believe that the principles of the Word of God have to determine our conduct of life.

The system of Christian philosophy that we have presented was originally developed in Holland more than thirty-five years ago and has since become known throughout the world.

In Holland the members of this school have done much in practical life to provide many people with a Christian answer to problems which are constantly encountered in everyday life.

It has made the layman aware of the dangers which arise out of a non-Christian or anti-Christian outlook. And it has stimulated many to advance the Kingdom of God in all aspects of life.

Since the second world war America is called upon to lead the free nations. Let us hope that the leaders of America and the American people will seek first the Kingdom of God. And we trust that this Christian philosophy may be used by God, for it has no other end than to glorify Him.

We will finish this summary of Christian philosophy with a final remark.

A scientific theory or a philosophical conception can never be "the end of all contradiction," an unchangeable word, an eternal truth. For it is always a work of men, who are erratic, feeble and subjective. "We know in part," the

Scripture says. This is also in force for this system of philosophy.

That means: the theses here explained have to be critically considered, and — if necessary — revised.

As for this, Prof. Dr. H. G. Stoker, a famous Christian philosopher from the University of Potchefstroom, South Africa, also an adherent of this philosophy, has proposed to distinguish — next to both cosmic dimensions of modalities and structures of individuality — a third dimension of events. Among "events" he reckons not only what occurs with and by men, but also, what occurs with matter, plant and animal and with the whole cosmos. In this dimension, Stoker says, "We meet with arising and decay, actual motion and change, genesis, development and history; all that can be conceived as occurring in time." He sees the time as the *form of running down* of events.

Hence it follows, that this "dimension of events" is a replacement for our dimension of cosmic time together with our historical modality. Therefore both are dropped in the conception of Stoker. We feel this proposal is worthy of our consideration.

We call attention to still another thing. It concerns a view of Prof. Dr. K. J. Popma, a well-known Dutch philosopher. He propagates of late years, that the human *faith* is not one of the many *functions* of man like feeling, thinking or love, but it lies on a deeper level. Faith belongs to the *transcendent dimension*, there where all cosmic modalities converge in the human heart. Faith is therefore the *direct religious activity of our heart*, which is the root of life.

For this he produces many Scriptural reasons. Some of them we will mention here. Christian faith is so little a function, that it possesses in the Holy Scripture many names, among other things: hypostasis (bearing-level), the new life, a new creation, names that we cannot think together into comprehensibility. Another reason is this: we can act as father, citizen, scientist, etc. But never can we do anything *exclusively* and *restrictively* in our quality as believers. For a Christian is *always* a believer in all his actions as father, citizen, and so on. Every human act and deed becomes achieved under the leadership of faith. This cannot be said about one of the functions. Therefore, faith itself is not a function. It is on the contrary the religious background of our whole functional life, the deepest religious driving-power of our existence. We believe Prof. Popma is right in this respect.

In this way philosophy goes on through many alterations. If this occurs by the light of the Word of God, in mutual cooperation, we may expect that our labour is not vain in the Lord, but will further the coming of His Kingdom. "For now we see in a mirror, darkly; but then face to face; now I know in part; but then shall I know even as also I have been known" (I Cor. 13:12).